ISLAM
The Ideal Way of Life

ENCYCLOPAEDIC SURVEY OF ISLAMIC CULTURE SERIES

ISLAM
The Ideal Way of Life

Edited by
MOHAMED TAHER

ANMOL PUBLICATIONS PVT. LTD.
NEW DELHI-110 002 (INDIA)

ANMOL PUBLICATIONS PVT. LTD.
4374/4B, Ansari Road, Daryaganj
New Delhi-110 002

Islam: The Ideal Way of Life

First Edition 1998
ISBN 81-7488-937-X

PRINTED IN INDIA

Published by J.L. Kumar for Anmol Publications Pvt. Ltd., New Delhi-110 002 and Printed at Mehra Offset Press, Delhi.

Contents

Preface

The *Encyclopaedic Survey of Islamic Culture* is a unique reference source. This series seeks to anthologise the most important primary and secondary materials on a wide variety of topics and writers of Islamic culture and civilisation. The scholar, the student and the layman will find in various volumes not only a generous selection of reprinted articles, but original essays, bibliographies, and other materials brought for the first time in a comprehensive and exhaustive fashion.

The need for this collation grew out of our awareness that there is no comprehensive source of information for the study and research of the field. Other published works are too specialised in the topics discussed or neglect the institutional as well the individual role which the Islamic system plays. Few encyclopaedic works do exist, and few anthologies also have appeared. Fewer books, again, have systematically covered such topics as Islam in Africa, Islamic sociology, Islamic polity, Islamic thought, etc. Although these topics have been addressed separately, no attempt has been made to discuss them as part of a united treatment of the literature of the field.

Islam brought a total change in all spheres of life. It revolutionised many societies, both in the east and the west. But this is not always accepted and acknowledged. To quote Major Arthur Leonard from his work: Islam; her moral and spiritual value:

"Never to this day has Europe acknowledged in an honest and whole hearted manner the great and everlasting debt she owes to Islamic culture and civilisation. Only in a lukewarm and perfunctory way has she recognised that when, during the dark ages, her people were sunk in feudalism and ignorance, Muslim civilisation under the Arabs reached a high standard of social and scientific splendour that kept the flickering members of European society from utter decadence.

"Do not we, who now consider ourselves on the top most pinnacle ever reached by culture and civilisation, recognise that, had it not been for the high culture, the civilisation and intellectual, as well as the social splendours of the Arabs and soundness of their school system, Europe would to this day have remained sunk in the darkness of ignorance. Have we forgotten that the Muslim maxim was that, the real learning of a man is of more public importance than any particular religious opinions he may entertain, that Muslim liberality was in striking contrast with the then intolerant state of Europe? Does the magnificent valour of the Arabs, inspired as it was by a theism as lofty as it was pure, not appeal to us? Does not the moderation and comparative toleration shown by them to the conquered, notwithstanding the fierce and burning ardour to regenerate mankind that impelled them onward to conquest, also appeal to us? Does it not all the more appeal to us when we contrast this with the bitterness of the attitude of the Christian sects towards one another? Especially when we consider that in Christendom, as it was then constituted, extortion, tyranny and imperial centralisation, combining with ecclesiastical despotism and persecution, had practically extinguished patriotism, by substitution in its place schismatic and degenerate Church?"

Further the same writer continues to say:

> "Is it possible that Europe is unmindful of, and has the ingratitude to ignore the splendid services of the scientists and philosophers of Arabic? Are the names of Assamh, Abu Othman, Alberuni, Albeithar, Abu Ali Ibn Sina (Avicenna) the great physician and philosopher, Ibn Rushd (Anempace) besides a host of others but dead letters? Is the great work that they have done and the fame they have left behind them in their books to be consigned to the limbo of oblivion, by an ungrateful but antipathetic Europe?

"It cannot be that already we have lost sight of the amazing intellectual activity of the Muslim world during the earlier part of the `Abbaside' period more especially. It cannot be that we have quite forgotten the irrecoverable loss that was inflicted on Arabian literature, and on the world at large, by the wanton destruction of thousands of books that was promoted by Christian bigotry and fanaticism? It cannot be surely said of Christian Europe that for centuries now she has done her best to hide obligations to the Arabs; yet most assuredly, obligations such as these, are far too sacred to lie much linger hidden."

This is one side of the story. The other side is that the West has definitely absorbed much of the Islamic contributions and is "unaware." To quote Marcus Marby and William Underhill "Bold new visions from ancient landscapes" (*Newsweek*, May 29, 1995): Christian and Islamic civilizations have been in conflict for most of their history. But as often as they have clashed, they have enriched each other. In this ninth century, Moors brought advanced architecture, astronomy and medicine to occupied Spain. While Europe lingered in the Dark Ages, courtly poetry from Persia inspired the troubadours, whose verse evolved into the literature of the early French Renaissance. Even whiling away hours over coffee and conversation—the basis for the cafe—came from Arab culture... France's most popular dish today is not escargots but couscous. French slang is peppered with Arab words like kif-kif (50-50) and Insha Allah (God willing). The hottest new music is Arab-inspired rai" (p. 28). The list of Arabic borrowed words in English and Western usages are many more, not mere algebra, alchemy, azimuth, albatross, timbal, zenith, etc.

There is, in short, a lot of misinformation and incorrect representation about Islam. And more so there is a need today to describe and interpret the issues and express in clear terms what this thought actually deals with. Due to social and cultural changes, the salient aspects of the field require examination. The post cold war era has left the world with a unipolar political system. Islam is a system which promises the world that if applied in toto it would solve the multi-dimensional problems of the modern era. But is there any one who wishes to test this module and try it in a space and time to see the truth of the statement?

The primary purpose of this encyclopaedic survey is to serve as a basic handbook on significant topics of Islamic culture. To facilitate an understanding of the field, the series presents a survey and an analysis of the various socio-cultural forces that shape both the structure and functions of the field as well as by the way this society has changed. We also analyse the larger forces outside the community, such as assimilation and acculturation, and forces inside the community, like, role of the leadership, role of the social and cultural groups and the so much alleged 'imbalance' in the theory and practice of the faith.

We are confident that this work will make a permanent and significant contribution to the study of Islam. Its style is simple, and it is presented in a style accessible to a wide audience. Its target audience is faculty, students, and all concerned with the understanding of the faith of the second largest following in the world. While it has scholarly materials, it is nevertheless also of use to those who have no knowledge of the field, as well as to those who are working in related and allied fields. Most important, we hope that this series will be useful in teaching and learning as an educational resource in the academic world.

The series is planned to be both, multi-volume and multi-faceted set, which will run into hundreds of numbers. The compilation of such a huge set is a gigantic task and requires the support and encouragement of all concerned. It requires feed-back and also support from the literary market place and literary circles all over.

A collection of articles, or an anthology, has many benefits, like, it renews our acquaintance with literature which we have neglected, it reveals to us material of which we were ignorant, and it exposes relationships where we did not suppose them to exist. This is the ultimate purpose of our efforts and we wish and pray that this is fulfilled.

A word of acknowledgement is due to the inspiration of the idea of a comprehensive, commulative and compact set of literary works on the Islamic culture. These inspirers are from all walks of life and their efforts must be acknowledged which includes contributors, authors and editors, as well as the publishers who have graciously contributed to this project and we duly acknowledge their cooperation. The well wishers are many more and listing all the concerned by names is impossible here. Each must be duly rewarded for this gesture, and this is our sincere prayer.

—Editor

1

Islamic Studies and the European Imagination

AZIZ AL-AZMEH

(Abstract: I will take up two interconnected issues, the first is the way in which a particular notion of Islam is conjured up by the European orientalist imagination and in turn, second, its contribution to Islamic studies as a scholarly discipline within orientalism with conceptual and categorical baggage which I repudiate).

It was customary for medieval Muslim scholars and divines, as it is customary in Exeter today, to deliver a public lecture marking the transition to a professorship. The purpose of this rite of passage was not entirely ritual nor necessarily frivolous, and need not be so today. It gave the incumbent the chance publicly to announce the provenance of his learning, to declare the direction of his scholarship, to inventorize his stock-in-trade, and to scrutinize the state of his field. Such formal statement of scholarly patrimony and intent is salutary. Reflection is always creditable; and taking up a chair, like the mid-age crisis, is a good vantage point for reflection, and I am perhaps fortunate in that the two do not coincide in my case. Without reflection, scholarship will become and remain captive to the unaided native intelligence, the truest companion error, and of course prejudice: prejudice shared with one's fellow professionals and with society at large.

I wish to continue this tradition; but I am acutely aware that an antique tradition such as this can only persist if subjected to change. So I shall invert the venerable order of things. I shall not assert the antiquity of my scientific pedigree. Neither do I propose to underline my faithfulness to my profession of orientalist, nor do I wish to celebrate what commonplace prejudices I might share with this profession and tradition. What I intend my reflections this evening to do is to scrutinize the condition of my orientalist profession and patrimony, and perhaps to perform an act of patricide. This against has an illustrious pedigree, going back to the very beginning of time when Cronos, time himself, neutralized his father Uranus. But whereas Cronos used a flint sickle, I shall deploy only words. I will take up two interconnected matters. I shall first discuss the way in which a particular notion of Islam is conjured up by the European orientalist imagination and how this has provided and still provides Islamic studies as a scholarly discipline within orientalism with conceptual and categorical baggage which I repudiate. Let me add here a word about orientalism: I understand by orientalism the deliberate apprehension and knowledge of the orient; I see orientalism as an ideological trope, an aesthetic, normative and ultimately political designation of things as oriental in opposition to occidental. It endows such things with changeless, "oriental" properties, some repellent and others charming, that go beyond history, that violate the changing nature of things, and that infirm them in a distant and irreducible specificity transcending the bounds of reason and forever valorizing common phantasy and folklore. To complement this first line of reflection, I shall briefly indicate major orientations for the dissolution of this orientalist category of Islam, and for the reconstitution of the study of Islam on the solid grounds of modern historical scholarship.

Allow me first to recall a predecessor, who to my knowledge was the first orientalist at Exeter. In 1704, Messrs Philip Bishop and Edward Score, of the Exeter High Street, published a book entitled *A True and Faithful Account of the Religion and Manners of the Mohammedans*. The author, one Joseph Pitts, was born in Exeter. In 1678 at the age of 17, he fell victim to his King's rapacious activities in the Mediterranean, when the ship on which he served his apprenticeship was overwhelmed by Algerian Corsairs. Nobody thought him worthy of a ransom, and he spend the next fifteen years in slavery, during which time he converted to Islam and made the pilgrimage to Mecca, but finally escaped and returned to spend the rest of his days in Exeter.

The book was quite a success; it went into at first four editions, and was reprinted in London as late as 1774; and his success was fully deserved, as the book almost completely confirmed the expectations of its readers, and there are strong indications that it was actually written according to printers' specifications. With the exception of such fantasies as could be falsified by tangible observation—such as the assertion of countless generations of Europeans and Muhammad's tomb in Medina was suspended in mid-air—the book rehearsed the usual repertoire of folkloristic absurdities current for centuries, absurdities which arise from a fundamental structure of all orientalist discourse; namely, that observations, and judgements without reference to observation, constitute two separate registers, with hardly any means of contact between the one and the other except for the possibility of the latter (judgements) given the guise of the former; such are, of course, the possibilities of phantasy. Thus Islam was still for Pitts, as for medieval Europeans and a number of young orientalists today, "a miscellany of popery, Judaism, and the gentilism of the Arabs." The Turks—the quintessence of Islam for Pitts and his contemporaries—are so much given to sodomy that "they loath the Natural Use of the Woman" and Muhammad could be nothing but "a vile and debauched imposter." The Koran for Pitts, needless to say, is but "a Legend of Falsities, and abominable Follies and Absurdities."

That observation is incapable of correcting prejudice was not a matter confined to semi-literate personalities such as Joseph Pitts. A still more staggering contrast is observable between Voltaire's nearly modern and historical view of Islam in his *Essai sur l'histoire generate*, and the dark medievalism of his tragedy, *Le Fanatisme ou Mahomet le Prophete*. That Muhammad was an imposter dominated by ambition and lust, and that he was therefore a worthy inspiration for Islam, is a medieval view which was shared by Edward Gibbon as by many until very recently. This medieval canon on Islam was fully formed by the end of the 12th century, the offspring of two independent but remarkably parallel traditions of anti-Islamic polemic, the one Byzatine and the other Mozarabic. This canon, both theological and literary, was remarkably impervious to observation. Marco Polo's descriptions are largely based on literary and theologica conventions which were astonishingly resistant to the observation of reality or to the reading of original Arabic sources which were already available in translation from the time of the Cluniac collection in the middle of the 12th century. And replete with factual information as they were, the medieval romances, the "histoire chante" of the time, were yet unremitting in their subordinaion of fact to propaganda and literary convention. It appears that Crusaders and others who were in direct contact with Muslims learnt nothing about them, and only borrowed from them the arts of gracious living. For the rest, the Islamic orient was a source of phantasy, the Land of Cockayne, and the source of military antagonism. It is not the individual contents of knowledge that matter, but the conformation of contents, and this was oriented to a specific warring phantasy. In this, the truth of individual statements is incidental.

The overriding need was to speak ill, and knowledge of Islam was a kind of defensive ignorance. Referring to Islam, Guibert de Nogent said in the 12th century that "it is safe to speak evil of one whose malignity exceeds whatever ill can be spoken." Such evil as was and still is spoken in very tangible survivals of medievalism is not purely arbitrary. It belongs to a repertoire of images and aesthetic judgements—judgements of value. Every culture thrives on establishing difference from others, and pursues this establishment of savage difference with particular energy in situations of serious external conflict or internal flux and uncertainty. It is often repeated that Jews in Europe were considered as tokens of evil and as scapegoats for issues with which they had no connection. Yet it is Islam and other orientals in this tokenist mode which has been most pervasively construed as an emblem of repellent otherness—it is not for nothing that Moses Hess, an early Zionist, took offence from the remark made by Bruno Bauer that the Jews were orientals. For a person such as myself, whose vision of history is one of radical mutations, it is a strange matter indeed to observe such instances of an archetypal collective memory, of a dark areas of cultural life live with continuing folkloristic emblems—a study of recent Spanish clinical psychology, for instance, has revealed the pervasive and obsessive presence of the Moor in Spanish fantasies. This of course involves a process very commonly met with in psychological and ideological phenomena, the process of displacement, where one image stands for another to which it has a certain normative continuity, or where one image or name is substituted for another with which it shares a certain property—in this case, unspeakable evil and horror. It is in this same emblematic mode that hysterical reactions are almost automatically triggered off today by such virtually interchangeable tokens of evil as communism, Shi`ism, Islam, terrorism, Arabism, Qadhafi, the PLO, and a host of other phantasms nightly brought to our attention on television and in the other media, not to speak of fundamentalist Christians and media firebrands. Witness, for instance, the so-called Prophecies of Nosterdamus now in currency, where an apocalypsc is constructed from Qadhafi, the Soviet Union and anti-Zionism.

These persistent images are really less in direct continuity with the medieval image of the Saracen than mutant restatements of political and cultural antagonism. In the Middle Ages, they were born of the conflict between Islamic lands and Christendom—both before and after the Crusades, when Christendom became a unit of political thought, of geographical demarcation, and of cultural self-consciousness: the salient dates are the conquest of Sicily in 1060, the fall of Toledo in 1085 and the occupation of Jerusalem in 1099. Of this conflict were born the categories of Saracen and Moor. They, the observable instances of Islam, became the indices of a class of phenomena which are different, negative, fearsome. Orientalism, as a cultural mood and a component in a negative aesthetic repertoire, naturally had to be expressed in the prevailing literate cultural idiom of the times, and it is, therefore, not surprising that medieval orientalism represented Islam in terms of religious polemic, as religious idiom was the terrain where both antagonism and concord were encoded.

Thus, the Saracens were explained in terms of Biblical legend as being of Hagarene descent, and Muhammad was thought of as a cardinal with frustrated papal ambitions; earlier, he had been thought of as one god among others worshipped by the Saracens, which included Mars, Pluto, Apollo and what was termed Alkoran. In the plays and romances of the Middle Ages, Saracens came to be regarded as an index of repellent difference pure and simple. The term "Saracen" was applied indifferently to Muslims as to North European heathens, to Roman emperors, and to various disagreeable personalities in the Bible. William the Conqueror seems to have thought that he was engaged in battle with the Saracens of Britain. It is not surprising, in the light of this general indexical function that shaped the categories of orientalism that Muhammad should be endowed with sweeping evil universality. In Canto 28 of Dante's *Inferno*, he is relegated to the 8th of the nine circles of Hell, as a sower of schism and scandal, outdone in this by only Judas and Brutus.

Dante was a scholar; scholarship, in the Middle Ages as today, is inseparable from the cultural politics of its day, and knowledge never was, and will never be, an innocent endeavour, but was, and is, utterly sullied. Scholarship is the enunciation, in specialised terms for a specialised audience, of generally accepted principles which are, in scholarship, identified, concretized, categorized, ordered, and concatenated. Medieval scholars of Islam conceived it as a form of Arianism; most notably, it was thought of in terms of Biblical prophecy. Eulogius and Alvarus, not to speak of Nicetas, saw it as the preparation for the final appearance of the Antichrist, and such a view has been peculiarly resistant to time, change, rationality or progress. Duncan Black Macdonale, a jewel among orientalists, could still state in 1933 that Islam was a second-hand Arian heresy. In 1597, an English Catholic exiled to the Continent spoke of Calvino-Turkism, in response to which the Anglican Matthew Sutcliffe spoke of Turko-Papism. Such attitudes had noble precedents. John Wycliffe had already seen Islam as the name for evil within the Church, and Luther himself, in a foreword to the 1543 edition of William of Ketton's Latin Koran, had declared that, whereas the Pope was the head of the Antichrist, Islam was his body. Throughout the Reformation and well into the 19th century, Islam was seen as the lesser of the two horns of the ram made famous by the 8th Chapter of the Book of Daniel, the greater hornide -ntified with Pope. I myself witnessed such anti-Arab apocalyptic propaganda in Britain during the 1967 war. Hopeful crusading clercs even took heart from the appearance of Genghis Khan and his attack on Islamic domains; they saw in him a new David destined to fulfil the prophecies of Ezekiel.

Let me remind you again that these conceptions existed among the learned public despite exact scholarship. In the shadow of the defeated Crusades, the Council of Vienna had, in 1312, ratified ideas previously canvassed by Roger Bacon and Raymond Lulle, which called for the learning of Arabic—this was in keeping with the times, as the receding Crusades were giving way to another way of carrying on the war, by missionary effort. These attitudes persisted despite the fact that chairs of Arabic were established in Pairs and Oxford in 1539 and 1638; that the language was taught in Leiden from 1593; that the Arabic grammar of the Dutchman Erpenius and the dictionary of his student, Golius, existed from the early 17th century.

We are not talking of two separate types and domains of knowledge about Islam, one for the scholarly elect and another for the rude masses, but of the coexistence within orientalism of two substantially concordant registers, one of which—the scholarly—has greater access to observation, as I have already indicated, and which looks all the more abject for this. Regardless of access to real or specious facts, and facts are always constructed and their construction is invariably culture-specific, orientalist scholarship is a cultural mood born of a mythological classificatory lore, a visceral, savage division of the world, much like such partisanship as animates support for football clubs. As in all myth and in primitive logic, difference gives way to antithesis in a play of binary structures. All cultures operate in terms of antithetical typologies of culture and savagery, of normalcy and disnature. It is in terms of these structures that Islam and things Islamic are construed, categorized, divided, and connected, and it is such parameters that dictate the terms of discourse on things Islamic. It is quite inevitable that one's own culture is taken for the norm whose terms and whose language become the metalanguage of a cultural typology in which other cultures appear not merely as other, but as contrary. What happened during the long emergence of the bourgeois-capitalist order which Christendom became was that the evil which was Islam gradually became a wants, a deficiency in the natural order of things which was this order itself seen, from the Englightenment onwards, as the culmination of universal history. Islam, once evil vying with good, thus became an anachronism, a primitive stage in an emergent historicist notion of things.

This was certainly a derogation, and it was a derogation in terms of might. It was made possible by the actual superiority in terms of political, economic, and technical power, which the bourgeois-capitalist order came to feel as a result of its universal expansion. Fear of the Saracren, of the Moor, of the Turk, once "the terrible scourge of the world," gave way to contempt, and the Ottoman Empire was soon to become the Sick Man of Europe; but it also gave way to enjoyment, which had become politically and culturally possible. Let me indicate, though, that European collective representations were not all nightmarish—a prurient fascination with things Islamic had titillated the libido of medieval monks no less than that of Lady Mary Montagu and of Alexander Pope.

Exoticism, frivolous or aesthetic admiration, is of course premissed on an unreflected notion of utter otherness; it is a mode of consuming an object, of employing it for decorative and other purposes, in a context other than its own. Exoticism is a pleasant way of subjugating one's contrary, and ran closely parallel to the changing fortunes in the power relations between Europe and the domains of Islam. As early as 1454, at a banquet in Lille, a centrepiece of the entertainment was a tower carried on the back of an elephant led by a gigantic lurk. An art historian has spoken of the "oriental mode" in the work of Durer, Bellini, and others, and indeed this persists today in illustrated editions of the Bible. Turkish and Persian carpets were in great vogue in the 16th and 17th centuries. Later, Charles II of England adopted Persian dress in court, in order to stop imitating French courtly costume. Samuel Pepys recorded that the new garment was quickly discarded as the King of France promptly ordered his footmen to be similarly dressed. There were more durable results of this exoticism, the containment and enjoyment of the bizarre; Islamist oreientalism was to have a great artistic impact—I mention, at random, Marlowe's *Tamburlanie*, Goethe's *West-Ostlicher Diwan*, Mozart's *Entfuhrung aus dem Serail*, the art of Delacroix and Ingres, and the Brighton Pavilion. at close quarters, exoticism ceases to amuse and gives way to the barbarism that underpins it. Take, for example, the village of Ayn Hud in occupied Palestine; it is a village for Israeli artists, and its title to special exotic privilege is one of characteristic grossness; it is the fact that its colourful houses in which the artists live have been left as they were when their owners and inhabitants were driven out in 1948. In effect, the village is exotic in much the same way as lamp-shades made of human skin that citizens of another racialist regime are reputed to have manufactured.

Decorativeness is thus superimposed on subordination, one that is premissed on eradicating the reality of the exotic. There is hardly anything Moorish about Othello but for fatal magic handkerchief given to his mother by a witch, who was, incidentally, only Egyptian. Corneille criticized Racine for putting common Frenchmen in Turkish dress. This list can be extended at will. Otherness is always the context of deploying one's own concerns. Such was the admiration for Islam, however sullied and ambiguous, of, say, leibniz and Condorcet, who considered it to be a natural religion in contra-distinction to superstitious Christianity. Such is also the substance of artistic exoticism. For Durer or Bellini, oriental themes and images were no more than visual frames for the depiction of Biblical themes. The languid odalisques of Ingres are really derived from antique sculpture, and they are given an oriental context and texture by motifs derived from the writings of Lady Mary Montagu and Montesquieu. Ingres had never been further south than Italsy, and the same schematization in terms of genre and fancy is evident in 19th century "ethnographic" painting of the Middle East.

By the Enlightenment, therefore, Islam was no longer invariablly and necessarily evil. It had also become something bizarre, distant, occasionally ridiculous. It had become a deficient order of things, and an order of deficient things. Deficiency is, of course, a polemical notion. It implies a requisite completeness, a consummate plentitude, in relation to which deficiency is measured. But this involves not only measurement: the correct order of things causes others to be seen and judged in its terms and on its own terms. The discourse involved is one of contrasts, very much like the primitive logic that underlay medieval and early modern conceptions. Alongside the continuing contrast of good with evil, orthodox with heresy, moral probity with libertinism and sodomy, the Englightenment scheme of things required the presence of other players in this game, which it could call its own. These were reason, freedom, and perfectibility, the three inclusive categories of the present epoch. Along with this, the birth of modern orientalist scholarship in the Englightenment was accompanied by the secularization of the profession. Clerics gave way to traders, dilettantes, gentlemen of leisure, and to consuls. In the course of the 19th and 20th centuries, journalists took the place of the dilettantes, salaried academics that of gentlemen of leisure, while colonialists and sundry spies joined the ranks of all these categories. As scholarship always follows the flag, Napoleon's invasion of Egypt was accompained by an army of scholars who produced the monumental *Description de l' Egypte*, and the French invasion by Algeria led to a prodigious scholarly effort. The *Journal Asiatique* was founded in 1823, the *Journal of the Royal Asiatic*

Society in 1834, and the *Zeitschrift der deutschen morgenlandichen Gesellschaft* in 1849.

The polemical structure of modern orientalist discourse is precisely premissed on the definition of things Islamic in terms of contrasts of reason, freedom and perfectibility. These yielded three major characteristics of things Islamic and from the topical clusters thus generated can be derived all the topics of orientalism and of Islamic studies, in an essential form complete and hardly altered since the mid-19th century. Those of you who are familiar with orientalist Islamic scholarship will readily recognize these topics. To reason corresponded enthusiastic unreason, politically translated as fanaticism, a major concern of 19th century scholars as of today's television commentators. This notion provided an explanation for political and social antagonism to colonial and post-colonial rule, by reducing political and social movements to motivations humans share with animals. Montesquieu, Hegel, and many others saw Muslim politics as life in the whirlwind of fortune, and intensely sensuous life in which passion, that low manifestation of nature, reigns supreme. Such passion according to this paradigm has two outlets: fractious and predatory politics, or else vice. In both, we have an abstract enthusiasm. Energy in the secular world is geared towards negative purposes only and is incapable of setting up a mature political order. Thus politics of communities designated as Muslim are amorphous and infinitely pliable. Muslim cities are seen to be formless and fissiparous and Muslim conquests and movements directionless and utterly wild. Muslim history is an absurd succession of events, time without duration, described by dynasties which Hegel said were "destitute of organic firmness," which belong "to mere space." The corollary of this is a wretchedly dogmacentric life, a total abandonment of individuality to the exclusive worship of an abstract God. Another corollary to this, and the political analogue of this abject subjection of mind, will and person to God, is the subjection of individuality to collectivity, the oriental mirror-image of freedom and its antithesis. From the 18th century, this topic was designated as oriental despotism, the irredeemable, immediate and unbridgeable gap between total tyrannical power on the one hand, and anarchy on the other. This theme, developed by major thinkers like Montesquieu, has been applied by minor intellects to the study of Arabic and Islamic polities and political theory.

These two primary categories for the apprehension of things Islamic—unreason and servitude—posit Islam as a creature in diremption, as the unlikely coexistence of sheer animality on the one hand, and an abstract, hence forever forced and repressive, principle of order on the other. Nothing mediates the relation between the war of all against all on the one hand, and the Leviathan on the other; nothing mediates between God and the world; one of them only is triumphant at a given moment. Civil society, the realm where individual needs are rationally coordinated, and that which brings forth the state, is unthinkable. It is little wonder that a variation of this theme has come increasingly to prominence. This is a characteristically dismal orientalist adaptation of the social sciences, one which views clan, tribe, locality, sect, or ethnic group as a natural entity, one whose sole determinant is virtually a seminal pre-determination. It is at once a natural entity which refuses to be subdued by a higher principle of order such as the State, and a unit whose connection to its members is irrationally obligatory, and therefore despotic. Social groups, rather than be regarded in terms of sociological categories, are looked upon as no more than involutions upon some infra-historical essence which does not admit of historical study except in the most banal sense, an infra-historical order which is ever-present and which explains present day events. These groups—sects, ethnic groups, and other *dramatis personae* which populate orientalist discourse, which fill the pronouncements of experts and which come to us nightly on our television screens in stories of irrational carnage and outrage—are seen as irreducibly specific, hence naturally antagonistic, endowed with a congenital propensity to factionalism. Thus communalism, which is a very recent phenomenon, is thought to be primordial. The title under which this animal existence is officiated is "identity," a hugely mystifying notion of great incidence and preference in expert opinion. It is this pathetic notion which is responsible for much of the nonsense one hears about the supposedly primordial antagonisms of Lebanon, about the conflict between Arabs and Berbers or between sedentary and tribal folk which animated French colonial historiography of North Africa.

The third category out of which things Islamic were identified and categorized is perfectibility. In the course of the 19th century this term, though not its meaning, fell out of use and was absorbed in the wider senses of evolutionism and historicism. And indeed, the evolutionary schemata of world history, be they that of Condorcet, of Auguste Comte, of Hegel, Marx or of Herbert Spencer, as of such theories as underline development theory and the disastrous policies of the World Bank—all these theories can accommodate accounts of the specific differences which distinguish the oriental-Islamic from the occidental-normative. Normative and terminative correspond to one another in the evolutionist-historicist Eurocentric scheme: Islam, as anomaly, as a flaw, is seen to be an anachronism. Its characteristics—despotism, unreason, belief, stagnation, medievalism—belong to stages of history whose inferitority takes on a temporal dimension.

It is quite striking how the antithetical structures in terms of which Islam is apprehended run parallel to the manner in which teudalism has traditionally been regarded, and indeed the notion of primitivism shares many features with both the orient and feudalism. But over and above the explicit insertion of Islamic history within evolutionist schemes, such as the unusual position it occupies in Hegel's *Philosophy of History*, or the peripheral position to which it is relegated in terms of the Asiatic Mode of Production, the historicity of Islam in terms of the philosophy of progress has been dubious. No properties of things Islamic were seen as contributory to the topical thematics of progress and evolution. Islamic history was and still regarded as, at best, an accidental vehicle for the transmission of Greek learning to the West.

As for its proper historicity, it is regarded in terms not of progress, but of decline; it is seen as an irrational irruption onto the canvas of history, an irruption which, for those of a generous disposition, carried a number of creditable principles. But it could only decline. Its original irrationality is implicitly seen in terms of either a doctrinal or a racial inadequacy. On assuming power, on founding an empire, and sponging the wares of superior civilizations, this unworthy beginnings can only realize its nemesis by very rapid corruption, sensescence and atrophy. And this rapid fall is implicitly reducible to the discordance between the loftiness of which some generous scholars ascribe to Islam's original impulse, and the dead weight of the Muslim's original irrationalism, their animal enthusiasm, the abstractness of their power, the formlessness of their societies. Whatever is construed as itself rational never goes beyond the bounds of the singular event to which it relates. Islamic history thus becomes, at best, a ponderous tragedy, at worst a soap opera, and in all cases a mis-adventure. Decline thus becomes not a fact of the historical order, but a predictable event of the metaphysical order. Decline is here not essentially an historical fact, but is natural given the antithetical conception of Islam employed: the antithesis of normalcy and nature is anomaly and disnature. Decline becomes metaphysically necessary, a foregone conclusion underlined by an actual disparity in might. That racist stereotypes and historical justification are concordant comes as no surprise.

Such are the schemata according to which modern orientalism conceives things Islamic. They should be recognizable to anyone studying the standard textbooks. They did not, and still do not, appear as simply the products of a collective imagination steeled with colonialism. On the contrary, they appeared, and still appear, as the result of direct observation and of scholarly endeavour. What gave them this prerogative was another result of the Enlightenment, and the backbone of Islamic studies: this is philology. Let us not forget how this philology grew, what fecund intellects worked in its establishment, and to what simplistic degradations it was subjected by orientalist Arabic philology. It was not only an outgrowth of antiquarian research; its beginnings were a rich web of antiquarian learning, and of criticism of the Biblical text—Richard Simon's unconsummated work stands out, as does the more comprehensive albeit historically less influential work of Spinoza. Phiological work on Sanskrit and its later development into comparative Indo-European philology by Bopp are also crucial, as were the later momentous development on Biblical criticism and textual hermeneutics by the likes of Schleiermacher and, in a different direction, of Friedrich Strauss. The luxuriant writings of German romantic constructions are also germane. In general, philology sought, with Spinoza, the separation between the sense of a text and its truth, a truth which had been typologically or otherwise pre-given in traditional Biblical exegesis. Philology rested in its decipherment of the world in the example of Vico, for instance, not on irreducible difference, but in similarity, hence accessibility to understanding on the basis of a humanity commonly shared by the philologist and by his charges.

But altogether orientalist philology in its Islamic studies mode retained from this revolution in the historical sciences only two rudimentary elements. The first is the positivism of incipient philology—and I use "positivism" in the generic epistemological sense, without reference to evolutionist doctrine. Positivist philology was and is a discipline with a decidedly moralising stance, a somewhat devotional sanctimoniousness, one which was described by one of the greatest classical philologists of the 19th century in terms of asceticism and self-denial, which he contrasted with Nietzsche's *Birth of Tragedy*, a text which provoked the outburst I am quoting. Let us not forget that morality has no business in a world devoid of infamy, and that consequently the other side of this technicalist purity is technically accomplished fraud: in fact, the 18th and 19th centuries were the golden age of scientifically authenticated fraud. I need only remind you of Macpherson's Ossian, or Chatterton's medieval poetry, and of the Chronicle of richard of Cirencester, not to mention the Hitler diaries which received the highest historiographical expert authentication. These textual contrivances are of the same type as taxidermy, also perfected in the 19th century, and both taxidermy and positivist philology aspire to an ideal of the same order.

This pedantic aspect of positivist philology was not infrequently the object of ridicule; the original Larousse dictionary, for instance, stressed this matter, but equally underlined the value of the discipline. This resided, and still resides, in its pursuit of sense of a text; it is a sort of ethnography of the past. In the field of Arabic, the tone was set by Antoine Isaac Sylvestre de Sacy, the father of Arabic philology in the West, who brought the full burden of his Jansenism to bear on his material. In his work as in that of his numerous students and of subsequent generations, somewhat critical editions of Arabic works have been established, lexica produced, the main factual outlines of Islamic history sketched in Western languages, the manuscript holdings of various European libraries inventorized—a process which was incidentally accompanied by the plunder of libraries in Muslim lands. Positivist philology aims at the "scientific" study of texts, of the meanings of their words and sentences, of the referents to which the text belongs: these are, according to a standard 19th century textbook, historical facts, cultural life, religion, law and society.

This exactitude of information and of designation, which fired whatever spirit positivist philologists may have had, has animated by a typical Enlightenment motif, and was aimed at the seizure of the real without the intervention of passion. It is a form of vernacular realism. This realism does not yield the truth; it only yields discrete items of information, factoids, according to implicit criteria of selection was are fundamentally inhibitory, which work by a sort of censor principle not unlike that of the naturalistic novel. Naturalism is fundamentally a censor, a defence against passion, and positivist realism is essentially antiseptic. In the field of philology, it is the scholarly counterpart of bureaucratic rationality. It produces a disorganized array of these factoids according to a rudimentary principle of positivist epistemology, that the linguistic sign and the real signified can be made directly to correspond without any mediation—this view is contradicted, of course, by linguistic science, by cognitive psychology, and by the history of art.

Semantics thus gives way to an abstract lexicalism, and the infounded supposition is made that the meanings of words, of terms, of beliefs, of doctrines, no less than of dogmas, of texts, and of statements are univocal and can therefore be uncovered once their origin has been exposed. The cardinal principle in the face of which positivist phiology flies is an ancient principle of rhetoric, now brought back to prominence by linguistics and discourse analysis; namely, that all things that involve words have to deal with the technical problems of words. And the key to these is neither the lexicon nor the grammatical compendium, but the properties and rules of semantics, the structure of texts, the construction of discourse, the infinite resources of language, the rhetoric of meaning and reality, the boundless ambiguity of the text. No text has an intrinsic and univocal objectivity of meaning; it is always context-specific, internally and externally, and thus open only to structural analyses.

What positivism thus seeks to establish is not scientific knowledge, but naturalistic apprehension. Its entire project is based on the notion of verisimilitude which is ultimately a visual metaphor, and vision is, of course, the most primitive of cognitive means. Knowledge is modelled on a sensuous paradigm of immediacy, as a mimetic rendition of "reality" full of the concreteness of immediate life. Such a project in fact is far from a consummated naturalism, and is closer to the romantic notion of poetry, albeit unspeakably inferior to it.

Thus, positivist philology is a genetic mode of study, an indication by a term of it origin. I do not call it historical because it iacks the totalizing orientation of modern historical scholarships. It seeks to describe past events—words, occurrences, dogmas, or whatever—according to the famous but unremarkable and not very profound aphorism of Leopold van Ranke, that he wrote history "wie es eigentlich gewesen" a teasing phrase which, with or without justification, has come to embody the historiographical utopia of the 19th century. This genetic investigation seeks the explanation of things in terms of their origins, and produces inventories of correspondences which are then served up as casual chains : texts fragmented and their parts reduced to other texts, events explained by single antecedents, fragments of dogmas explained by scriptural fragments, totally without respect to the fact that, even if, let us say, dogmas are explicitly set out in terms of Scriptures, this does not mean they are derived from them except in the banal sense that a Scripture, like any other text, is almost infinitely interpretable, and universally deferred to. The true meaning of a text, by contrast, his historical: a text has no sense outside the various and contradictory traditions that appropriate it. Even fundamentalists invoke the original text to the exclusion of commentary in order to substitute their own novel glosses. No end in really prefigured in its beginning. The resulting picture is of scholarship which is almost entirely enumerative, enumerating instances of an origin and variations therefrom, a very extreme form of philosophical realism totally oblivious to the fact that, even if it were possible to identify origins, and this is a very dubious proposition, it is surely impossible to make an exhaustive inventory of beginnings and thus arrive at an approximation of the Truth—genetically conceived, of course. The event and the explanation of the event are therefore of the same order: the order of narrative is t the same time the order of explanation and comprehension; vision and reason are united in a poetic reverie in the guise of an exacting Phiological severity.

Thus, orientalist scholarship piles fact upon fact and date upon date in an order ostensibly blind to all but real succession. But this research is always geared towards the discovery of origin. It is not at all surprising that the over whelming volume of orientalist research into Islamic matters has investigated beginnings, historical beginnings and Koranic textual beginnings. It has claimed to find in these beginnings the fount, origin, and explanation of the whole sad story of Islamic history, institutions, societies and thought. From the Koran this scholarship has derived the principles of economic life and the supposed failure of capitalism. From the same text it seeks to explain the actual source of history. From the principle of *jihad*, holy war, one of the most eminent orientalists in Britain derived all political activity in India, Turkey, the Levant, Iran, Spain, and the Sudan over twelve hundred years. From the conflict of 'Ali and Mu'awiyah, orientalist scholarship seeks to explain the war between Iran and Iraq. If you looked at the "explanations" of the Iranian revolution and of the Iran-Iraq war, you would find yourselves in the company of much discussion of the so-called "martyrdom complex" of Shi'ism, of the death, nearly 1400 years ago, of Husayn. You will find hardly any discussion of Iranian history over the past 100 years or so. Islamic studies is thus a cluster of pseudo-casual chains. These chains are meant eventually to be reducible to the irreducible essence of Islam, which really performs an explanatory function very much akin to that of Phlogiston in 18th century chemistry. The result is that elusive origins are sought, and the actual course, outcome, institutions and processes of Islamic history and culture are ignored except under the metaphysical auspices of the study of "decline."

This is of course a retrospective construction, a casting of the origin in the light of subsequent events, which flies in the face of the most elementary principles of historical scholarship. Scholars working in this field have always sanctimoniously claimed objectivity; yet their procedure is imbued with a vast meta-historical principle, an origin of origins, the pseudo-cause of other pseudo-causes, which is presupposed in Islamic studies. An irreducible substance is posited, one to which all occurrences in Islamic history are reducible—other occurrences are decreed anomalous and of non-Islamic origin. What we witness is not a genuinely barren agnosticism, in which many orientalists take pride, what we find is not literally a display of what Croce called the "sumptuous ignorance" of philological history, nor simply what Lord Action praised as "colourless" writing. What are at play in the naturalism of Islamic studies, in the censor principle mentioned, are enunciations which are not formless, nor simply polemical and directed outwards, nor again devoid of passion. Islamist discourse is thoroughly and irredeemably structured by implicit ideological notions, notions which identify things as Islamic, as original, and which organize the world of things Islamic in terms of European imagination, and of the colonialist and neo-colonialist meanagement of the world. It is not only that the unreflected and uncritical ssortment of factoids must be the victim of implicit ideologies, folkloristic images, and racist stereotypes. These facts have to be identified as relevant. others have to be rejected as irrelevant, sequences of putative influence have to be judged as plausible, other as unthinkable, all in the name of the naturalistic mode.

History is, thus, captive to metahistorical schemata; it is structured by a poetics, according to the terms of Hegel's analysis of history, epic and poetry in the third book of his *Aesthetics*. It is structured by the three metahistorical notions I spoke of: unreason, despotism, and backwardness. Each is in fact a class of topics, of criteria of selection, and of relevance, and together they set the boundaries of that which is thinkable. It is assumed that there are a number of intrinsic substantive qualities which characterized a changeless, or only superficially changeable *homo islamicus*: a creature born of distance, not only of the antithetical distance I have spoken of, but of the accompanying political established by colonialism.

I have already spoken about the character of this *homo islamicus*, of how he is defined by the inversion of the three cardinal notions through which the bourgeois-capitalist epoch conceives of itself: reason, freedom and perfectibility. To this schematization of the self corresponds the schematism of the other. Each of these-schemata is a topic which is invariably called forth to schematize things that are observed Islamic. Thus, there are "Islamic cities" unlike all other cities, "Islamic economies" to which economic reason is inapplicable, "Islamic polities" impenetrable to social sciences and political sense, "Islamic history" to which the normal equipment of historical research is not applied. Facts are dissociated from their historical, social, cultural and other contexts, and reduced to this substantive Islamism of the European imagination. Accurate detail becomes local colour, a mere enhancement of naturalism, a "reality-effect." This is why orientalism in its Islamist mode is a mode of perception and apprehenson, not of knowledge. It identifies things as Islamic, and does not know them as historical. It names things as Islamic, and at the same stroke endows them with the changeless and ageless characteristics of the *homo islamicus*. This is another reason why Islamic studies is, as I have already said, exhaustively enumerative: the identification of things as Islamic by their reduction to a textual Islamic origin is what it considers to be its proper task. Things Islamic, when so identified with reference, add nothing to their origin. They have no specificity defined in terms of their historical circumstances and apart from the metahistorical specificity of their origin. This accounts incidentally for the dull repetitiveness which many scholars believe they see in Islamic history; it accounts even more so for the implicit uneventfulness and lack of real change in which is premissed this genetic study, this egraded form of historicism. All in all, things Islamic are uniform, indistinct, isomorphous. This is, of course, a thoroughly unhistorical view. Revolutioanry Iran is as far from Saudi Arabia as 10th century Islam in Spain is distinct from contemporary Iran. One needs to substitute "Christianity" for "Islam" to see how ridiculous the picture will look: it is true that Bantu messianism and revolutionary Nicaraguan Jesuitism are both Christian. But this is a far cry from assuming their essential identity, or from assuming their indistinctness except in appearance from say, atavistic Catholicism in Poland or the politics of the Rev. Ian Paisley, or for that matter, from Maronitist politics in Lebanon. Anyone who assertes the essential identity of Cathars, Flagellants, Rasputin, and the Dutch Reformed Church will surely be pronounced mad. Euroepan scholars of Islam are in a strange league with Muslim fundamentalism. Both espouse a savage essentialism, a changeless a historical irreducibility, a mythical "real" Islam independent of time and existent only at the beginning of things Islamic and at its pristine fount. Both insist that a rigourist form of religiosity is the characteristic, the real, of which Islam is in places as different as 20th century Turkey and 10th century Canton are mere avatars, any difference between these two Islams, or between aspects of them and the supposed pristine condition, is relegated to mere incidentals. Both fundamentalism and orientalism therefore eliminate the major part of history: rigourist fundamentalism was only very seldom espoused, and always by very small minorities, and the historical reality of Islam, as of other religions, is the normal course of events in which fundamentalist moments are incidental. One cannot use the brand of Christianity propagated by the Rev. Jerry Falwell as an explanatory principle with which to unravel the reality of Philip II's Most Catholic dominion. Fundamentalists realize the wildest fantasies of orientalism; for the former, as for the latter, the striving is for a myth of origin.

Yet the Islamism of things Islamic is only convincing because it is a classificatory token upon which scholarship is superimposed, a token of political and cultural otherness. In this otherness, things are levelled for ideological convenience. Things Islamic, therefore, duplicate each other. Studies have shown how this takes place, how the structures of society duplicate those of theology, how theology structurally duplicates the essential features of despotic devotions, how these themselves duplicate the structures of power and of morality, how the whole of history is deployed to show the changeless integrity of the *homo islamicus*. Orientalist discourse on Islam indeed presents it through "a set of representative figures" a vocabulary and a repertoire of plastic images which are invariably encountered—much like the reperotire of plots, textual units and their permutations which account for the repetitiveness of science fiction, folk tales and pornography. All that cannot be made liable to reduction to these topics and notions of orientalist Islam is denied to Islam: thus Arab-Islamic philosophy is seen as only nominally so; Sufism, spiritually rich, is forced into the modes of heresy and non-Islamic provenance; the celebrated Ibn Khaldun was made into a precursor of positivism and other European doctrines, or, in extreme cases, a representative of the Berbero-European anti-Arab spirit, all by virtue of his supposed modernity. Indeed, virtually the whole of Muslim intellectual history is written in terms of a supposed conflict between Reason and Belief, the one foreign and the other native. This is not really very different from certain medieval process of throught: some of you might know that medieval writers, in awe of and in admiration for Saladin, explained his excellence by asserting that his mother was one Countess of Pontieu.

In effect, the orientalist rendition of Islam is only putatively historical. The rejection by traditional orientalist scholarship, as by 19th century historical and philological scholarship, of what it termed "speculation" is really the counterpart of this. It was only natural that emergent disciplines should distance themselves from others; the 19th century was the professionalisation of history, and the attempt to suppress its rhetorical status. Chairs of history were established in Berlin in 1810 and in Paris in 1812, but in Britain it was only in 1866 that a chair of history was established at Oxford. Great historians like Guizot and Michelet were dismissed for teaching "ideas" rather than "facts." But one can clearly see that the rejection of positivism, idealism, and romanticism in 19th century historiography and orientalist philology was nominal and institutional, not conceptual. Orientalist philology, as I have tried to show, is nothing but thoroughly structured by positivist epistemology and an essentialist category of Islam. Instead of the antiquarianist ideal, the result of this is the enemy of antiquarianism, what it derisively termed *histoire romanesque*.

Thus, in the orientalist study of Islam are aborted both the full possibilities of positivism and of historical study. The possibilities of positivism are aborted because the field of relevant facts is severely circumscribed, and the facts themselves severely schematized. The possibilities of historical study are aborted because of the genuinely a historical character of the genetic reductionism I have spoken of. Historicism is used antithetically; it does not seek to look for genuine changes and transformations, to chart the course of history, but to fix distance, to affirm the Islamism of Islamic history, i.e., to reduce it to its schematized metahistorical components, which affirm the antithetical difference of things Islamic from things normal. This is why orientalist Islamic studies have been so peculiarly resistant to the acquisitions and advances of modern historical, including social, sciences and to the normal procedures of phiological and historical study today. This is also why many of my fellow professionals in this field work on history in total oblivion of historical methodology, or literature in total innocence of critical theory or even any inclination to literature, on grammar with hardly any awareness of linguistics. This is so much the case that there is hardly any perceptible change in the essential categorical, thematic, and conceptual baggage of Islamic studies in more than a century; works supersede each other only by the addition of detail. But the features I have outlined, and the profound anti-intellectualism which animates the profession of Islamic studies, are essential for the survival of Islam as a category of orientalist discourse. The profession lumbers on with the disquieting confidence of its anti-intellectualism. It is still not unusual to take such library skills as are requisite in the edition of manuscripts and the collation of sources to be adequate indications of consummate scholarship. It is equally unusual in view of this involuted cultural homelines to regard some form of contact with Muslim countries to be adequate for intellectual mastery of the area, and thus to hold experience as an adequate substitute for study and exposure to Islam as perfect substitutes for scholarship. Not at all unlike sympathetic magic, contagion is seen as the cause of effectiveness, and partial contiguity in space is taken for mastery of the whole. Again, not unlike magic, this is a technique of control, Expertise in Islamic or Middle Eastern matters is, thus, unrelated to learning; learning is one thing, and expertise is quite another matter, connected less with knowledge than with belonging to particular circles which politicians and businessmen endow with oracular qualities, less because of reliability than because of a unity of practical purpose—diplomacy, war, subversion and profit with the occasional tinge of romanticism. The context of practical expertise in which studies of Islam and of the Middle East find themselves is premissed on the protean quality of Islam I have spoken of, and can only be preserved with the systematic resistance of the discipline to the present conditions and requirements of historical and sociological scholarship.

The Islam of Islamic studies is not "out there," but is a politico-cultural canon. Without it, many people would find themselves out of a job.

Thus, abandoned to the native intelligence, to folkloristic images, to a spurious notion of objectivity, the very premises of Islamic studies are radically and thoroughly unsound; their very foundation, the identification and the construal of relevant facts, is based upon a political and cultural imagination. This corresponds to what has been called the "intoxicating Orient of the mind," a "state between dreaming and waking where there is no logic—to keep the elements of our memory from attracting each other into their natural combinations." Thus, the only possible attitude for historical scholarship towards the entire tradition of European Islamic studies is one of a very radical scepticism. One may be preapred to accept some bibliographical and text-critical results of this tradition. But any proper writing of Islamic history has to rest on the dissolution of Islam as an orientalist category. It will have to start with putting into question the very notion of objectivity itself—or rather, to regard it as an historical category and discursive problem. It will have to come to terms with the great intellectual revolution inaugurated by Marx. It will have to take account of the fact that narrative, born out of fiction, myth and epic, is on the wane in the study of history, and that not reality, but intelligibility is the cornerstone of moddern historical scholarship. It will have to take full account of the discovery of historical discontinuity and bear out the consequences thereof, as of the rejection of "origin." Full account has, moreover, to be taken of modern philology and rhetoric, and the simplifications of notions such as "influence," and gear itself towards "fields of sense" and associated categories and towards the acquisitions of modern critical theory as in the work of Benjamin, Frye, Barthes and others and the theory of discursive formations. It has to liberate itself from Islam, and scrutinize Islamic histories, societies, economies, temporalities, cultures and sciences with the aid of history, of economics, of sociology, ciritical theory and anthropology. Only then will Islam be disassociated, and reconstituted as historical categories amenable to historical study. In this, positivist philological research is axial. But this is only in the sense that it is to be presupposed: like literacy, it is the elementary beginning, not the end of research and study.

REFERENCES

1. N Daniel, *Islam and the West*, Edinburgh, 1960.
2. R W Southern, *Western views of Islam in the middle ages*, Cambridge, 1962.
3. D Metlitzki, *The matter of Araby in medieval England*, New Haven.
4. B P Smith, *Islam in English literature*, Delmar, 1977.
5. E W Said, *Orientalism*, London, 1978.
6. E W Said, *Covering Islam*, London, 1981.
7. M Rodinson, "The western image and western studies of Islam", in *The Leagcy of Islam*, ed. J. Schacht and E Bosworth, Oxford, 1974.
8. A Laroui, "The Arabs and cultural anthropology: Notes on the method of Gustav von Gruenbaum" in Idem, *The Crisis of the Arab Intellectual*, Berkeley, 1976.
9. My article, "The articulation of orientalism," *Arab Studies Quarterly*, 3 (1981), pp. 384-402.
10. T F Glick, *Islamic and Christian Spain in the Early Middle Ages*, Princeton, 1979.
11. D. B. Macdonald, "Whither Islam?", *Muslim World*, 23 (1933).

Revised and edited; originally published in Islamic Culture, Jan. 1987.

2

Philosophus Autodidactus: Lineage and Perspective

SAMI S. HAWI

(Abstract: While clearing Ibn Tufayl's thought of some misinterpretations to which it was subjected in this connection, I shall argue and explain that a comparative analysis of tales preceding *Philosophus Autodidactus* will show that the Andalusian philosopher did not adopt the philosophic ideas underlying these tales. At most he seems to have adopted the names of his characters from Avicenna's recitals and nothing more. Any attempt to find more significant resemblances between the two authors in this respect is, in my view, an overplay of scholarship).

A. Preliminary—The Question of its Originality

(i) An Evaluation of Gauthier's Position

The patient vigilance and skill of a scientist, refined by artistic vision and poetic genius, are the stuff of which Ibn Tufayl composed his *Philosophus Autodidactus*. He had studied and assimilated most branches of knowledge of his times; he invested this rich knowledge in this work and fashioned it into an organically knit synthesis which, besides its encyclopedic character bore the marks of his originality and revealed his own philosophic understanding of things.

Ibn Tufayl's ideas, like the ideas of most thinkers, are historically conditioned by the cultural and philosophic categories of his age. But if these ideas distinctly show elements of the thought of his predecessors, it does not necessarily follow that he is not philosophically creative. The fact that he adopts, mentions and quotes sympathetically from the works of other Muslim philosophers does not properly permit one to construe such a work as *Philosophus Autodidactus* merely as an amplification and elaborate exposition of the thought of his times.

For instance, Leon Gauthier does not seem to consider Ibn Tufayl's work original. This may explain why, despite his outstanding scholarship, he did not carry out of serious philosophical analysis of *Havy Bin Taqzan*: "Ibn Thofail n'a jamais vise une veritable originalite philosophique." Gauthier supports his points by noting that Ibn Tufayl indicates at the end of his Introduction that he borrowed his doctrines from al-Ghazzali, Avicenna and his contemporaries: "... qu'il emprunte le fond de ses doctrines a El-Ghazzali, Avicenna et accessoirement, a des philosophes recents de moindre importance." In my opinion Gauthier misunderstood the whole point and translated certain key passages from Arabic wrongly. Ibn Tufavl does not say that he borrowed (*emprunte*) his ideas. These are Ibn Tufayl's words:

> "The purity of the truth and the scope of the knowledge we possess have been attained by carefully pursuing (*tatabbu'*) the arguments of al-Ghazzali and Avicenna, checking them one against the other, and comparing the results with the views which have appeared in our own times... until the truth became clear to us, first by critical examination and theory, and now by some brief taste of it (truth) through (mystical) experience."

Thus, it is clear from this passage that Ibn Tufayl is telling us that he pursued and compared the discussions of al-Ghazzali and Avicenna until he was able to find "clearly" the truth for himself. "...Then we found ourselves competent to set down a view to be preserved in our name..." Accordingly, Ibn Tufayl did not "borrow" his ideas from al-Ghazzali and Avicenna, or acknowledge that he is only presenting the views of these thinkers in his work. The utmost that one can infer from his words is that the two thinkers had a definite influence on his thought. The works of al-Ghazzali, Avicenna and others served him better to find the truth and to express his own independent view of things. After all, didn't Aristotle and Avicenna do the same thing with their predecessors? This process is necessary for whoever wants to apply himself to the search for truth. Gauthier's statements, therefore, cannot be accepted as a fair judgment of Ibn Tufayl's work.

The passage also shows that Ibn Tufayl does not abandon us to a state of darkness and wonder as to his historical and philosophic sources. His method of systematic examination and criticism, and the candour with which he acknowledges his sources must fairly be considered to his credit, not as a mark of unoriginality. His Introduction, which must be considered an integral part of his work, imbues the latter with philosophical seriousness and methodical value. Had he not written this, a great amount of scholarly labour and historical investigation would have been required to trace the historical and intellectual threads with which *Hayy Bin Yaqzan* was uniquely woven. Thus, it was Ibn Tufayl's sincere and imaginative intellect in its search for truth and in its bold attempts to comprehend the mystery underlying the myriad natural and transcendental episodes that led him to a patient and critical study of al-Farabi, al-Ghazzali, Avicenna and Ibn Bajja. He mentioned their works, and confidently stated that he benefited from them. But in so doing he did not admit any lack of originality and an utter dependence on their thought as Gauthier and others would have us believe. Appearances should not deceive: Ibn Tufayl was large enough to realise the worth of methods employed by philosophers who preceded him. He did not, for instance, hesitate to use the names of characters from tales by Avicenna, nor did he hesitate to tell us that in *Hayy Bin Taqzan* he intended to present the secrets of "illuminative philosophy" mentioned by Avicenna. But in all this he took care to leave room for his own thought, by *not* saying that he intended to disclose the secrets of illuminative philosophy *exactly* as Avicenna described them. Ibn Tufayl's work shows a meticulous skill and a competent command of terminology. Such a philosopher does not employ a term or construct a sentence without knowing very well what he means by it or what function it performs in his conception of things.

(ii) The Sense in which Ibn Tufayl's Work may be considered Original:

However, in claiming that *Philosophus Autodidactus* is an original work one should have a distinct idea of what "originality" means. For one thing, in this connection it does not mean that the whole work leaped out of Ibn Tufayl's mind in its present form, *ex nihilo*, as it were. As it is in nature, so it is in thought; there is no creation from absolute nothing nor are there wide gaps in the long line of intellectual creativity. This is rarely a discontinuous process. Philosophic insights develop gradually as a result of contributions by many minds over a considerable period of time.

"Originality" of any intellectual or material product denotes one of two things: discovery or invention. A "discovery" is the result of obtaining knowledge of some existing entity that has not previously been perceived. Vitamines and viruses were discovered, not invented; whereas an invention is a modification or fusion of pre-existent ideas, insights, practices, so as to generate a different form of ideas or action. In this sense one ought therefore to deal with altered patterns of thought and action. In is in this latter sense that Ibn Tufayl's work on the whole can be considered original.

Consequently, it is natural to perceive a long lineage of tales and philosophical thought preceding Hayy Bin Taqzan, and Ibn Tufayl draws out attention to this fact. He had no scruples in adopting one of these tales and many of these philosophical ideas. At first Ibn Tufayl followed the traditional elements available to him. However, when his ideas reached a critical point, his own philosophic and creative impulses began to flow brilliantly.

Of course, he modified and expanded the inherited elements to suit his purpose; after all, didn't Plato and Shakespeare transform events and characters to conform to their scheme? What would remain of the Shakespearian Brutus and Marc Antony if we shrank them to their historical dimensions? What would remain of Plato's Socrates if we stripped him of the intellectual fluidity and artistic genius of Plato? It is easy to recognize the nature and source of the stones of a beautiful building, but it is hard to recapture and creativity of the architect who combined them into their present form.

Thus, the substances of which *Philosophus Autodidactus* is made is a matter not of absolute novelty but of a unique creative synthesis by a mind that dared to face the consequences of its reasoning and of its concrete observations, and to utilise the facts already known.

From the preceding remarks one can infer the following:

(a) In his work Ibn Tufayl utilised and fused significant elements of the thought of former philosophers.

(b) Ibn Tufayl derived the characters of *hayy Bin Taqzan* from antecedent literature. He employed these characters to express his own views.

Since I have treated point (a) at length elsewhere, I shall here develop point (b).

B. Use of a Tale, Fiction or Allegory

(i) The Employment of Tales and Man's Adaptation to the Environment:

As was remarked earlier, Ibn Tufayl informs us that he adopted the names of his characters from the Sheikh Master Abu 'Ali Ibn Sina (Avicenna). The names of Asal, Salaman, and Hayy Bin Yaqzan were used by Avicenna in two different recitals. However, neither Avicenna's nor Ibn Tufayl's employment of them is entirely novel.

Man, instinctively, perhaps, used an allegorical interpretation of phenomena long before the inception of pure philosophic and scientific thought. That imagination is the inexhaustible source of inspiration for all human endeavour is nowadays regarded as an incontrovertible fact. It is the bedrock and substance from which all novelties spring, be they artistic, religious, philosophic, or otherwise.

People of early antiquity were confronted with the struggle for existence and the necessity of adapting themselves to their environment, and, when faced with the many puzzling phenomena that their "understanding" could not analyse, their imagination came to the rescue. With the aid of imagination they could devise plans to satisfy their practical needs and better their lives; they could also lessen their awe and perplexity by bringing imagination into play. They observed thunder and rain, the changes of seasons; they rebelled against mischief inflicted by humans on humans, they were gratified by good deeds. Man's physical and intellectual adjustment to his environment and that of the environment to him was a labourious and painful process which he sought to mitigate. Consequently, poetry, myths, tales and religions were created, instrumental to his intellectual satisfaction and psychological needs.

Burdened with man's dual nature, good and evil, the early Greeks, for instance, established the cult of Dionysus. Originally a deity of wine, intoxication and fertility, Dionysus was brought from Northern Greece to Thebes, where his cult was elaborated and imbued with sophisticated theology. Fathered by Zeus, he was slain and devoured by the evil Titans. But his heart was saved; this Zeus at and begot him again from a human mother. Dionysus was now proclaimed by Zeus the Lord of the World, and the source of life and death. Zeus then murdered the Titans by a thunderbolt and created Man from their ashes. Consequently, man is a duality of "good" and "evil", his body composed of the evil element of the Titans and his soul of the divine and immortal fragments of Dionysus. This theme that the body is base, a means of man's bondage and that the soul is divine, a means of man's liberation and access to divinity, rang through the entire heritage of Greek and Christian philosophy and still reverberates in the literature of modern times.

Thus Ibn Tufayl's background rests upon *a primitive archetype of creativity founded in one of the most intimate aspects of man's nature in responding to environmental episodes* Rationality is not man's only basic differential. He is essentially an animal "symblicum":

in responding to stimuli man uses speech, symbols, fiction, science, and religion.

Cassirer points out that man's understanding of the environment and his response to different stimuli are different from those of the other primates in that man's responses can be integrated, controlled, slowed down or enhanced voluntarily: while in the primate kingdom the recoil to stimuli is mechanical, immediate and most often guided by the tyranny of instinct. The heart of this interiorised and controlled process in man's source of conceptual understanding, poetic vision, formation of narratives, and origination of scientific hypotheses. In this process lies the impulse behind such works as *Hayy Bin Taqzan,* Plato's *Phaedo*, Goethe's *Faust*, and Kant's *Critique of Pure Reason.* Hence the apparent narrative from of *Hayy Bin Taqzan* belongs to a whole species of similar philosophic and poetic creative works that came before and after it.

(ii) The Hellenic Tradition

For instance, the preceding discussion brings to mind the modes of writing in which the Presocratic philosophers gave expression to their ideas. Xenophanes, Parmenides, Empedocles and the Pythagoreans used explanatory narratives and myths in imparting knowledge. In their response to surrounding phenomena, their imaginative insights and intellectual apprehensions were integrated and then disseminated in narrative and allegorical form. For example, Parmenides begins his Way of Truth with an attractive allegorical introduction in which his poetic vision carries him on a steed to an imaginary place nearest to his heart's desire; a goodness takes him in her right hand and leads him to learn the well-rounded truth that lies far "from the beaten track of men." After his imaginative tale Parmenides presents his views by means of a series of unprecedented logical deductions.

Similarly, Ibn Tufayl's imagination takes him to an island with a most temperate climate near the equator where men are born without fathers or mothers. Finishing his imaginary account, Ibn Tufayl provides us with rigorous inductive and deductive inferences about Hayy's progressive knowledge of nature.

With Pythagoras and the Pythagoreans the story is not much different. Pythagoras cloaked his teachings of mathematics with Orphic practices and legendary themes. His followers made of him a legendary figure and attributed to him all their scientific and religious knowledge, whereas Ibn Tufayl ascribed the whole history of *Hayy Bin Yaqzan*, overflowing with all his profuse knowledge of science, philosophy and theology, to his "blessed and good ancestors."

These instances of expressing fact through fiction point to one inescapable and significant conclusion: Parmenides, the Pythagoreans and Ibn Tufayl *did not acknowledge the allegories or poetic medium to be of their own creation.* They are their and not theirs at the same time. Considered this way the narrative form plays a double function: on the one hand it dramatically emphasises the detached and objective truth of their doctrines and shows that these doctrines, judged by other minds, are found tenable and true; on the other, it constitutes a good strategy for the writer in conditions of stress or intolerance by permitting him to repudiate his views at will and consequently relieves him of possible social and political repercussions.

In addition to the Presocratics, Plato's extensive use of allegories and myths cannot be overlooked. His dialogues, especially the early ones, most frequently end without a positive statements as to what Plato himself believed. His dialectic drama, in which the dynamic and rich display of ideas takes place, is effected by his characters as living personalities who appear to speak for themselves about individual views of life and who acquire a being independent of their author. In the same manner, bearing important differences in mind, Ibn Tufayl's characters, Hayy, Asal, and Salaman, appear to be invested with independent personalities, each having an outlook to life quite different from that of his author. Thus there seems to be an implied attempt by both Plato and Ibn Tufayl to disown their characters.

With Plato this attempt in much more pronounced than with the Presocratics or Ibn Tufayl. For instance, when the rational discursive discussion reaches its apex, Plato normally continues on another level, that of fable and myth: "... I am certain that this (tale) is not an invention of my own..." says Plato's Socrates. Plato may ascribe the story to "The Wise"—under such a name he refers to the Pythagoreans or, as in the *Republic*, to "... a sort of Phoenician tale; something that has happened era now in many parts of the world..." In the *Laws* the myth is a tale we have received from the "Sidonian Cadmus." Most important is Plato's attribution of his ideas to the mind of this Master, Socrates.

This resemblance in narration and origination of Plato's myth to the beginning of Ibn tufayl's account of Hayy Bin Yaqzan may be a matter of chance and free association; but the fact that Muslim philosophers before Ibn Tufayl had translated, commented upon and assimilated a tremendous amount of Greek philosophy brings to mind the *possible* influence of Plato of Ibn Tufayl. If however, this resemblance is not due to a direct influence it may have been indirect through the work of Muslim masters.

Furthermore, the consequences of the moral of the Allegory of the Cave introduced in the *Republic* draw Ibn Tufayl nearer to Plato than is ordinarily assumed. Man's imprisonment in the world of shadows, the tyranny and dictates of the senses, make human enlightenment and salvation slow, difficult and distressing. Hayy Bin Taqzan's ascension, the release of his soul from the bonds of his "animal faith" and from the darkness of his immediate and instinctive needs, was no less perplexing and painful. The sudden death of the roe compelled him to search in anguish for the immediate cause: an initial link in the long chain of causes leading to the almighty One. In the Cave the rescuer was a man, a kind of Hayy, who was painfully dragged through the long rugged path, losing his ignorance and cognitive daze, to reach the company of the sunlight and its illuminated entities. After discovering God, to his great pleasure, Hayy contemplated His Beauty, Glory and Joy and turned away his attention from heavenly bodies and earthly things: for it these God appeared "like the forms of the Sun shining in rippling water."

Hayy was determined to gaze directly into the sun, where "he caught sight of himself as a disembodied subject." Plato's released prisoner, on the other hand, was able to last to look at the sun and contemplate its nature, not as it appears when reflected in water or an alien medium, but as it is in its own domain. This contemplation gave him everlasting happiness and produced in him pity for his imprisoned companions. After his long journey Hayy saw himself as a disembodied being while Plato's prisoner, guided by a human rescuer, a kind of Socrates, finally beheld the charm and beauty of the disembodied world—the Ideas.

This distinct and significant resemblance between Plato's Allegory of the Cave and Ibn Tufayl's *Hayy Bin Yaqzan* does not stop at this point. Plato laid necessary imperatives on all human "prisoners" in the "bigger cave," the world, to study ten years of mathematics before discussing moral ideas and ascending through them to the world of Forms. If their intellect had not been trained in this manner, Plato's prisoners would have drifted into the yawning chasm of illusion. Ibn Tufayl allowed Hayy fourteen years—from age twenty-one to thirty-five of training in strict observation and abstract reasoning before he was able to shatter his dream world and unenlightenment and reach the immaterial Agent. Only men of Hayy's caliber or that of Asal are allowed to think of things the way they really are. Ordinary men such as Salaman, in the lowest stages of cognition, should learn through parables and the projection of images, otherwise they land in error.

Furthermore, Plato's released prisoner was mocked and laughed at when he went down again to the darkness of the Cave, painfully attempting to educate his friends; they resented him and if they had been able to lay their hand on him they would have killed him. Hayy's attempts to do the same in Asal's inhabited island were no more successful. Both Hayy and Plato's former prisoner became extremely reluctant to manage the affairs of men and retreated to the contemplation of the truth alone.

Also, the mastery of mathematics alone does not lead us to an intuitive face-to-face confrontation with the Good which Plato sought; similarly Ibn Tufayl introduces his original metaphor of the blind man to demonstrably affirm this fact. This knowledge of the natural world acquired through inferences and syllogistic deductions compared to the intuitive knowledge of the sublime truth is, according to Ibn Tufayl, like the knowledge of a town acquired by a blind man. By practice and training the blind man learns to recognise houses and landmarks well enough to stroll through the city without a guide. Now if his sight were restored the would walk the town without finding any contradictions to what he had previously believed, but there would be two profound changes, the one conjoined to the other: great vividness and tremendous joy.

Thus if one cannot establish a direct historical relationship between the Andalusian philosopher and the Athenian sage, it is still worthwhile observing the profound affinity between *Hayy Bin Yaqzan* and Plato's diffusion of myths, notably that of the Allegory of the Cave. Of course, employing a story form undermines neither the quality of the writings nor the originality of the thought of either philosopher. Even Aristotle maintains that "... the lover of myths is in a way of lover of wisdom; for myth is made up of wonders."

(iii) The Muslim Tradition

Thus far, this inquiry has been directed to the possible factors behind the origination of tales and myths and their employment by the presocratics and Plato for disseminating philosophic ideas. These tales, together with Ibn Tufayl's, were discussed *only as media independent of their doctrinal commitments*. The latter were dwelt upon in passing only to elicit the former.

A closer look at the more immediate lineage preceding Ibn Tufayl's story in the Arab Muslim tradition reveals that simply as an idea and a tale it was not entirely new. It is found in skeletal non-philosophical form in an old Arabic tale of Iskandar (Alexander) dhul-Qarnain and also in a story mentioned by Hunain Bin Ishaq. Later than these two version are Avicenna's recitals of *Hayy Bin Yaqzan* and *Asal and Salaman*. A comparative analysis of these tales will show that apart from the names of his characters Ibn Tufayl did not adopt the ideas embedded in the stories preceding him. This analysis will also show that Avicenna's recitals are not entirely his own creation. Arab folkloric tales and Hellenic elements were the source. Ibn Tufayl seems to have adopted the names and nothing more from Avicenna.

a. The Story of Iskandar dhul-Qarnain

This story seems to be much older than Hunain's or Avicenna's. Garcia Gomez carried his study of the tale to the third century B.C. He came across a tale found among the manuscripts in the Escorial which in his opinion could be the original source of the story form of Ibn Tufayl's *Hayy Bin Taqzan* and Avicenna's two tales. One aspect is slightly similar to Ibn Tufayl's story; the rest is entirely different.

In essence the tale has two main aspects: the story of Alexander dhul-Qarnain, and the story of the Idol, the King and his Daughter. It is this second part that is relevant to our discussion: it tells how Alexander reached as island where he found an impressive idol bearing an inscription. When a learned man deciphered the inscription Alexander discovered that it told the story of the man in whose memory the idol was erected. This man, the son of a king's daughter, had been cast upon his birth into the sea; by some miracle the waves carried him to an island where a roe picked him up and took care of him. The boy grew up without achieving philosophical wisdom or mystical knowledge, until a man came to the island and taught him the habits, ideas, and knowledge of traditional society. This man happened to be the boy's father; eventually a boat passed by and carried both to an inhabited island.

This agrees with one of Ibn Tufayl's versions of the birth of Hayy. The rest of the story, which is long and tedious, focuses on themes that have no direct bearing on Ibn Tufayl's work.

b. Hunain Bin Ishaq's Version

Hunain Bin Ishaq translated from the Greek the following story:

Once in olden times there existed a king called Hermanos who exercised sovereignty over Byzantium, Egypt and Hellas. He was very pious and knew well the influences of the heavenly bodies on earthly creatures. He resented the company of women and refused to take wife, lest she conspired against him and distracted his mind from his duties. A friend of his, a sage, counselled him to father a child, an heir to his glorious and vast kingdom. Consequently the sage under suitable planetary forecast obtained some of the king's semen and placed it in a congenial container. The substance in the container through astronomical and alchemical processes grew to a favourable disposition and received the form. In this manner the child was born, and disposition and received the form. In this manner the child was born, and he was called Salaman. His father engaged a beautiful nurse to take care of him; her name was Absal. When Salaman grew up he fell madly in love with her. His love estranged him from his princely duties, and from seeking the highest level of truth and wisdom. Both the king and the sage tried their best to talk him out of this behaviour and to divert him from sensuality and worldly temptation. But all was in vain; Salaman was not dissuaded by their efforts and decided to escape with absal for beyond the sea. The king, who was versed in the knowledge of cryptic sciences, annulled the spiritual beings that inspired their sexual desires. Consequently they experienced the greatest pain and misery; despite their inflamed passions they could not reach each other. Weary and desperate, Salaman and Absal hurled themselves into the sea. Salaman was saved from drowning by the king's order and Absal was abandoned to die. Salaman's grief, overwhelming him with inward turbulence and confusion, drove him insane. Upon instructions from the king, the sage tried to help Salaman. Through continuous fervent prayers and supplication he enabled Salaman to see Absal's image every day. She appeared to him continually and Salaman was consoled by her company and conversation until one day the image of Venus appeared to him instead, radiating beauty and perfection. Salaman instantly fell in love with her, forgetting his love for Absal, and addressed the sage thus: "O Sage, lend me you hand; I want naught save this women." Accordingly, the sage made it possible for Salaman to see her constantly. Henceforth

Salaman's wits were restored and he was able to devote his time to the pursuit of truth and the ruling of his kingdom.

c. Some Comments on the Story

It is possible that the tale owes its genesis to Hellenic-Neoplatonic circles Furthermore, while 'Ibn Tufayl's *Hayy Bin Yaqzan* is *not* predominantly symbolic— as I have argued elsewhere— Hunain's translated talem in order to have any philosophical import at all, *should be considered as a symbolic fiction wanting interpretation;* otherwise it would be nothing more than a purely aesthetic composition, whose fountainhead is organised fancy and whose meaning is frivolous, touching only the surface of things. In brief, therefore, the story revolves around one basic Neoplatonic theme: the darkness and misery that man commits himself to when yielding to the intoxicating pleasures of senses, while his redemption and bliss lie in annihilating bodily temptations by rising to the heights of contemplating the Ultimate Good. In other words, man should focus his life on the *eternal* aspects of his nature while suspending his *temporal* component in order to achieve lasting self-integration.

Other interpretations of the story unjustifiably tend to burden it with detailed Neoplatonic profundities that are mostly weary weavings of the interpreter's own mind. This excessive interpretation led scholars such as Tusi to almost infer from it a whole Muslim Neoplatonic system. The reason for this is its imaginative form, which renders the deciphering of its symbolism subject to different themes and ramifications. While this imaginative form may explain the beauty and artistic charm of the tale it also shows that one should exercise caution in deciding where to establish the bounds of interpretation.

The following aspect of Tusi's detailed interpretation seems relatively plausible: The king is supposed to be the Active Intellect; his friend the sage is the emanation of truth which the Active Intellect receives from the higher intellect; Salaman is the rational soul that emanates from the higher intellect and frees his soul from bodily attachments; Absal is the corporeal animal faculty and Salaman's love for her is the rational soul's inclination to sensible pleasures. The escape of the two lovers tar beyond the sea is their surrender to transient sensuality and remoteness from truth; their punishment represents the soul's tendency despite the ageing of the body. The attempt to kill themselves by drowning the Salaman's eventual survival signify the soul's immortality after death and the dissociation of the body.

Tusi presents additional details in unravelling the symbols of the story. His interpretation is construed in terms of the philosophic schemes and terminology of the Muslim Neoplatonic philosopher such as al-Farabi and Avicenna. He himself after his arduous attempt concedes that his interpretation of Avicenna's intentions does not ring true. His mistake, in my opinion, was the following: *As the story was originally written in Greek, the author could not have had the terminology and themes of Muslim philosophy in mind, for these did not arise until later*. Such terms as "Active Intellect" and the "emanation of truth form higher intellect" are clearly Farabian and Avicennian, and are not normally found in the writing of Plotinus. It was al-Farabi's attempts to infuse Neoplatonism with elements of the Peripatetic School and to enlarge its hierarchical structure that brought forth the notion of series of intellects and made it known to Muslim scholars. Tusi committed the fallacy of accident by dilating and overmphasising the unintended similarities between the symbols of the tale and Avicenna's philosophic system. If the tenor of the story is clearly neoplatonic, it is clearly not intended to be of the Avicennian type.

Anthropologists studying the genesis of tales and myths tell us that certain tales may travel not only from one country to another but indeed around the globe. They are a product not so much of the inventive talent as of the re-arrangement of elements by omission, combination and addition, in order to express a particular subject in a particular period. Hunain's story may not have girdled the globe, yet apart from its Neoplatonic themes, it served in different Muslim countries as a medium for transmitting the visions and ideas of Muslim mystics such as Ibn el-Farid and Jami. The latter, a Persian mystic poet, composed a well-known suggestive epic poem entitled *Absal and Salaman* which centres on mystical allusions and oblique forms of expression.

Exploring the mystical undulation of the story Henry Corbin writes:

> "Essentially our task is to decipher the indications registering the successive phases of one and the same consciousness, that to the adept: first the tearing asunder of his pre-initiatory existence, then his initiatory birth..finally his attainment of the *royal dignity* of Perfect Man...The king father is the world of traditional consciousness, the masculine World of the Day, the world of the official normal and strict imperative of reason. Absal typifies the feminine world of premonitions, of coming births, of the polygenesis still closed in fecund Night, with no norms except the spontaneities of love. Between these two universes, these two forces of soul, consciousness is rent constantly asunder... So long as the mystical child born of the Mandragora has not succeeded in integrating these two with its being, the lamentable vicissitudes and failures described by the recital will be repeated. The integration is the outcome not of a rational dialectic but of terrifying and painful experience...The decisive episode in the initiation occurs when Salaman and Absal cast themselves into the sea...

It is not perhaps difficult to agree with Corbin about certain aspects of his *Ta'wil* of the story, nor is it difficult to grant his inferences and even go beyond them. The difficulty with his *Ta'wil* is that is employs a psychogenetic approach which, if it aspires to objective conclusions on the one hand, may be arrested on the other by the subjective and introspective states of the writer's own imagination. One may even add to Corbin's conclusions by urging that the sage is a kind of psychotherapist who aids his patient to integration by slowly and painfully ridding him of the intense libidinal fixation which led to the dramatic rupture of his personality. Thus the sage helped Salaman to unite his dispersed energies, permitting his soul to strive and reach for the truth.

This *Ta'wil* may be feasible, and the Freudian analysis and synthesis of literary symbols have become nowadays a vogue and a fashion. Yet, despite all the available methods for *Ta'wil*, there remains only one simple, direct and clear fact: that is, the story denotes the toils and bitter pain that the soul encounters in attempting to leave the world of darkness and error for the world of illuminated and illuminating Truth.

d. Avicenna's Two Versions and that of Alexander

Avicenna's versions of the tale seem to have more cohesion with Avicenna's general system than Hunain's version. One will not be led astray it one interprets its symbolism in terms of the detailed Avicennian cosmic view of things. Two of Avicenna's symbolic tales command our attention here: the tale of *Salaman and Absal,* and that of *Hayy Bin Yaqzan*. The characters of these two tales obviously appear in Ibn Tufayl's *Hayy Bin Yaqzan*; I shall take up each tale in turn.

Salaman and Absal were brothers. Absal, the younger of the two, grew up under his brother's care and guidance to be handsome, sensible, knowledgeable, courageous, and a man of ardent resolve. Salaman's wife became infatuated with him and convinced her husband to talk Absal into marrying her younger sister. The night of the marriage Salaman's wife placed herself in her sister's bed. Due to an abrupt change of weather, a dazzling bolt of lightning gave Absal a glimpse of her face, and he turned her down insultingly. Now Absal decided to mobilise an army to conquer the East and West and subdue his brother's enemies. Having accomplished this, he brought both loot and glory to his brother. However, Salaman's wife bribed and instigated the army officer to betray Absal and consequently, in another battle, they let him down and he was left wounded, taken for dead, on the battlefield. It chanced that a wild animal sympathised with him, fed and cared for him till his health and powers were restored. Meanwhile Salaman was encircled and humbled by his enemies, and longed fervently for his brother. Absal came to his rescue, took up arms against the enemies, destroyed them and consolidated his brother's rule. This time Salaman's wife conspired with the cook and the chief who poisoned Absal's food and killed him. Salaman's grief for his brother knew no bounds. He abandoned his kingdom and withdrew to perpetual prayer and invocations. God revealed to him the truth, whereupon he ordered the connivers to drink poison and die.

In his second tale Avicenna makes Hayy Bin Yaqzan the main character. The narrator says that once he happened to go with his companions to a place of recreation near his residence. As they were walking at a leisurely pace a sage appeared greeted them with a smile and presented himself as Hayy Bin Yaqzan. The impact of years was evident on him, yet he had none of the qualities of old age except his penetrating wisdom. Also, he had the appearance of comeliness and youth. The sage spoke thus to the narrator: "Your companions are evil companions. They lead you to untruth and are the cause of your ignorance and bondage."

REFERENCES

1. Ibn Tufayl, Hayy bin Yaqzan, ed. and trans. into French by Leon Gauthier, Beirut, 1936.
2. See my article "Ibn Tufayl's Hayy bin Yaqzan: Its structure, literary aspects and method," *Islamic Culture*, July 1973, pp. 191-211.
3. See my article, "Ibn Tufayl's appraisal of his predecessors and the influence of these on his thought," *Int. J. Middle East Stud.,* (in press).
4. Ibn Sina, *Allusions and intimations,* tr., Dunya, Cairo, 1958.

Revised and edited; originally published in *Islamic Culture*, Oct., 1974.

3

The Place of Rumi in Muslim Thought

IMTIAZ AHMAD

(Abstract: Throw some light on the place of Rumi as a Mutakallim, one who is an expert in Kalam or theology.

Mawlana Jalal ad-Din Rumi is best known for his great work, the *Mathnawi*, one of the most significant mystical poems in world literature. It is a compendium of the teachings of the Qur'an and the Sunna, and also of sufism. The greatness of Rumi does not lie solely in his teachings on mysticism, for he was also a *Mutakallim*, that is to say a Muslim theologian. Many scholarly works have been written on the subject of his mysticism and of his poetry, but very little has been said regarding his role as a *Mutakallim*.

The *Mathnawi* is certainly a monumental work of *Tasawwuf* and *Tariqat* but it also makes an important contribution to the study of *'Aqa'id* and *Kalam*. Many of the characteristic topics of Islamic mysticism—love, renunciation, submission, meditation and seclusion—are dealt with, but Rumi writes also, with great depth, and uncommon lucidity, of the doctrines concerning Allah *ta'ala*, the Prophethood, the Hereafter, Freewill and Predestination.

In dealing with these subjects Rumi departs from the path adopted by his contemporaries. He follows neither the rationalist' philosophical method of pure reason and dialectical argument nor the traditional method of compulsion and dogma. Indeed he criticises both these methods and shows the way to a new treatment of fundamental topics. Thus instead of bolstering his view-point with the logic and rationality of the Mu'tazilites or demanding that people accept his views, he appeals directly to the heart, mind and imagination of his reader in a style that is uniquely effective, so that often the reader feels as though his own deepest beliefs were at last being put into words of compelling eloquence. From this point of view, Rumi's arguments need no other proof of their veracity, and yet and conviction they carry is enduring.

Existence of God

The problem of the existence of God has always been a fundamental issue, both for theologians and philosophers. Yet the arguments advanced to prove the divine existence have, for the most part, been purely logical, and similar arguments may be used to refute belief in God. Since the issue is a metaphysical one, such arguments, of the senses, can never provide a satisfactory solution. Ultimately the subject is beyond the reach of such external sources of knowledge. Such rational arguments seldom answer man's need for total conviction; and the traditional theologians have felt no need to provide such proofs of the existence of God but have confined themselves to commanding Muslim to believe in the divine, since this is what the Qur'an commands. For many rationalists this viewpoint has seemed inadequate.

Rumi has tackled the issue of God's existence from a new angle. Not only does he employ arguments used in the Qur'an, but he presents these arguments in the actual manner of the Holy Book.

To prove the existence of God, the Qur'an invokes the pure and primordial nature of man, while drawing our attention to the innumerable signs of the divine which pervade the whole universe. The Qur'an urges us to meditate upon the designer and controller of this perfectly designed and totally controlled universe.

The Prophet is commanded to ask: "Can there be any doubt about Allah — Creator of the Heavens and the Earth." The Holy Book is filled with examples of the signs which convince men of the divine existence, proving the Creator by means of the created.

Rumi sets out to prove the existence of God along the same

lines. Numberless events, he says, take place around us in the world, but we fail to perceive the One who is their ultimate Cause. The effects are visible to us, but the Cause is hidden from our eyes. From the Rumi infers that, "the fact that something is happening necessarily proves that someone causes it to happen from behind a curtain", and "the movement of a thing necessarily implies that a power exists which moves it." Similarly, he emphasises man's need to discover God through His universal signs, since man is incapable of seeing God in Himself.

Rumi draws further arguments for the divine existence from the natural laws which govern the universe. The astonishing regularity and uniformity which we perceive in the midst of such an immense variety of conflicting forces and conditions leads Rumi to conclude that the whole universe is controlled and regulated by a Controller, a Regulator, a Reckoner and a Measurer.

Rumi also considers the issues of God's existence from another angle, taking into consideration the particular properties of the material objects contained in the universe. He divides these objects into two categories: material (objects of the senses) and non-material (including ideas, emotions, memory, and so on). He then states that material objects possess different degrees of *kathafat* or density. Some, he says, possess a great deal of this quality, others very little. He adds that there are certain objects which possess so little of this density that in certain cases their presence is virtually imperceptible, while at an even higher level things are totally devoid of this quality of *kathafat*.

Rumi remarks that objects possessing a great amount of *kathafat* are more visible than those which possess less. By extension of this argument, he concludes that, the higher and nobler an object, the less visible and less perceptible it is. Explaining this by an example he says that the human being has three different levels: those of the body, the soul (life) and the intellect. The first of these, being at the lowest level, is clearly visible and immediately perceived. The second, which is higher, is more hidden, for its presence becomes evident only when there is some movement or activity in the body. The case of the third level—Intellect of *'Aql*—differs from the other two: the simple movement of the body is not sufficient to indicate its presence; to be aware of intellect we must perceive order and purpose in the body's movements. The movement of a lunatic's body proves that he is alive, but he cannot be considered a person possessing intellect in view of the abnormal behaviour and movements of his body. *'Aql*, being on a higher plane than either life or the body, is therefore the more hidden.

From this hypothesis Rumi draws an argument to prove the existence of God, applying the principle that "the closer and less sophisticated a fact, the less visible and more hidden is the cause." Since the Controller of the universe is the highest and most sophisticated Cause, He is imperceptible to our senses. By this argument Rumi also explains the nature of the body and the soul, comparing the former with the sleeve of a shirt and the letter with the hand within. The body is visible, he says, while the soul is invisible, just as the sleeve is apparent whilst the hand is hidden. In his treatment of God's existence Rumi surpasses the Mutakallimun; while they had attempted to prove that God was the Cause of all causes (*`illa al-`ilal*), he proves, with copious illustrations, not only God's existence but also His freedom from attributes (*tanzih*), as also from all that is material (*Bari can al-madda*). At the same time, he refutes in this respect the theories of the naturalists (*Maddiyun*).

Prophethood

Rumi's method is equally original when he comes to treat the question of Prophethood. Once again he avoids using pure logic and dialectic arguments, invoking instead the assistance of man's inner consciousness. First, he distinguishes between the animal soul and the human and the prophetic soul. He maintains that, just as the human soul represents an elevation of the animal soul and differs from it fundamentally, so the prophetic soul is different and ever higher, and he divides this prophetic soul into higher and lower categories.

Like other Sufis, Rumi holds that the word *Wahy* may be used with reference to inanimate as well as to animate objects and, among the latter, to animals as well as to human beings. Then, so far as human beings are concerned, it may be used with reference to the inspiration of pious men as well as Prophets and Messengers of God. According to Rumi, the prophetic *wahy* is a state in which a prophet passes from a human condition to one which is superhuman, a state in which he is capable of hearing the divine speech either through the mediation of the angels or directly.

Throughout his treatment of this issue, Rumi emphasises the importance of man's inner experience as against his sense-perception. He attributes to man five inner senses in addition to the five external sources of knowledge, and he uses allegories to explain these senses and to prove the supremacy of the Inner to the External, comparing the former to red gold and the latter to copper.

As for the proof of Prophethood, he does not seek to make use of logical arguments. But considers man's inner awareness (or *wijdan*) as the best arbiter in determining the truth or falsehood of Prophethood. According to him, the Prophets' Message is so unique and so extraordinary that the hearer, provided he is free of insolence, has immediate proof of it and is convinced of its truth. Such a claim may seem unfounded to students of Islamic history. The might ask: Had this been the case, why did the Prophets in general and the Prophet Muhammad in particular meet so much opposition in propagating the divine messages? The answer to the question is to be found in the *Mathnawi*, where Rumi explains that the prophetic message penetrated only those who have a true desire to seek guidance. As for those who are disobedient and have no desire to know the truth, such messages are meaningless to them. In other words, sincere desire and a genuine urge are prerequisites for appreciating the truthfulness of a Prophet's message, which is put to the test by man's inner awareness. Rumi illustrates the point by saying that, just as the property of water (whether it is drinkable or brackish) can be discovered only when it is tasted, so the property of a prophetic message can be known only by this inner awareness, accompanied by a true desire to seek the truth. This Rumi holds that true seekers for knowledge have no need for rational proofs of the Prophethood. He says that a thirsty man (provided that he is genuinely so) never demands proof as to whether the cup he is offered contains water or not., and, similarly, when a mother calls her child to feed him he runs to her without demanding proofs of her motherhood. Both the thirst man and the hungry child hasten to their benefactors because of their genuine thirst and hunger. Speaking of the effect of the Prophetic Message on believers who are sincere, rumi says that their hearts move spontaneously and willingly to accept the call. This, in his view, is why Prophets do not depend upon miracles to provide proof of their messages. Miracles, in his view, do not fully convince the rational mind. Their effects are therefore short-lived. Thus, we see that, rather than attempting to prove the prophethood through rational arguments based on the uncertain evidence of the senses, Rumi relies upon the intuitive powers of the human soul and man's inner awareness.

The Hereafter

The problem of the Hereafter is directly related to the question of the soul. According to the Naturalist philosophers (*Maddiyun*) the soul dies when the body dies. The Mutakallimun, on the other hand, while accepting this viewpoint, add that, in the Hereafter, the soul will be recreated in a resurrected body. As against this, Rumi holds that the soul is immortal where as the body is transient and mortal. The relation of soul to body is, according to Rumi, that of a craftsman to his tools. Just as the loss of his tools has no effect on the craftsman as such, so the annihilation of the body does not affect the soul.

Like other Sufis, he regards the life of this world as a child's game. The true life comes after bodily death, so that this life may be regarded as no more than a prologue to the life eternal. Every evolution, he says, in the result of a preceding extinction or destruction. He remarks, in this connection, that treasure is found only when the earth is dug up, and a new house is not built until the old one is demolished. He says, "Even the fool writes on a slate only after effacing what is already written there, and water gushes forth from the earth after it has been dug up."

Rumi concludes that, since man is always in the process of evolution—changing from a lower state to a higher one— this life must be followed by a life that is everlasting. Typically, he explains such metaphysical problems by illustrations taken from our everyday life.

Freewill vs. Predestination

The issue of *Jabr* and *Qadar* is amongst the most intricate and controversial ones. Ever since the rise of philosophy in Islam, this question of Freewill and Predestination has been a favourite topic among scholars. In Rumi's time, independent schools of thought had developed and their theories were well-established. The Qadarites argued in terms of power (*Qudra*) and choice (*Ikhtiyar*) in man. While the Jabrites held that man's actions are totally dependent upon the Divine Will, the community was divided into two opposing camps upon this issue: those believing in Freewill, and the Determinists (or advocates of Necessitarianism). The Ash'arites had reduced the rigidity of the determinist theory by introducing the idea of "acquisition" (*kasb*), but they still laid the ultimate responsibility for all man's actions on God. The author of *Musallam ath-thubut* has rightly, therefore, described *Jabr* and *kasb* as "twin brothers". So far as their main outlines were concerned, there were really only two schools of thought on the subject in Rumi's time, and most of the Sufis inclined towards the Jabrite view. Rumi might have been expected to follow in their footsteps, but a close study of his writings shows that his was not the case, indeed they suggest that he inclined more towards the theory of the Qadarites. Nevertheless, he presents both the Jabrite and the Qadarite viewpoints in the *Mathnawi*.

The Qur'an contains verses which may be taken to support either of these theories. Similarly, in the *Mathnawi*, we find couplets in support both of *jabr* and *Ikhtiyar*. In support of the determinists' theory, Rumi compares man with a musical instrument played upon by God. In another phrase, he compares out life to a mountain within which we hear, not out own voices, but the echo of the word of Allah. Elsewhere, to demonstrate man's total dependence upon the Divine Will, comparing us to helpless pawns upon the chessboard of life, with every move depending upon the Divine Will alone. Yet again, Rumi illustrates man's relationship to God in terms of a painting and the artist who paints it. Just as the painter has full control over his work, so God has full control over human actions.

In the story of the Sabians, Rumi quotes a number of arguments devised by the determinists in support of their views. They say, for example: "If for a hundred years you went on asking a stone to turn into a jewel; if you asked the old to become new again a hundred times over; if you asked soil to become water; if you asked water to turn into honey or milk; or if you wished that counterfeit money should become real—in none these cases would your wishes be fulfilled."

Rumi cites so many arguments in support of determinism that one might readily infer that he held, like other contemporary mystics, to the doctrine of predestination; and yet a considerable number of verses in his great work show that Rumi was strongly opposed to the theory of *jabr*. These verses suggest that he regarded determinism as a form of escapism and self-deceit and regarded its adherents as lazy and irresponsible people, averse to shouldering responsibility. He warns them by a Prophet tradition that if they continue pretending to be sick they will, in the course of time, become so. He says that man uses his power of choice and his freedom of will to mould the course of his life and to improve his own character, acts which are not contrary to the Divine Will but in complete conformity with it.

He shows that those who claim to believe in absolute determinism are in fact deceivers for, while exercising choice, they react differently according to whether they are responding, on the one hand, to the call of reason and conscience, or, on the other, to the call of their animal desire. In the former case, they appear to be helpless creatures, inactive so far as the performance or their religious and moral duties is concerned; in the latter case, they become masters of their own actions and satisfy their desires.

Rumi provides a number of arguments to support his contention that freedom of will is an indivisible part of human nature. Citing examples from our everyday life, he remarks that when a roof falls on someone's head they show no anger against it, or, when someone's property is devastated by a flood, they do not rage against the water. Similarly, when a man's turban is blown away he does not scold the wind. The reason for this, he says, is that we know that these inanimate objects are without free will. But the case of human action, he points out, is quite different. All the actions performed by men are accountable, since man is expected to possess the faculty of choice in his actions. Rumi further elaborates this point by saying that inanimate objects are devoid of will and no one looks for friendship or enmity from stones. Man, on the other hand, is praised for his good deeds and blamed for his evil ones. The very fact that commendation and condemnation are restricted to man alone proves that the possesses, by his very nature, freedom of will.

Rumi ridicules the Jabrites in the story of the fruit thief and the owner of the garden. In the tale, a thief climbs a fruit tree and begins to pluck the fruit. When the master of the garden asks him what he is doing, the thief replies: "The garden and the fruit are God's property. If one of God's slaves takes something from God's garden, what is wrong with that?" Hearing this, the owner tied the thief to the tree with the thick rope and began to beat him severely. The thief cried: "Fear God for punishing an innocent man!" The owner replied: "You should submit to the will of God; just as the garden belongs to Him, and not to you or me, so this rope by which you are tied, the stick by which you are being beaten, your flesh and your body all belongs to God. We, therefore, have no control over them. Moreover, I am the obedient servant who is following the command of God; similarly, it is God's stick that is falling on a body which belongs to Him; your complaint against this punishment is therefore meaningless, since it is being given by the will of God."

In Rumi's view, the problem of free will and predestination does not call for dialectical argument, for it is so simple an issue that it is comprehensible even to animals. The dog, for example, when hit by a stone never chases the stone; instead, it turns upon the man who threw the stone; or again the camel that is goaded with a stick becomes angry with the driver, not with the stick. Rumi concludes: "When animals are aware of the possession of free will, should not man feel ashamed of his belief in the theory of determinism?"

Rumi also tackles the Jabrite theory from another angle. He points out that God's Commands (*Awamir*) and Prohibitions (*Nawahi*) themselves indicate that man possesses freedom of choice. Were this not so, he would not be held accountable for his deeds. From this evidence, it may be seen that Rumi appears to inclined rather towards the theory of free will, whilst striking a balance between *Jabr* and *Ikhtiyar*.

Let us now consider the motives of our poet-philosopher in evolving his characteristic, illustrative style. In considering his writing (particularly his masterpiece, the *Mathnawi*), the reader is likely to ask why he chose to employ this particular style in the treatment of metaphysical subjects. It is possible that the religious and mystical aspects of his life may provide an explanation. We not that he had acquired a deep and thorough knowledge of *'Ulum Zahiri* and *'Ulum Batini* under the able guidance of Ash'arite theologians and scholars such as Baha al-Din (his father), Sayyd Burhan ad-Din Muhaqqiq and Kamal ad-Din b.al-Adim al-Halabi. In *Tasawwuf*, he was particularly influenced by the great mystic Shams-i-Tabriz, as he himself acknowledges.

It is known that during Rumi's time different school of thought had developed and dialectical debates were common among orthodox scholars and the rationalists. At this time the intelligentsia of the community seem to have upheld the views of Ibn al-Arabi, Imam Razi and other in opposition to the teachings of Imam Ghazali, and their inclination was to employ reason and logic in the treatment of theological issues. But the rational approach of the Mu'tazilites was adopted only by the intellectual sector of the community. The masses still held fast to the traditional Islamic preaching by religious leaders, many of whom possessed only shallow knowledge of their faith. The masses practised *Taqlid* and followed without question what was preached from the pulpit by the 'Ulama. In fact, the rationalists and the Traditionalists remained at opposite extremes and had drifted from the straight "middle path" recommended in Islam. Rumi could not be an indifferent spectator in this situation. Equipped both with traditional and rational arguments, he struck a point between the two extremes, exposing (with the sarcasm) the attitude of the *Muqallidin* while pointing out the defects in the theories of the theologians.

In dealing with metaphysical issues, Rumi's method was to elucidate problems by the sue of illustrations from common experience. Throughout the *Mathnawi* his arguments are enforced by means of allegories, and this lends them a very particular strength. It may be asked why Rumi adopted this approach. It can be said that he was inspired by the style of the Qur'an itself, aware that the teachings of the Qur'an are intended for humanity as a whole. He therefore believed the these teachings should be presented in simple and easily understandable language. It is not surprising, then, that he accuses the 'Ulama' of having only a shallow knowledge of religion and of misleading the masses by their complex eloquence. He discourages blind following of *taqlid* and exhorts his readers to make a deliberate efforts to acquire religious knowledge for themselves. Rumi's aim was to demonstrate the teachings of Islam among the mass of the people, and this seems to have been his principal motive for making such extensive use of allegory, fable and anecdote in his master work, the *Mathnawi,* which has sometimes been described as "The Qur'an written in the Persian language."

REFERENCES

1. Abul Hasan Ali Nadvi, Tarikh dawat wa azimat, vol.i, 3d ed., Karachi, 1976, p. 486.

2. Shibli, *Sawanih Maulana Rum*, Lahore, 1961, p. 135.
3. Rumi, Mathnawi, 7th ed., Lahore, 1906.
4. A. Hakim Khalifa, *Hikmat-e-Rumi*, 2d ed., Lahore, 1906, p. 87.
5. Khalifa, Tashbihat-e-Rumi, 2d ed., Lahore, 1977, p. 32.

Revised and edited; originally published in *Islamic Quarterly*, vol. 15.

4

Neoplatonism and its Impact on Muslim Thought

MOHD. NOOR NABI

(Abstract: Traces the origin and development of new-Platonism, and links it with the harmony between philosophy and religion. Presents an exposition of Neoplatonism and its impact on Muslim thought).

Neoplatonism is a philosophical movement. Originally it was a movement in which an attempt was made to reconcile the thought of Plato with that of Aristotle and side by side to preserve the Greek theology and mysticism but in a rational and systematic manner. This movement is above creed, and religion and it would be reasonable and just to call it a humanitarian movement.

Modern age is an age of conflict and unrest. We have made great scientific discoveries, but alas! we are still not in a position to live like human beings. Today the world is at the verge of destruction. Terror and anguish are the features of the day. There are many social problems like, apartheid, social unrest and insecurity. In this critical juncture such ideas as humanitarianism, altruism, universal love, brotherhood and religion, and international organisation of peace and welfare of humanity at large sound attractive and appear beautiful and soothing to the sorely suffering men and women of today.

Though Ammonium Saccas (185-250 A.D.) was the founder of Neoplatonism yet credit must go to Plotinus (205-270 A.D.) who established Neoplatonism as a school of thought. His 'Enneads' are the primary and classical document of Neoplatonism. It was the privilege of Porphyry, the illustrious disciple and the biographers of Plotinus, who collected the disconnected jottings of his teacher and after, to some extent shaking and pruning, arranged a series of fifty-four essays into six divisions of nine each, each division being called an 'Ennead'.

Plotinus was a great mystic but his mysticism did not come in the way of his rationalism. On the contrary he made rationalism the indispensable discipline to attain the final 'ecstasy' of immediate union with the 'Primal one.' Plotinus observed meditation and passed through the various stages of the rigorous discipline, such as the political virtues, the cathartic virtues and lastly the atonement of the soul with God. Through this discipline "he was in his personal character one of the purest and most pleasing of all philosophers, ancient or modern." (Mozley). Porphyry tells us that four times in a state of ecstasy he was made one with God. He is also said to have been ashamed that he had a body. The last words of Plotinus were, "Now I seek to lead back the self within me to the All-self."

It is significant to note that Plotinus never associated himself with any of the organized systems of worship. "The Gods," he said, "must come to me, not I to them." Their dwelling was not in temples but in the human heart.

The Platonic philosophy created a great gulf between the supernatural and phenomenal worlds on the one hand and between man and God on the other. Aristotle by bringing the "Theory of Form and Matter" tried to bridge the gulf between the two worlds but so far as the relation between man and God is concerned, it remained quite dry and barren. It provided, to some extent, a relief to mind but human heart remained restless. The greatness of Plotinus lies in providing comfort and peace to both mind and heart. Plotinus erected the imposing and charming structure of his philosophy by incorporating the most imaginative and picturesque elements in the Platonic philosophy such as, the presentation of the idea of God in the likeness of the sun shedding being the life throughout the universe, the theological drama of creation in the Timaeus, the doctrine of the fall and re-incarnation of the soul and her possible release from the wheel of birth and rebirth and mystical re-union with her divine source, the opposition of the spirit to the flesh and its salvation by flight from the world to a higher sphere.

The main points of Neoplatonism are as follow:

a) The One or the Real

The Real, according to Plotinus, is that which is uncreated, indestructible, unchangeable, motionless, indivisible and therefore unextended, simple in quality, simple in essence, without taint of variety, multiplicity and alteration. Applying this standard, Plotinus disqualifies, one by one Matter, Soul, Mind and even the Aristotelian Active Reason as suitable candidates for the position of Ultimate Reality. The Ultimate Reality, in his opinion, is one. One is absolute Unity, simple, indivisible, homogeneous, unalterable, uncreated and indestructible. Its original essence is pure Being and absolute causality. It is also the "Good" in so far as every thing finite is to find its aim in it and flow back into it. It has no attributes at all. One should not even call it existence. It is something above existence and above goodness, and at the same time an operative force without any substratum.

After defining the ultimate Reality as one, the Absolute Unity Plotinus tries to explain 'Many', the multiplicity and to establish a relation between One' and 'Many'. This he does by presenting the 'Doctrine of Emanation'. The doctrine of Emanation is the procession of all things from One, but this procession is not a procession in time, it is logical and not the chronological order of being. Plotinus explains it on the analogy of spring or light. The first source of all being, he says, is compared to an overflowing spring which by its excess gives rise to that which comes after it or a central source of light which illumines all things. But the moment the effusion of being has separated itself from its source it becomes other than, different from, and less than the One. This separation gives rise to an act of what Plotinus calls 'epistrophe' or turning back and yearning towards its source. On the basis of this doctrine Plotinus asserts that from the One, the first emanation is 'Nous' or the Divine Reason or the Universal Mind; from Nous came the World Soul; from the World Soul, the Individual souls and lastly the physical universe.

Nous brings the distinction between subject and object. It has a dual nature. On the one hand, it strives for pure unity and closeness to individual One and on the other it is the sheet of multiplicity. It sees the world process not as a temporal succession of events but under the aspect of eternity. Its act of knowing the truth knows once and for all everything that there is to know about the past, the present and the future. It contains Ideas or Forms of particular men, as well as an Idea of mankind in general.

The One itself no more exists than it thinks or can be thought of Existence can be predicated of the Divine Reason and of the rational order of the Universe it enshrines.

b) World Soul

The relation of the World Soul to the Nous is the same as that of the Nous to the One. It stands between the Nous and the phenomenal World, is permeated and illuminated by the former, but is also in contact with the latter, It embraced innumerable individual souls and possess the freedom either to be ruled by Nous or to turn aside to the sensual and lose themselves in the finite (Harnack). It can attain her goal only by being reabsorbed into the Divine Reason and ceasing to be herself.

A very significant point is to note at this stage, is that the One, the Nous and the World Soul, all the three are co-eternal, there is no question of temporal succession. The time comes into origin when the individual soul proceed from the World Soul.

c) Individual Soul

The operation of Individual Souls takes place in time. She thinks of one thing after another, perceives one event after another and the functions she sustains go on. Plotinus lays equal stress upon the unity of the World soul and the multiplicity and variety of individual soul. Individual souls, he emphasizes, must be separate and distinct, else we should all experience one another's sensations, desires, thoughts and the like, and for that matter everything that occurred anywhere in the Universe. But on the other hand, all particular souls are inter-related and all partake of the nature of Soul in general. This apparent contradiction of the general and individual soul, Plotinus solves on the logical basis by giving the notion of science.

d) Physical Universe

Physical Universe is corporeal or spatial. In physical universe there is diminution of divine light. The white light of the One begins to fade in the material univerial universe.

e) Immortality of the Individual Souls

Plotinus argues at great length about the immorality of the individual soul. He rejects the position of the materialists, the Pythagoreans and even the Aristotelian contention regarding soul and categorically affirms the independent existence of soul from body. He says that soul is an incorporeal essence, the source and the substance of life and motion. Plotinus declares not only the retional parts of our soul immortal but also the sensitive and the vegetative parts, which are portions of the sensitive and vegetative powers of the World soul, and at death return to their source.

f) Re-incarnation

Being ever lasting out souls must exist before birth as well as after death. Plotinus tells us that the heavens are full of souls, possessed not only of reason but also of the sensitive and vegetative faculties, and dominated, as the case may be, by one or another of these three powers. When these souls fall into the body and become incarnate, the propensities of the individual they inherit, are determined by their dominant characters. The process of reincarnation is directed in the same way. Persons living on the level of sense become wild and lustful animals, the stupids become plants—absent minded philosophers into soaring birds. Good all round men become men again.

This reminds us of the theory of Re-Birth or Doctrine of Metempsychosis of the Hindu Philosophy and the theory of 'Involution' and 'Evolution' put forward by a great Indian thinker of the 20th century, Shri Aurbindo.

But re-incarnation for Plotinus is only episodic-like passing, he says, from dream to dream or sleeping each night in a new bed.

g) Salvation

Prof. R. Baine Harris has rightly remarked that Plotinus may be described as a rational mystic or perhaps a 'metaphysical mystic', since he believed in the necessity of logic and metaphysical understanding as a means to-mystical experience. This becomes explicit when we go through the doctrine of salvation of Plotinus.

Salvation, Plotinus says, begins with self-purification and the practice of ordinary moral life. The practice of moral life is not only to avoid sin but it is to do good positively. This leads to the freeing of the soul from all bodily desires and worldly goods and to fix its attention upon the Nous. And this is possible through dialectics which for Plotinus is a form of philosophical analysis or the discipline of philosophic thought wherein logic is used as a tool for the analysis of reality. Through this analysis the soul progressively sees itself as soul, then as Nous and then eventually as an element of the Ultimate. Now and now only is soul prepared for the final ecstasy of re-union with the One. At this stage the soul beholds God not as sovereign good but adores Him as sovereign Beauty.

Ecstasy is the consummation of reminiscence. It is to release the soul from everything except God which is possible through meditation. It is a state of the soul which transforms it in such a way that it then perceives what was previously hidden from it. This state will not be permanent until our union with God is irrevocable. Here, in earthly life, Ecstasy is but a flash. It is a brief respite bestowed by the favour of Deity.

Dr. Radha Krishnan interprets it as the attainment of Vision. He says, "The soul is then in a condition of complete passivity and rest, a state of intense concentration and complete forgetfulness of all things. It then sees God, the source of life, the principle of Being....... The vision is attained and then the soul touches and gazes on the supreme light".

Fuller would say, "It cannot be called a beatific vision. It is rather "some other kind of seeing, ecstasy, and simplification and self-surrender." The soul is identical with God as the centres of two concentric circles are identical."

Porphyry (232-304 A.D), the compiler of Enneads, followed mainly the tenets of his master, Plotinu, and popularised it. He replaced the logic and categories of Plotinus with those of Aristotle and made the aim of Philosophy the salvation of the soul. He and some of his followers allowed nature to be affected by the capricious actions of daemons. He also advocated some prohibitions such as pleasure of every description and eating meat.

Iamblichus (250-326) founded the Syrian school of Neoplationism which especially emphasized 'theurgy' as a means of salvation.

Proclus (409-417 A.D.) developed the Iamblichaen brand of Neoplatonism to its logical extremes by developing many more triads within triads for Plotinus' three emanations. He was quite zealous in his religious activities, worshipping the sun three time a day, observing all the Egyptian holydays, and spending part of the night in prayer, praise and making of sacrifices. His work is the culmination of the speculative movement extending over five centuries which was motivated by mainly religious interests. He found a place for Gods above the Nous and immediately below the One. He also accepts ecstatic experience.

Muslim Neo-Platonists

Neoplatonism, then, was a movement. The Greek Neoplatonists tried their best to bring harmony between Philosophy and Religion, and to provide a solid ground for this harmony, they made communion with God or the vision of God, the highest end of Religion subservient to the discipline of philosophy. This solemn motto of Greek

Neoplatonism was adopted, to a great extent, by a majority of the Muslim philosophers such as Al-Kindi, Al-Farabi, Ibn Sina, Ibn Miskawaih, Ibn Tufail, Ibn Rushd and even by Imam Al-Ghazali. Al-Kindi, Al-Farabi, Ibn Miskawaih and Ibn Sina not only adopted the prime motto of Greek Neoplatonism but they also presented their thought in Neoplatonism fashion. To explain the relation between One and Many, between the Creator and the creation they presented the theory of Emanation as it was put forward but the Neoplatonists. They advocated, like Plotinus, the Independence of the soul from the body, the immortality of the soul and the communion with God. As Greek Neoplatonists were loyal to the religion of their land, i.e. Greek Theology, in like manner the Muslim thinkers were committed to their religion, i.e. Islam.

Credit must go to Abu Yusuf Ya'qub Al-Kindi (801-873 A.D.), the first Arab philosopher who transmitted the Neoplatonic thought to the Muslims for the first time. He revised the Arabic translation of an anonymous Neoplatonic work called 'Theologia Aristotelis, which was in fact a paraphrase of the fourth, fifth and sixth Enneads of Plotinus. Al-Kindi directed Muslim Philosophy towards an accord between Philosophy and Religion and thus reconciling Hellenistic heritage with Islam, he laid the foundation of a new philosophy which remained for a long time the chief feature of Muslim Thought.

On the Neoplatonic pattern Al-Kindi defined God, 'The true One (al-Wahid al-Haq) the First, the Creator, the Sustainer of all that' He has created. He is transcendent and can be qualified only by negative attributes. He has no matter, no form, no quantity, no quality, no relation, nor is He qualified by any of the remaining categories (al-maqulat). He has no genus no differentia, no species and no accident. He is immutable........ He is, therefore, absolute oneness, nothing but oneness (wahdah). Everything else is multiple. This definition clearly shows that Al-Kindi presents Islamic conception of God in Neoplatonic form.

In a short treatise on soul, Al-Kindi borrows the idea from the Enneads. The soul, he says, is a 'simple entity and its substance emanates from the Creator just as the rays emanate from the sun. It is spiritual and of divine substance and is separate and distinct from the body. When it is separated from the body, it obtains the knowledge of everything in the world and has vision of the supernatural. After its separation from the body, it goes to the world of the intellect, return to the light of the Creator and sees Him.

A good man is defined by al-Kindi as one who gets away from the pleasures of the body and lives most of his life in contemplation to attain to the reality of things and such a man is very similar to the Creator.

Another treatise of al-Kindi on 'Intellect' played a vital role in Muslim Thought. In this treatise Kindi has explained the different kinds of 'Intellect' ('Aql) such as the potential or material intellect ('Aql Hayula), the habitual or acquired intellect ('Aql Mustafad), the active intellect ('Aql bil Fa'il) and the agent intellect ('Aql Fa'al) and shown how knowledge is obtained.

After Kindi we now come to Al-Farabi.

Al-Farabi (870-950 A.D.) was quite familiar with the works of Plotinus and Porphyry and he also wrote a commentary on the 'Isagoge of Porphyry.' His cherished ideal was to maintain that philosophy is essentially one unit; therefore, there shawls be only one school of thought, the school of truth. Like Al-Kindi he too formulated that religious truth and philosophical truth are objectively one.

In his book, "Risalah fi Ara Ahl al-Madinat, al-Fadilah" al-Farabi presents the `Theory of Ten Intelligences' to explain the relation between One and Many, heaven and earth and mutable and immutable and his theory is quite similar to the theory of Emanation of Neoplatonism.

Al-Farabi holds that the One, i.e. God is the Necessary by Himself. He is both intelligent and intelligible. Nothing is like Him.

From the Necessary One flows or emanates only one another by virtue of its self-knowledge and goodness. This emanent is the first intelligence. The first intelligence is possible by itself, necessary by another; and it thinks the One as well as itself. It is one in itself an many by virtue of these considerations. From thinking by first intelligence of the One flous another intelligence. By virtue of its thinking of itself as possible to itself flow the matter and form of the first heaven because every sphere has its specific form which is its soul. In this way the chain of emanations goes on so as to complete the ten intelligences and nine spheres and their none souls. The tenth and last intelligence, or agent intelligence, is that which governs the sublunary world. From this intelligence flow the human souls and the four elements.

This theory of Emanation of Farabi reflects his effort for the Unity of Truth and for reconciliation between Neoplatonism and Islam. It further shows the influence of the lamblichean brand of Neoplatonism developed by Proclus.

Like al-Kindi, al-Farabi too divides Intellect ('Aql) into four kinds, but his explanation of Acquired Intellect basically differs from that of al-Kindi and is at par with the intuition and inspiration of Plotinus. The Acquired Intellect, al-Farabi says, is the level where human intellect becomes disposed to conceive abstract forms which have no connection with matter. It is a kind of intuition and inspiration, or in other words, it is a kind of immediate apprehension. This is the noblest level of human apprehension and it is reached only by the few. This Acquired Intellect rises to the level of communion, ecstasy and inspiration.

Here we find a close affinity between the thought of Plotinus and al-Farabi.

Human knowledge, al-Farabi further says, depends on a radiation from the separate intelligence, and agent intelligence stands in the same relation to human intellect as sun to our eyes. Our eyes depend on daylight, and in the same way out intellect is capable of comprehension only when it is unveiled by the agent intelligence which illuminates its way.

Thus, we see that like Neoplatonism, mysticism is fused with philosophy and rational knowledge coincides with ecstasy and inspiration in the system of al-Farabi. And on the basis of this theory of knowledge Farabi explains revelation and prophecy and concludes that religious truth and philosophic truth are both the radiation of divine illumination through imagination or contemplation.

Ibn Miskawaih (d. 1030 A.D.) owed much al-Farabi. He also expressed his indebtedness to Porphyry and Proclus in the book "Al-Fauz al-Asghar.' He benefits specially from the book of Proclus entitled "Kitab Sharah Qual Flatun fi al-Nafs Ghair Maitah." His definition of God, theory of Emanation and psychology are in complete unanimity with those of Neoplatonists. But unlike Neoplationism he is against all forms of ascetic life. He poses a question both in "Al-Fauz al-Asghar" and "Tahdhib al-Akhlaq, "How can he who retires from men and lives in isolation be temperate, just, generous and courageous?"

Like Ibn Miskawaih Ibn Sina (980-1037 A.D.) too is greatly indebted to al-Farabi and when we go through his book "Kitab al-Najat" it seems as if it is the reproduction of "Al-Madinat Al-Fadila" of Al-Farabi. Therefore like al-Farabi Ibn Sina also may be estimated as a great Neoplatonist.

Ibn Sina's 'doctrine of Being' like that of Plotinus is emanationistic. Like Farabi he shows that from God the necessary Existent flows the first intelligence alone and then from 1st intelligences flow one after another the ten intelligences and nine heavens. The 10th intelligence, Ibn Sina says, is called by the majority of the Muslim philosophers and Angel Gabriel. In his book Kitab al Shifa' Ibn Sina categorically states that for concrete existence not only form and matter are necessary but God also is indispensable because both form and matter depend upon God and here Ibn Sina follows a Neoplatonic line instead of the Aristotelian one.

Essence, in the opinion of Ibn Sina, exist in God's mind (and in the mind of the active intelligence) prior to the individual existents exemplifying them in the external world. The essence is neither universal nor particular but it is just an essence. Both particularity and universality are "accidents" which happen or occur to the essence. Both the universal and the particular issue from the active intellect by an act of direct intuition. Ibn Sina goes to the extent that at every stage intuition is involved in the origin of knowledge, and of all intellectual knowledge, more or less, it is not so much true to say 'I know it' as to admit `It occurs to me'. The effort is necessary on the part of man; the response is the act of God or the active intellect. Here we find the Neoplationian fusion of rationalism and mysticism. Like Plotinus Ibn Sina insists that the soul is independent of the body. He discusses in detail the influence of the mind on the body. Plotinus explained the principle of 'Sympathy' in which the mind-body interaction was explained, but Ibn Sina also explains phenomena like magic, suggestion and hyponosis on the basis of this principle which were accepted in Hellenism as exceptionaly occult. And this shows an advancement of Ibn Sina on Greek Neoplatonism.

Unlike Neoplatonism Ibn Sina rejects the doctrine of the absolute identity of subject and object in intellectual operation, for, he argues, in the case of normal consciousness, there being a succession of ideas, if the mind became identical with one object, how could it then become identical with another. In this connection he criticizes Porphyry for his 'mystical and poetical statements.'

He also categorically rejected the transmigration of souls and the idea of the possible identity of two souls or the ego becoming fused with the Divine ego. On the contrary, he emphasizes that the survival must be individual. He categorically says that it is a primary fact of experience that each individual is conscious of his self identity which cannot be shaken by any kind of argument. He further says that even the qualitative nature of the intellectual operations in different individuals may be different. These arguments show the originality and the intellectual genius of Ibn Sina.

Thus we see that al-Kindi, al-Farabi, Ibn Miskawaih and Ibn Sina not only incorporated the main Neoplatonic doctrines in their philosophical system but also advanced them and purified them from the baser elements. After Ibn Sina, Imam Al-Ghazali (1058-1111 A.D.) gave a death blow to the emanationistic theory of Neoplatonism but retained the independence of the soul from the body, the immortality of the soul and the philosophic and mystic discipline of the soul for the vision of God. And from Al-Ghazali onwards Sufism (Islamic mysticism) became the dominant feature of Muslim Thought and developed its doctrines independently, some of them similar to the doctrines of Neoplatonism.

REFERENCES

1. B A C Fuller, *A History of Philosophy*, 3rd ed., Oxford, New Delhi, 1969, p. 309.
2. *Selected Works of Plotinus*, trans. by Thomas Taylor, ed., by G R S Mead, London, G Bell, 1929, pp. XIX,XX.

Revised and edited; Originally published in *Islamic Culture,* April 1979.

5

Al-Ash'ari and Mu'tazilites on Evil

MOHAMMED YUSOFF HUSSAIN

(Abstract: The question is whether God is Justice or Injustice since He creates everything in the world, including evil. Al-Ash'ari (d. A.D. 935) held that God is the real Creator of the Universe including all human actions. Mu'tazilites maintain that God creates only the compulsory, not the voluntary actions, that God creates only the good but not the evil. Examines the distinction between al-Ash'ari and the Mu'tazilites regarding the problem of evil and its relation to the justice of God).

The Mu'tazilite on the Creation of Evil

The Mu'tazilites from the very beginning, tried to maintain the justice and the absoluteness of God. To associate God with the creation of evil is against the claim of the justice of God. If God creates evil, it follows that God is evil. If God is evil, He must be unjust to His creatures. So, the main point of the Mu'tazilites is to avoid 'attributing evil to God.' This does not mean, according to the majority of them, that God has no power over evil. Only Ibrahim al-Nazzam (d. A.D. 845) held that God has power over evil, which distinguishes him from other Mu'tazilite scholars.

Before we elaborate the Mu'tazilite position in general, it is worth mentioning some scholars among them who have different interpretations of this problem. To begin with, it is interesting to consider the interpretations of Abu al-Hudhayl al-'Allaf (d.A.D. 841) who is said to have the following position:

> That God has power to do evil, but that He did not actually do it because of His wisdom and compassion. Alternatively he

argued that evil proceeds from deficiency, that there is no deficiency in God, and that therefore it is impossible to suppose His doing evil.

Abu al-Hudhayl's reasons for avoiding attributing evil to God are twofold; firstly, the nature of the acts of God or God Himself; and secondly, the nature of evil. Since it has been agreed that God is wise and His works are works of wisdom, it is impossible to suppose that God is doing evil which is regarded as contrary to the work of wisdom. Moreover, it is impossible to suppose that God has power to do evil due to the nature of evil itself, that is, 'evil proceeds only from deficiency.' From these two reasons, Abu al-Hudhayl concluded that it is impossible to maintain that God, though He has power over evil, creates it.

Al-Nazzam, however, has a different interpretation of the problem of evil. He said that God neither has power over evil, nor creates evil. His position is based on two considerations, firstly, the nature of evil itself, and secondly, his idea of God. As to the former he said that evil is the essence of a thing, therefore, the power to create it is itself to be regarded as evil. From this argument, it is obvious that he is trying to avoid the following statement, that "if God creates evil, God Himself is evil." As for the latter, he argued:

> If God has power over evil, then the occurrence of evil is possible, and as the supposition of the occurrence of a possible thing entails no impossibility, let us suppose that evil did occur. Now, God might or might not have had knowledge of the evil which occurred. If we say that He did not have the knowledge of it, it would necessarily follow that He was ignorant; and if we say that He did have it, it would necessarily follow that He was in need of this evil; for had He not been in need of it, He would not have created it. When a person is not in need of a thing and knows its inherent evils, he will have nothing to do with it, if he it wise.

This argument comes mainly from the theory of the works of God. Since it has been proved that the works of God are the works of wisdom, therefore, it is unreasonable to suppose that God is in need of creating evil. Moreover, it has been proved that God knows; then to suppose that God is ignorant of the occurrence of evil (so that we can suppose that He is not in need of evil) is also unreasonable. This conclusion which can be drawn from al-Nazzam's argument is quite simple. Since God is not ignorant, the occurrence of evil is in His knowledge, therefore, He is in need of evil. But on the other hand, since God's works are regarded as works of wisdom, surely, He is not in need of evil. God is wise and so He has nothing to do with the creation of evil.

Another Mu'tazilite scholar who had a different interpretation of this issue was 'Abbad b. Sulayman (d. A.D. 864) He argued:

> All that God does is right. There cannot be anything profitable for man which He does not do; if there were, He would be unjust. He does not create unbelief but gives the unbeliever power not to believe. He does not create anything which we call evii or bad, like hunger or sickness; even the pains of hell are not evil, either really or metaphorically.

His doctrine of uncreatedness of evil is based on the distinction he made between 'power over evil' and 'power to do evil' An example of this distinction would be a wife's conception of a child. W.M. Watt elaborates this examples, stating that 'Abbad was influenced by Mu'ammar.

> Just as a man has power over his wife's conception of a child, although he himself does not have power to conceive a child, so (thought Mu'ammar) God may have power over movement (that is, can cause men to move) although He Himself does not have power to move, and likewise may have power over evil (sc. the evil doing of men) but not power to do evil.

The main problem to deal with is the 'attributing evil to God' and 'the power of God,' From this doctrine, 'Abbad is on his way to avoiding 'attributing evil to God' and at the same time asserting that 'God is all powerful.' As to the question of the unbeliever, he argued that since unbelief is evil, and God does not create evil, therefore unbelief is not the creation of God. From this argument, he draws the conclusion that God does not make a man to be an unbeliever, because unbelief is an addition to the man who is an unbeliever.

'Abbad's interpretation of evil was opposed by al-Jubba'i (d. A.D. 915). He said that the distinction between 'power over evil' and 'power to do evil' is invalid. He maintained that from this distinction it would follow that God is weak though He has power, because He is not the agent of such action. As to the example given by 'Abbad, al-Jubba'i is reported to have said:

> If God brought about conception in a woman, he said, then he was 'one causing conception' (*muhbil*), although this was the word which would normally be applied to her husband.

Regarding his interpretation of evil and the reward in the life of hereafter, al-Jubba'i is well-known for his failure to give a satisfactory answer to his pupil, al-Ash'ari, on the theory of *salah wa al-aslah,* i.e 'God is bound to do the best for His creatures.' His failure to explain this theory is regarded as one of the causes of al-Ash'ari's separation from the school of the Mu'tazilites.

From these brief observations on the Mu'tazilite doctrine, it is obvious that though they differ in interpretation they are alike in their main aim, i.e., to maintain the justice of God and the uniqueness of God. On the basis of this similarity, we shall in the following paragraphs examine their arguments in general to see the problem clearly.

The Mu'tazilites believed that God's Will is not related to everything, for the following reason:

> God's volitions are in time, say that God wills His particular acts in the sense that He purposes to create them according to His knowledge. His will precedes the act by a moment. He

wills that the good acts of His servants should come to pass and that the evil should not.

From this proposition, they argued: "If God's will is related to everything, He wills evil...If He wills evil, He is evil." From this argument, arise two fundamental questions: if it is not God who creates evil, then who is the creator of it? And why does God not create evil?

Their answer to the first question is based on the assertion that voluntary actions are made by means of human capability given by God. Good and evil actions are described as voluntary. Therefore, they said that good and evil are made by man's capability given by God. It is false, according to them, to hold that evil is created by God.

Regarding the second question, the Mu'tazilites based their answer on the goodness of the creation of God. They held that God is only bound to do what is best for His creatures. They argued:

> A wise man only does a thing for a wise purpose: and action without purpose is useless folly. The wise acts for his own advantages or to profit someone else. Since God is exalted above profit obviously He must act for the profit of others, and all His acts must be salutary the best for His creatures.

In the connection, the Mu'tazilites fall into two different groups. The first hold the opinion expressed by the Mu'tazilites of the Bahgdad section. They asserted that, in providing the greatest possible powers of mind and body of man, God was bound to do the best for them; even the punishment in the life hereafter is the best for them because when man is released from Hell, he is fit for Heaven. The second opinion was that of the Mu'tazilites of the Basra section, who hold that creation was the result of grace and favour. Moreover, God is bound to avoid weaknesses in man and do the best for them. Both of these sections are right, as far as their doctrine of *salah wa al-aslah* is concerned. Both sections believed that God is bound to do the best for His creatures. This position followed from another interpretation of the unbeliever or the disobedient.

> If God knew that a people would be disobedient to His commands through an apostle, His knowledge would restrain His from willing their performance. If He knew that men would disbelieve and pe :sh, their well-being would turn Him from His wish. It is as thought one let down a rope to a drowning man, knowing that he would strangle himself with it.

Al-Ash'ari on Evil

The Mu'tazilite position on the problem of evil was totally rejected by al-Ash'ari. The idea of maintaining the justice of God by attributing the creation of evil to an agent other than God, according to al-Ash'ari, would only raise another fundamental problem, i.e., it would comprise the sovereignty of God. If God is not creator of evil, then God would not be all— powerful. Evil exists, and to deny this would mean denying the reality of our history. Now, if the occurrence of such evil has nothing to do with God, then it would entail two alternatives: either (a) it exists by itself, or (b) it exists through an agent other than God. As to the former, al-Ash'ari argued that every existing being does not exist by itself. This is in contrast to Mu'ammar's view that 'human actions need no creator' but exist by their nature through the 'body'. Though Mu'ammar emphasized human actions, the same point is also applied to evil because evil is regarded as an accident, and every accident must be ascribed to the action of bodies themselves. Since, the first alternative has been proved to be false, we conclude that evil exists through another agent. If this agent is not God, then it would lead to a concept of dualism; which is contrary to the Islamic concept of God and creation.

Al-Ash'ari develops his doctrine to maintains that God is the creator of evil, yet He is a just God. In other words, according to al-Ash'ari, to say that God is the creator of evil does not at all lead to the conclusion that God is not a just, all-powerful God. First of all al-Ash'ari argued that evil, like all other things, is the creation of

God. The in his reply to the Mu'tazilite position he said the God's actions are without purpose. Again, to avoid any confusion with the Mu'tazilites, he maintained that God creates evil to be the evil of another being distinct from Himself.

(i) The Createdness of Evil by God

It has been argued by al-Ash'ari that God creates everything in the universe, including the human actions, compulsory and voluntary. This claim leads to another, that good and evil are believed to be the creation of God. On the other hand, the Mu'tazilites maintained that God creates only good but not evil, because God does what is best for His creatures. Then the question arises, if God is not the creator of evil, who is the creator of it? If it is created by some one other than God then it will follow that the agent (other than God) must be an effective power in the sense that he can create things contrary to God's creation. This is certainly a dualistic position.

Regarding the theory of effective power, al-Ash'ari claimed that "if God wills a thing, it is, and when He does not will it, it is not." Here we will elaborate it in order to see how it applies to our present discussion. Al-Ash'ari put forward two alternatives regarding the theory of effective power:

> Which is the worthier of the attributes of effective power; he of whom it is true that, when he wishes a thing to be, it must certainly be and when he does not wish it, it is not; or he who wills it to be and it is not, and what he does not will, is?

He then claimed that the Mu'tazilited are in favour of the second alternative, then they support an untenable conclusion. And if they were in favour of the first alternative, then they would have admitted that Satan is worthier of effective power than God. From this argument, al-Ash'ari is trying to oppose the Mu'tazilite position that evil was created by an agent other than God. This agent must be regarded as an effective power to will and create evil. This certainly follows from their position that Satan is more effective than God, since what he (Satan) wills, is, and what he does not will, is not. Moreover, this argument deals directly with the problem of the eternity of God's knowledge and His eternal will. Al-Ash'ari recognizes the eternity of God's knowledge and will. From this assertion, he argued that 'God eternally knows' will be true at a given time, and His will which is eternal will also be at that same time. Consequently, what He knows will not be eternally, nor what He eternally wills. Therefore, He wills what He knows in eternity.

The indirect consequence of this position is that, since God's will is eternal, like His knowledge, there is no reason to maintain that the creation of evil is without His will, for what He eternally knows will be and what He eternally wills will be; and what He eternally knows will not be, and what He eternally wills will not be, will not be. Therefore, from this argument, there is no reason to maintain that evil is not created by God, for He knows it to be and wills it to be. The majority of Muslim scholars agree that God is the only effective power in the universe, which leads to the following conclusion:

> When God wills a thing, it is, and when He does not will it, it is not because He is the worthier of the effective power.

Then, it is certain that another agent is not regarded as an effective power. If he is effective, this would lead to dualism. Since another agent is not effective in power, therefore, to claim that evil is created by an agent other than God is meaningless and invalid.

The Mu'tazilite position in maintaining that God only creates good but not evil was reckoned to be similar to the dualistic concept of Zoroastrianism. In the teachings of Zoroastrianism, the world was regarded as the battle-ground of good and evil. The good was led by Ahura-Mazda and the evil was led by Angra Mainyu, also known later as Ahriman.

Regarding the Mu'tazilite position, al-Ash'ari argued that, it they held that God created only the good, not the evil, they would fall into the dualistic concept of God and creation as was found in the teaching of Zoroastrianism. Since the Mu'tazilites would not accept the Zoroastrian position, the only alternative remaining to them, according to al-Ash'ari, was to maintain that God creates the good as well as the evil. This certainly will not fall into dualism but recognizes the power of God.

However, just as surely, the Mu'tazilite conception of Creator and creation is far different from that of Zoroastrianism. But al-Ash'ari maintained that the idea of separating the creation of good and evil is similar to the doctrine of Zoroastrianism. This claim was made by the later follower of al-Ash'ari, ibn al-Murtada, especially in his comment of Mu'ammar's position. Ibn al-Murtada stated that: "Mu'ammar has been exposed to gnosticism and Zoroastrianism."

(ii) God's Actions Without Purpose

It has been mentioned before that the theory of *salah wa al-aslah* (God creates the best for His creatures) maintains the goodness and justice of God. From this theory, it was concluded that God is bound to do the best for His creatures. It also states that God does not create evil, for creating evil is surely contrary to the goodness of God. Al-Ash'ari's reply to this theory was reported by al-Shahrastani.

Al-Shahrastani used the term 'orthodox' to refer to a school including al-Ash'ari, opposed to the Mu'tazilite position. The argument is elaborated as follows: If God is bound to do what is best for His creatures due to the fact that God who is regarded as wise must do and act for a wise purpose and an action without purpose is unthinkable as held by the Mu'tazilites, then it would follow that the Creator is absolutely dependent. Firstly, this argument is a direct reply to the position of the Mu'tazilites in general, especially with regard to their theory of *salah wa al-aslah*, by which they argued that "a wise man only does a thing for a wise purpose: and action without purpose is useless folly." Secondly, it deals with al-Nazzam's position in particular, who argued that if we say that God did have knowledge of the evil, it would necessarily follow that He was in need of this evil, for had He not been in need of it, He would not have created it.

Regarding al-Nazzam's argument, though he does not say that God was in need of evil, he used the premise that if, for example, something exists, God had need of it. The phrase 'had need' shows that God's works have purpose. The orthodox said that God's actions are without purpose, therefore, al-Nazzam's premise in his argument in invalid. As to the theory of *salah wa al-aslah* which involved the use of the phrase 'God's action is with purpose, the orthodox claim that the Mu'tazilites' theory is invalid, because to claim that God's action is with purpose would entail that God is dependent. If He is in need of something as the end product of His actions then He is indeed dependent and not self-sufficient. According to the orthodox. God's action embrace good and He does not destroy the world. However, this does not mean that He is in need of gain and advantage from His actions. Al-Shahrastani concluded that.

> There is a difference between a good consequence following divine operation, and attributing good and utility to the disposition of those acts, just as there is a necessary difference between a perfection which necessitates a thing's existence and one which merely evokes it. The former is an excellence like an inseparable attribute; the latter an excellence like a provocative cause.

From the above argument, it is clear that according to al-Ash'ari and the orthodox, the Mu'tazilites' argument does not hold; since the premise used by them is proved to be invalid, the conclusion is also invalid. Therefore, the theory of *salah wa al-aslah* is meaningless.

Apart from the main aim to establish the doctrine of the justice of God. The theory of *salah wa al-aslah* to maintain that God's actions are the actions of good will and for the welfare of man. The theory is related to the idea of 'Providence' in Christianity. In this connection, it is of interest to compare these two ideas briefly. Regarding the idea of 'Providence,' John of Damascus has stated:

> The work of God are partly according to the goodwill of God

and partly according to permission. Works of goodwill comprise all those which are undeniably good, while works of permission are concessions.

With reference to these two theories, in Islam and Christianity, it is obvious that they are related in the sense they are similar in interpretation. To try to decide whether Christianity influenced Islam or Islam influenced Christianity in this matter, would to another detailed investigation. As far as the theory of *salah wa al-aslah* is concerned, it was developed by Wasil b. 'Ala' (d. A.D. 784). He was the earliest scholar of the Mu'tazilite school and is reported to have adopted this theory from the creed of Ma'bad al-Juhani (d. A.D. 699), Ghaylan al-Dimashaqi (died before A.D. 743), and John of Damascus (d. A.D. 750). It is uncertain whether Muslim scholars were influenced by the Christians in this matter. However, the similarity of these two is quite obvious.

Regarding the origin of these two theories, Sweetman reported that:

> Both Stoicism and Platonism emphasized the providential view of the world. The two great religions, quite apart from Greek philosophy which they came to use, strongly maintained the same belief. Neoplatonism was equally sure and its various exponents, while expressing themselves in various ways, saw the order of the whole cosmos as manifesting in different degrees the Divine Intelligence. In the school of Alexandria, generally speaking, there was an optimistic view of the world.

From this belief account of Greek philosophy concerning the 'providential view of the world,' it is obvious that the theory of *salah wa al-aslah* and 'Providence' are closely related to, and may have originated in Greek philosophy.

The Mu'tazilites, though they differ among themselves in interpreting the uncreatedness of evil by God, all agree that by disassociating God from creating evil, they establish the concept of Justice of God. However, al-Ash'ari accused the Mu'tazilites of borrowing from Greek philosophy and introducing it into doctrine. As far as al-Ash'ari is concerned, he is trying to abolish any external influence in Islamic thought, and he says that the Mu'tazilites are not free from such an influence in their interpretation of evil.

(iii) God Creates Evil to be Evil to Another Being Distinct from Himself

On the basis of the two sections discussed above, at least two conclusions could be drawn. Firstly, the controversial question of maintaining the justice of God (according to the Mu'tazilites) and sovereignty of God (according to the Compulsionists) remains unsolved. Secondly, it is evident that all Muslim scholars who deal with this issue lay more emphasis on the question of 'what God does' rather than 'what man does.'

Regarding the first conclusion, al-Ash'ari is closer to the Jabarites' position on upholding the sovereignty of God. They held that all actions are determined by God whether they are of good or evil. This must be regarded as 'attributing evil to God.' But al-Ash'ari, though he maintained the createdness of evil by God, argued that it did not follow that God is evil. Concerning the second conclusion, since God's action is the main subject to be discussed rather than man's action, it involved the question of 'God's decree.' The word 'decree' is translated as 'decision'. According to al-Ash'ari the term 'God's decree' is not co-extensive with the term 'evil' or 'unbelief'. In favour of this claim, he produced his philosophical arguments which lead to a middle path position between the two extreme schools, that is the Mu'tazilites and the Compulsionists (including the Jabarites).

It has been argued earlier that God is the efficient Creator of everything in the universe in the sense that He creates things as they really are, faith to be good, and unbelief to be bad and false. On the other hand, man, through experience, wants unbelief to be good and feels that faith is painful. Since God is the true producer of unbelief, He can never be the unbeliever, who desires unbelief to be good, neither can He be the producer of faith that is painful. Al-Ash'ari then argued:

> So if the one who produces unbelief as it really is cannot be the unbeliever, and if the one who produces faith as it really is cannot be the believer, then the intention of both must be God Most High, Lord of the Worlds.

The solution of the problem is therefore as follows: It has been shown that God is the producer (creator) of evil, as it really is. He cannot be the evildoer, who desires that evil be good (as contrary to its reality). Therefore, from this analogy, it follows that, according to al-Ash'ari, God creates evil to be evil for another, nor for Himself. He confirmed this claim by a statement: "But I maintain that evil is from God is the sense that He creates it as evil for another, not for Himself."

With respect to the position of Abu al-Hudhayl, who argued that evil proceeds only from deficiency, it is obvious that al-Ash'ari should agree with this statement, for al-Ash'ari said, evil is bad and vain. But he point on which they differ is derived from Abu al-Hudhayl's statement that 'there is no deficiency in God.' Al-Ash'ari should also agree with this statement, for he is in a position of maintaining the absoluteness of God. Their difference lies in their different understanding of the actions of God, especially with regard to evil. Al-Ash'ari argued that God creates evil to be the evil of another, not Himself and this certainly entails that evil proceeds from the evildoer (man), not God. Therefore, it is true that evil is a deficiency, but the second premise, 'there is not deficiency in God' is invalid because evil proceeds from the evildoer, not God. Since, according to al-Ash'ari. God creates evil to be bad and vain, whereas the evildoer wants it to be good.

(iv) The Justice of God

Al-Ash'ari argued in favour of the position that evil is created by God for another, nor for Himself, and God could not be held to be an evildoer or evil itself. However, this position does not directly answer the question whether God is just or unjust. At first sight, al-Ash'ari's position could easily be taken as establishing God as unjust to His creatures. Thus, the question of the justice of God should be dealt with in another way. To analyze this issue, we have to define the terms involved. Since, as has been mentioned before, all Muslim scholars emphasize the question of 'what God does' rather than 'what man does', the term 'God's decree' must play a vital role in dealing with this problem. Besides that, the term 'evil' and 'justice' should be clarified as to what al-Ash'ari meant by them.

Regarding the term 'God's decree,' Al-Ash'ari defined it in his reply to the question whether God decrees acts of disobedience. He answers, "Yes, in the sense that He has created them, and has written them down." From this statement, it is obvious that al-Ash'ari defined the term as co-extensivc with the term 'God's creation.' We have already discussed this position, maintaining that God creates all in the universe as it really is. And in this regard God is understood to have decreed all things in the universe including what is good and what is evil. Since evil is part of God's creation and is also to be regarded as part of what God has decreed, therefore, the term 'evil' is not co-extensive with the term 'God's decree.' It can be said that God's decree is co-extensive with God's creation. But since the existence of evil is only a part of God's total creation, it cannot therefore be said that evil is co-extensive with God's decree. From this clarification, it is unreasonable to claim that the existence of evil in the sense that God creates it, entails anything inconsistent with the term 'God's decree' for evil is not co-extensive with the term 'God's decree'.

Al-Ash'ari divided 'decree' into two kinds. First, decree in the sense of command, announcement and information; this is right. Secondly, decree in the sense of creation; this included right and wrong. But using the word 'unbelief' as an example of 'evil' he concluded,

> We are pleased that God has decreed unbelief as bad and determines it as false, but we are not pleased that the unbeliever is thereby unbelieving because God has forbidden us that.

It is obvious that, though al-Ash'ari believed in God's decree, it does not follow that he is content with the evil of the evildoer, for God does not command such acts.

As to the term 'justice,' al-Shahrastani stated the definition given by the orthodox including al-Ash'ari:

> Justice, in fact, consists in giving things their place, and this implies acting as Lord according to His own will and knowledge. The opposition is injustice and it is inconceivable that he should be wrong in His decision and unjust in His dealing.

The term 'evil' has been defined and discussed before and does not need to be dealt with again. Briefly, evil is simply bad and vain.

As far as al-Ash'ari is concerned, if we are to establish the 'justice of God' with respect of God's decree and the createdness of evil of Him, we are able to justify it through a correct use of these terms.

Al-Ash'ari has proved that God is the true and efficient Creator, for he creates things as they really are and God's decree in the sense of creation, involves what is good and what is evil. But it has been stated that God's decree in the sense of command is regarded as right, therefore, the term 'evil' is not co-extensive with the term 'God's decree.' Regarding the createdness of evil, God creates evil in the sense that He creates it to be vain and bad. This indicates that He is giving evil its place as bad and vain. Therefore, there is no reason to say that God is unjust, though evil is believed to be a creation of God, for 'evil' is created by God as it really is, to be bad and vain.

REFERENCES

1. W.M. Watt, Free will and predistination in early Islam, London, Luzac, 1948, p. 72.
2. Mir Valiuddin, "Mu'tazilism", in A History of Muslim philosophy, vol. I, ed. by M M Sharif, Wiesbaden Otto Harrassowitz, 1963, p. 209.

3. W C Klein, The Theology of al-Ash'ari, Beyrouth, Imrpimerie Catholique, 1853, p. 34.
4. Anwar G Chejne, "Mu'ammar ibn Abbad al-Sulami: Aleading Mu'tazilite of the eight-ninth century," Muslim World, 51 (1961) 313.
5. Mir Valiuddin, "Mu'tazilism," in M M Sharif, vol. I, p. 205.

Revised and edited; originally published in Islamic Culture, Jan., 1990.

6

Perfect Man according to Ibn Al-'Arabi

WILLIAM C CHITTICK

(Abstract: The Muhammadan reality, or, the ideal Prophet is what can be considered as Insan kamil in Ibn al-Arabi's terminology. Discusses the microcosm and macrocosm of the humane and the perfect person in Islamic usage, which is different from the common or forgetful 'man').

Ibn al-'Arabi discusses "man", as "perfect man" (*al-insan al-kamil*), that is, man as originally created and as he is exemplified in the persons of the prophets and the saints. He does not mean the forgetful (or common) man of our own acquaintance. Moreover, "perfect man" can be viewed from two fundamentally different points of view, since we have to distinguish between the human embodiments of perfect man and the "reality of perfect man." In the first case, we are talking about the prophets and the friends of God; in the second, we mean the eternal and immutable archetype of the individual perfect men. The situation is further complicated by the fact that Ibn al-'Arabi refers to the reality of perfect man by many different names. Four our purpose here, we can simply say that he often calls it the "Muhammadan Reality".

According to Islamic cosmology in general and Ibn al-'Arabi's teachings in particular, God created man as the last of the creatures, since He employed all the other creatures to bring him into existence. As the final link in the "great chain of being", man brings together and combines (*jam*) in himself all previous links. Not only does he have animal, vegetal, and mineral components, he also replicates the whole invisible and visible cosmic hierarchy, beginning with the

First Intellect and including the Universal Soul, Prime Matter, the Universal Body, the Throne of God, God's Footstool, the starless sphere, the sphere of the constellations, the seven planets, and the four elements. In some mysterious way, man contains everything in the cosmos.

Ibn al-'Arabi discusses the cosmological links between man and the various strata and creatures of the macrocosm in many contexts. In a brief overview we can do no better than to discuss the most fundamental determinant of man's existence, the fact that he was made in the divine image. According to the Prophet, "God created man in His own image," or, slightly more literally, "Allah created Adam upon His own form." It is important to note the use here of the divine name "Allah," which is called the "all-comprehensive name," since it brings together every other names, such as All-merciful, All-forgiving, Just, Creator, Generous, Powerful, Exalter, Abaser, and so on down the list of the ninety-nine, or 1001, or infinite divine names. No name other than Allah includes in itself all the names, since each of the other names has its own specific and limiting characteristics which sets it apart from the others. Only Allah is truly a universal name.

Since man was created "upon the form of Allah", he was also created "upon the form of" the other names. That is why the Qur'an says that God taught Adam "*all* the names". Hence man displays an indefinite variety of divine aspects or "faces" (*wajh*). If all human attributes and activities for the whole of human history could be brought together in one place, we would begin to have an idea of what manifesting "all the names" implies. It is precisely this human all-comprehensiveness which allows for every sort of human possibility, every imaginable attribute, every conceivable act, whether good or bad, high or low, just or unjust, compassionate or cruel. If, in contrast, Adam had been created upon the from of the All-compassionate, no human being would be angry or cruel; if he had been created upon the from of the Vengeful, no one would ever forgive his enemy; if he had been created upon the from of all All-mighty and the Glorious, he would never obey God or anyone else. But since he was created upon the form of all the names, any conceivable attribute can appear within him. For what are the divine names, but the archetypes of every possibility of existence?

Again, since man comprehends *all* the names, each human individual reflects every divine attribute to some degree. But during the course of a human life the divine names manifest themselves in all sorts of combinations and interrelationship which may or may not produce a harmonious and balanced individual. In the last analysis it is the mode in which the names display their properties within man which determines his destiny in this world and the hereafter. From the human point of view this mode is completely unpredictable, and thus our situation stands in stark contrast to all other creatures, since they are created within known and fixed stations (*maqam ma'lum*). But man has no fixed station, and he can become anything at all. His station does not become fixed until the moment of death.

Only one creature other than man was created upon the form of the name Allah—the cosmos in its entirety. "Cosmos" or "universe" (*al-alam*) is defined as "Everything other than Allah." God and cosmos include everything in existence, while each is the mirror image of the other. Hence every name of God is reflected in the universe. As Ibn al-`Arabi puts it, the cosmos itself is the sum total of all the "properties" (*ahkam*) and "effects" (*athar*) of the Divine Names. The fundamental difference between God and the total universe is that God exists by His very essence and has no need of the cosmos, while the universe has no existence in its essence and has every need for God. In the last analysis, says Ibn al-`Arabi, even to speak of the "existence" of the cosmos is a metaphor (*majaz*), not a reality. The cosmos only exists after a fashion, much as a reflection may be said to exist in a mirror. But God cannot not exist.

May and cosmos are similar in that each was created upon the form of God. However, the cosmos manifests the Divine Names in a differentiated mode (*tafsil*); as a result, each and every name displays its own properties and effects both separately and together with every other name and combination of names. Hence in its spatial and temporal totality, the cosmos represents an infinitely vast panorama of existential possibilities. In contrast, man displays the properties and effects of all the names in a relatively non-differentiated mode (*ijmal*); all the properties of the Divine Names are drawn together and concentrated within him. God created the cosmos upon His own form primarily in respect of the multiplicity of His names, but He created man primarily in respect of the unity of the names, the fact that each and every name refers to single Reality. Ibn al-'Arabi often expresses these ideas by employing the terms "small world" and "great world"—that is, microcosm and macrocosm. More commonly, he uses the expression "small man" or "micro-anthropos" for man and "great man" or "macro-anthropos" for the universe.

Since man is a part of the cosmos, the cosmos is not a complete divine image without him. Hence, at the beginning of the *Fusus al-Hikam*, Ibn al-'Arabi writes that man is the spirit of the cosmos, while the cosmos without man is like a proportioned and well-balanced body, ready and waiting for God to breath His Spirit into it, but lifeless as long as man has not appeared. It is for this reason that Ibn al'Arabi calls perfect man the "pillar" of the cosmos; without him the cosmos would collapse and die, which is precisely what will happen at the end of time when the last perfect man departs from this world for the hereafter. Cosmologically speaking, the corruption and decay of the natural environment is one of the outward signs of the fact that there are fewer and fewer perfect men on the face of the earth.

Though the cosmos is not complete without man, man is complete without the cosmos, since he himself is a total divine form and a total world; that is what perfect man loses nothing through death. Quite the contrary, when he dies he is released from the limitations of the spatio-temporal world and actualizes the full ontological expansion demanded by the Divine Form. He himself blossoms into a limitless world, independent of this world and dependent only upon God.

The Goal of Creation

That the universe without man is incomplete should be enough to alert us to the fact that the cosmos has no purpose in and by itself; its only purpose is to bring man into existence. For perfect man is the "Sought-after Goal" (*al-`ayn al-maqsudah*). God's reason for creating the universe. Ibn al-`Arabi writes.

> The whole cosmos is the differentiation of Adam, while Adam is the all-comprehensive book. In relation to the cosmos He is like the spirit in relation to the body. Hence man is the spirit of the cosmos, and the cosmos is the body. Through bringing together all of this the cosmos is the "great man" as long as man is within it. But if you look at the cosmos alone, without man, you will find it like a proportioned body without a spirit. The perfection of the cosmos through man is like the perfection of the body through the spirit. Man is "breathed into" the body of the cosmos, so he is the goal of the cosmos.

Man is also the goal of the cosmos because no other creature can truly known God. In the famous *hadith* of the Hidden Treasure, God says, "I was a Hidden Treasure and I wanted to be known; so I created the creation that I might be known." Every creature knows God after its own fashion, but only perfect man known." Every creature knows God after its own fashion, but only perfect man knows Him under the guise of Allah, the all-comprehensive name. Ibn al-`Arabi constantly quotes the Qur'anic verses that tell us, "Everything in the heavens and the earth glorifies God". This glorification, he says, is grounded in a knowledge of God possessed by each and every created thing. The creatures glorify God inasmuch as they know Him. Flowers glorify Him as the Lord of the sun, the earth, and the rain, while bees glorify Him as the Lord of flowers. Men glorify Him as the Lord of their goals and desires, whatever these may be. It is God who is Provider, Sustainer, Life-Giver, Merciful, and so on, and all people glorify Him by such names at least by making use of His bounties, whether or not they verbalize their glorification. But only perfect man glorifies God by the name Allah, a glorification which comprehends the glorification of all things.

Perfect man is the only creature complete in itself. Not even the cosmos is complete unless man exists within it. All other creatures within the cosmos are partial images of God and possess an incomplete knowledge of Him.

> Everything is the cosmos is ignorant of the whole and knows a part, except only perfect man, for God taught him all the Names and gave him the all-comprehensive words. So his form was perfected, since he combined the form of God and the form of the cosmos... God sees His own form in the mirror of man..., since all the divine names are ascribed to him.

To summarize: Man, or more precisely perfect man, is the microcosm, since he was created upon the form of every divine name and thereby contains within himself the realities which brought the whole cosmos into existence. The universe as a whole is the macrocosm, so long as perfect man exists within it, since without him it is but a body without a spirit.

As for the reality of perfect man, the "Muhammadan Reality", that is the Form of God in Himself, or the Divine Face turned towards the creation of both macrocosm and microcosm. In other words, microcosm and macrocosm are two Forms of God manifest (*zahir*) within the created order; but the reality of perfect man is the Form of God as nonmanifest (*batin*), or in other words, that which is designated by the name "Allah". Ibn al-'Arabi writes,

> Perfect man is sought after for his own sake, since he is the manifest of the Form of Allah. But god Himself is both the Manifest and the Nonmanifest.

The Path to Perfection

Because perfect man contains all the realities of both God and the cosmos, he recognizes God in all things. He sees with a vision whereby all veils are lifted. For him the words of the Qur'an are concretely realized: "Wherever you look, there is the face of God". For perfect man, everything is a divine Self-disclosure (*tajalli*). Ibn al-`Arabi writes,

> The original disposition (*firah*) of Adam is the original disposition of all the cosmos..., it is the Self-disclosure of Allah... So within him is the capacity (*isti'dad*) of every existent thing in the cosmos. Hence he worships by every religion, he glorifies God with every Self-disclosure—on condition that he fulfills his humanity and knows himself. For he does not know his Lord except through knowledge of himself. If anything of himself veils him from seeing the whole, he has committed a crime against himself, and he is not a perfect man... By perfection is meant knowledge of self, and knowledge of self is identical with knowledge of the Lord. Adam's original disposition was his knowledge of God, so he knew the original disposition of all things. That is why God says, "He taught Adam all the Names".

Achieving perfection depends upon knowing oneself, and to know oneself is to know Allah. In Ibn al-'Arabi's vocabulary, those who do not achieve perfection are known as 'animal man" (*al-insan al-hayawan*). Though Adam was created perfect, imperfection and animality have gradually come to be the dominating characteristics of his children. But we should not take man's present animal state as normative. Hence, it is incorrect to define man as a "rational animal", since, as Ibn al-'Arabi puts it, "Man is defined specifically by the Divine Form." He writes,

> A person who does not reach perfection in this world is a rational animal, a part of the Divine Form, nothing else. He does not reach the degree of man. On the contrary, he is related to man as a corpse is related to a human being, since a corpse is a man in shape, but not in reality; the corpse lacks all powers, just like him who does not reach perfection.

Ibn al-'Arabi refers to the process whereby human being come to possess the divine names in fact and not just virtually as "assuming the traits of the Names of Allah" (*al-takhalluq bi asma Allah*), or "assuming God's character traits" (*al-takhalluq bi akhlaq Allah*). He identifies this assumption of divine traits with the spiritual path. It is clear that the reason man must assume the divine trait is that he does not manifest them in his present situation, and it would be a terrible error to imagine that man is perfect simply by virue of being human. How then does one become perfect?

To summarize Ibn al-'Arabi's answer: one must follow the divine guidance, revealed through the prophets. Only in this way can man bring his beliefs, his thoughts, and his activities into conformity with the Divine Form upon which he was created. Ibn al-'Arabi often refers to this divine guidance as the balance of the Law (*al-mizan al-shar'i*); in other words, it is the Law or *Shari'ah* revealed by God and exemplified in its highest form through the Qur'an and the example of Muhammad. Only the external, formal, particular pronouncements of God can protect man from his own ego-centric ignorance and the whims and desires of others. Only a norm revealed by God Himself can allow man to assume God's character traits and names. The most ḍangerous course a person can follow is to fall back upon his own interpretation of the nature of things or upon an interpretation that is not firmly rooted in thc Balance of the Law. Many passages from Ibn al-'Arabi's works could be quoted to illustrate these themes. One examples will have to suffice:

> Beware of throwing the Balance of the Law your hand!... If you understand from the Law something different from what the people understand, such that your understanding prevents you from performing the apparent and exoteric statute of the Law, do not rely upon your own understanding! For it is the ego's deception taking a divine form but coming from a direction of which you are unaware.

> We have met sincere people... who were confused in this station. They preferred their own mystical unveiling (*kashf*) and their own understanding to the established statute of the Law, thereby nullifying the statute. They depended upon unveiling in their own case, and then they let other people observe the status exoterically. But in our view this unveiling

> is nothing... Anyone who relies upon it has suffered a dreadful confusion and has left the framework of the path of the People of God, thereby joining those who are the "greatest losers," those about whom the Qur'an says, "Their striving has gone astray in the present life, while they think they are working good deeds".

The Balance of the Law provides the only means whereby one can hope to assume the character traits of God, yet, paradoxically, following it does not mean that one actively strives "to assume God's character traits." In other words, one does not try to imitate God's generosity, His justice, His forgiveness, and so on. A little reflection upon the diversity and multiplicity of God's names should be enough to show that this sort of task is totally beyond the reaches of our forgetful human nature and that the very attempt to imitate God would involve a tremendous arrogance. The goal of striving on the pat is not to acquire God's attributes for ourselves, but to negate our own attributes. Man does not gradually grow in stature until he becomes a kind of demigod rivalling God Himself. On the contrary, man is gradually reduced in stature until there is nothing left of himself. But since nothing belongs to man in the first place, once he eliminates his own attributes and effaces his own self, there remains only that which truly is: the face of God turned toward creating him, the Divine Form, the Reality of Muhammad.

This explains why Ibn al-'Arabi often describes the station of perfect man in negative terms, since positive terms can only refer to the Self-disclosure of God Himself. On the metaphysical level, Ibn al-'Arabi explains that perfect man returns to his own immutable archetype, which is non-existent in relation to the cosmos. It is well-known that Ibn al-'Arabi speaks of the "Oneness of Being" and the fact that all true existence belongs exclusively to God. Our *existence* as separate creatures is illusory, since existence is God's; but our *reality* as separate creatures derives from the Eternal Divine knowledge, and so our reality is eternal and immutable. When perfect man negates his own existence as a separate creature, he returns to his non-existence, which is his true nature; but by the same token he dwells in eternity, at ease in the Being and bliss of God.

Humanly speaking the station of perfection is described by the term 'servanthood" (*ubudiyah*). As Ibn al-`Arabi often remarks, it is impossible to gain nearness (*qurb*) to God without being His servant. Perfect man is the utter and absolute servant of God; he does nothing on his own, since his separate existence has been negated. Whatever, he does is done by god through him. In many passages Ibn al-'Arabi speaks of servanthood as the highest human station, achieved primarily by Muhammad, the most perfect of the perfect men, who is known to all Muslims as "God's servant and His messenger" (*`abduhu wa rasuluh*). First Muhammad is God's servant, then only is he worthy to be His messenger. It goes without saying that in order to reach this extremely exalted station of servanthood, one must first follow the commands of one's Lord to the last detail. In other words, servanthood cannot possibly be actualized outside the framework of the revealed Law.

Ibn al-'Arabi tells us that he himself had actualised servanthood in imitation of Muhammad to the highest degree. He alludes to this point in many passages, and in some cases he is quite explicit. For example,

> On the night that I wrote down this chapter, I had a dream that
> filled me with joy. I awoke and I composed a verse....
>
> *Every age has a person through whom it soars—*
> *For the rest of this age, I am that one!*
>
> This is because, to my knowledge, there is no one today who has realized the station of servanthood more than I, though there may be my equal. For I have reached the utmost limit of servanthood. I am the pure and utter servant who knows no taste of Lordship!

One more point needs to be brought out. By now it should be

clear that according to Ibn al-'Arabi, being a perfect man is not only the *highest* possible human aspiration, it is also, properly speaking, the *only* human aspiration. If man does not actualize the Divine Form upon which he was created, he remains but an animal, less than human, no matter what sort of great deeds he may have accomplished in this world. The station of perfection is the mark of being human, and it has only been achieved by a relatively small number of those whom we normally refer to as "human beings." By reaching perfection man becomes the absolute servant of God, totally effaced as an independent individual but fully affirmed as a Divine Form. Perfect man lives in every situation exactly as that situation demands according to the Wisdom of God, not according to any human norms. Perfect man is fully and completely merciful, compassionate, forgiving, loving, generous, just, and so on, exactly as demanded by the Divine Reality Itself.

One could go on listing the attributes of perfect man indefinitely. I merely want of point out that the station of perfection as described by Ibn al-'Arabi is beyond out wildest fantasies of what it means to be human. If this is so, would it not be better for all of us to give up the idea of being perfect? Certainly not, says Ibn al-'Arabi, since in any case we have to live up to the Truth which is embodied within ourselves; in any case we owe it to God to follow the Balance of the Law, which He revealed to guide our activity; and in any case God has guaranteed happiness in the hereafter to those who follow the Law to the extent of their capacities, whether or not they reach perfection. But as human beings, we must always strive to attain to our true archetype, the Muhammadan Reality itself. I close with one further quotation from the "Greatest Master":

> You should think about the degree of animal man in relation to perfect man, and then you should try to understand which kind of man you are yourself. For you have the capacity to receive perfection, if you understand. That is why you have been admonished and notified by the whole world. If you did not have the capacity to receive perfection, it would be incorrect to admonish you, and letting you know about perfection

would be vain and useless. So blame only yourself if you do not reach that to which you have been called[2]!

REFERENCES

1. Ibn al-Arabi, Futuhat al-Makkiyah, Beirut, n.d.
2. Al-Quran, XIV: 22.

Revised and edited; originally published in Islamic Culture, Jan-april, 1989.

7

Methodology of Understanding Islam

BASHIR A DABLA

(Abstract: Presents a world view of Islamic studies, as given by Ali Shariati. Shariati emphasises on the fact that the analysis of approaches and methods of understanding Islam is of fundamental importance as they develop correct thought which is basic to true knowledge and that true knowledge creates sound belief).

Islam represents a world view which encompasses the whole of life. While it deals with personal matters, it also provides guidance in social affairs. According to Dr. Ali Shariati, Islam is "a school of thought that gives life to man, individual and society, and that is entrusted with the mission of the future guidance of mankind." He felt that Islam is universal, humanistic, scientific, innovative, creative, providing divine guidance to Muslims and humanity. It is for change and revolution and against exploitation and injustice; demands full commitment in theory and practice; and provides the model society (*Ummah*) and the model personality (Prophet Muhammad). He presented Islam in the historical perspective by observing that

> . . . Islam is not a new religion but an integral part of a larger stream which has flowed through the chord of entire human history. Various Prophets were ordained at different times to establish the universal religion in accordance with the circumstances of the age and the need of the era. Islam ... (is related) with other movements which, throughout history, have been launched to emancipate and ameliorate the lives of the people."

Shariati believed that the analysis of the approaches and methods of understanding Islam is of fundamental importance because they develop correct thought which is basic to true knowledge and that (true knowledge) creates sound belief. This analysis is of utmost importance because the Muslims, in general, and non-Muslims, in particular, lack the proper understanding of Islam.

In regard to the understanding of Islam, Shariati raised a question of fundamental importance, i.e., what is the correct method of knowing about Islam? He answered this question in detail. According to him, while trying to know the correct method, one must not fall into the trap of imitation of any European method—naturalistic, psychological or sociological. This is because the wholesale borrowing or borrowing with certain adjustments of the European methods distorts theoretical as well as empirical realities. So, he felt that in order to find a proper method to learn about Islam, one must be innovative enough in devising a new method, which may include some of the elements of the European method/s. The partial inclusion of the Western methods is necessary because new approaches have been discovered in the West for investigation of religion and its role in the society. He asserted that there may not be a unique method for understanding Islam comprehensively due to the fact that it (Islam) is multi-dimensional. So, the application of plural methods seems realistic. He said:

> Islam is not a religion based solely on the mystic intuition of man and restricted the relationship between man and God: this is merely one dimension of the religion of Islam. In order to study this dimension, a philosophical method must be followed because man's relation to God is discussed in philosophy, in the sense of general and unfettered metaphysical thought. Another dimension of this religion is the question of man's life of this earth. In order to study this dimension use must be made of the methods that have been established in the human sciences of today. Then, too, Islam is a religion that has built a society and a civilization; in order to study these, the method of history and sociology must be used.

Shariati held that there are two fundamental methods for learning Islam correctly. These methods are as follows:

(i) the study of the Qur'an, taking it as the compendium of the ideas and the scientific and literary output of the person known as 'Islam'; and

(ii) the study of Islamic history, taking it as the sum total of the developments in Islam from the beginning of the Prophet's mission down to the present.

He explained these two methods in the logic of equating Islam with the human personality. A religion, according to him, is like a person in the methodological context. In order to acquire correct knowledge about a great personality, the researcher adopts two main methods which are: (i) investigation of the intellectual, scientific, and written works of the individual concerned; and (ii) extensive study of his biography which includes all of his major and minor life-events. Similarly, the correct understanding of Islam can be achieved by the study of its original source, i.e. Qur'an and its historical development. what precisely he meant was as follows:

> The knowledge and understanding of the Qur'an as the source of the ideas of Islam, and the knowledge and understanding of Islamic history as the record of the various events that have occurred at different times—these are the two fundamental methods for attaining a precise and scientific knowledge of Islam.

Shariati felt that the degree of knowledge and understanding of both, the Qur'an and Islamic history, prevalent among the Muslims is very low. By implication, he meant that both of these original sources must be studied comprehensively for knowing Islam correctly.

Shariati presented another method, which is one of the widely used methods in Europe, for gaining knowledge and understanding Islam, i.e., the method of typology. The meaning which he attached to this method is that it consists of "classifying topics and themes according to type and then comparing them on that basis." In this context, he developed a particular method for studying religion, which is applicable to all religions. This method has got two important features: first, it emphasizes the identification of five distinctive characteristics of Islam; and secondly, it compares them with the corresponding features in other religions. He felt that the five distinctive and comparable characteristics of any religion are as under:

(i) the god or gods of every religion, i.e., the entity worshipped by the followers of the religion;

(ii) the prophet of each religion, i.e., the person who proclaims the message of the religion;

(iii) the book of each religion, i.e., the foundation of the law proclaimed by the religion, to which it invites men in faith and obedience;

(iv) the circumstances of the appearance of the prophet of each religion and the audience to which he addresses himself, for each prophet proclaims his message in a different fashion; and

(v) those choice individuals each religion nurtures and produces—the representative figures it has trained and then presented a society and history.

Shariati has operationalized this method in five stages in the case of Islam. We will explain these stages in the following:

1. The First Stage

One must examine the type, concept, features and characteristics of God discussed in Islam; one must refer to the Qur'an and words of the Prophet as well as the elite among those whom he trained; and one must compare Allah with the figures depicted in other religions as God, such as Ahuramazda, Yahwa, Zeus, Baal and so on.

2. The Second Stage

One must understand what kind of a book the Qur'an is, what topics it discusses, and what areas it emphasizes; one must study what matters the Qur'an treats and in exactly what fashion; and one must develop a comparison between the Qur'an and other religious texts, such as the Gospels, the Torah, the Vedas, the Avesta, and so on.

3. The Third Stage

One must concentrate on the personality of the Prophet in both human and prophetic dimensions; one must study the way in which he spoke, worked, thought, smiled, sat, and slept; one must observe the nature of his relations with strangers, with enemies, with friends, and with family; one must examine his failures and his triumphs and the manner in which he confronted great social problems; one must compare him with other prophets and founders of religions like Moses, Jesus, Zoroaster and the Buddha.

4. The Fourth Stage

One must examine whether the Prophet appeared without any preliminary and if anyone was waiting for him; one must know whether he anticipated and knew the mission; one must enquire about the extraordinary current of thought which began to flow through his mind totally changing his manner of speech and personality in such fashion that he initially found it difficult to bear; one must observe how he confronted men when he first proclaimed his mission; one must compare the circumstances under which the Prophet of Islam appeared with those under which other prophets such as Jesus, Abraham, Moses, Zoroaster, Confucius, Buddha and others appeared. A definite comparison is portrayed by Shariati among the prophets of the Abrahamic and non-Abrahamic lines. While all prophets of the non-Abrahamic line turn immediately to the existing secular power, hoping to propagate their message in society by means of that power, all prophets of the Abrahamic line from Abraham to Muhammad proclaim their missions in the form of rebellion against the existing secular power.

5. The Fifth Stage

One must choose to study Aaron in the religion of Moses, St. Paul in the religion of Jesus, and 'Ali, Husayn and Abu Dharr in the religion of Islam, as outstanding specimens of each of the religions.

During the study of the life of Husayn, one must try to know the principles for which he fought, his sensitivity with respect to social matters and the destiny of the people, and his devotion and self-sacrifice towards the Islamic cause. Shariati compares Husayn with Abu 'Ali Sina and Husayn bin Mansur Hallaj. Ibn Sina was a great philosopher, scholar, and genius, and an outstanding figure in the history of science and philosophy in the Islamic civilization. But he placed himself in the service of rank and power and never showed any concern with the destiny of men and the fate of his society. Similarly, Hallaj was a man aflame with the passionate love of God. He was constantly immersed in the burning invocation of God and this was a source of true exaltation for him. But, his 'spiritual lunacy' could hardly have any social impact.

Shariati felt that if Islam is understood through the adoption of the above-mentioned scientific methods, new realities will dawn upon observes, including laymen. In fact, the scientific study of Islam lead to new horizons of knowledge. He said:

> There are several important topics in the human sciences that I discovered with the aid of the Qur'an that have not yet been discussed by these (natural) sciences.

In order to prove his point, he gave the examples of the ideas of 'migration' and 'change and development.' He maintained that the study of these ideas in the Islamic context would divulge new realities which could not be discovered within the Western scientific framework. This type of study will also help in understanding many questions of history and sociology in a better, fresher and more precise fashion.

According to Shariati, migration (*Hijrah*) is not merely "a historical event" from the point of view of the Qur'an. It is rather a profound philosophical and social principle in the sociological and historical sense. It is because the development of all known civilizations is directly related to the process of migration. On the basis of his study of the Qur'an, Shariati concluded that

> All the civilizations in the world—from the most recent, the civilization of America, to the most ancient that we know of, the civilization of Sumer—came into being on the heels of a migration. In each case, a primitive people remained primitive as long as it stayed in its own land, and attained civilization after undertaking a migration and establishing itself in a new land. All civilizations are, then, born of the migrations of primitive peoples.

Similarly, Shariati discovered some very distinguishing ideas in Islam regarding the basic factors in the change and development of societies, the topic which has been debated in the human sciences for hundreds of years. In regard to this topic, the social scientists in the West have taken varying positions, often contradictory and one at the cost of the other. While one school considered accident to be the basic factor, another school believed in the human evolution in accordance with pre-determined laws that play exactly the same role in human society as the laws of nature in the human realm. In the same way, white some proclaimed that laws are no more than a tool in the hand of powerful personalities who always act as the guides for societies, others held the opinion that the people—the generality of society—do play the role in determining their destiny. Shariati comments that none of these theories could be found in Islam exclusively. After a detailed and careful study of the Qur'an, he concluded that

> While the people are those to whom the Qur'an addresses itself and they constitute the axis and fundamental factor in social development and change, and while they are responsible before God, at the same time, personality, chance and tradition also have been recognized as capable of affecting the destiny of society. According to Islam, there are then four fundamental factors of social development and change—personality, tradition, accident and *al-nas* (the people).

Among these four factors, he distinguished two—*al-nas* and tradition—as the most important. *Al-nas* represents the scientifically demonstrable laws which exist in society. The meaning, nature and implications of the above-mentioned fundamental factors are explained in the following five ways:

(i) Personality, according to Islam, is not a creative factor in itself. Even the prophets have not created new norms in society. Sociologically, their superiority over teachers and reformers may be explained in terms of their divine knowledge and the consequent behaviour. In the Qur'an, the prophet has been portrayed as the bearer of message whose duty was to show man the school and the path of truth. However, his message had a definite context. That is why, his personality had an important "role in bringing change, development and progress in building a future civilization and in changing the course of history."

(ii) Accident has no decisive role in Islam, for God intervenes directly or indirectly in all affairs. It has neither a logical cause nor an ultimate purpose. Moreover, accident cannot come in the way of Islam because it, as a scientific school of thought, believes that change and development stem from the societal dynamics which possess immutable and scientifically demonstrable norms. However, a certain form of accident exists in human fate. Shariati explained it by the example of Chingiz Khan who appears in Mongolia, comes to power in accordance with social norms, and assembles a large force around him. But, the defeat of Iran at the hands of Chingiz Khan is an accident; it was quite possible for it not to have occurred.

(iii) The historical fact is that those addressed by any school of thought, religion or prophet constitute the fundamental factor of social change. While the Qur'an is addressed to *al-nas*, the Prophet was sent to the same. Moreover, it is *al-nas* (the people without any particular class or social form), not the prophet, who are accountable for their deeds, especially for decline and degeneration. Thus Shariati claimed:

> Islam is the first school of social thought that recognizes the masses as the basis, the fundamental and conscious factor in determining history and society.

(iv) Islam appears to approach the theory of determinism in a particular way. While accepting the fact that change emanates in society on the basis of fixed patterns and immutable laws, the individual is equally responsible in determining society's fate. So, both—society and individual—are responsible for their destinies. Shariati says that

> Society... has been established on the basis of God-given norms and patterns, and its development and evolution is also founded on them. But at the same time man is responsible, and the cannot divest himself of his responsibility through reliance upon Khayyamian fatalism or historical determinism, thus ridding himself of accountability for the destiny of his society.

(v) The role and interaction pattern of these factors, mentioned above, is interesting. The proportional influence of these factors depends on the circumstances prevailing in society. In societies where *al-nas* is in an advanced stage of development in the cultural and educational fields, the role of personality gets minimized. In contrast, in societies that have a lower level of civilization, the individual emerges as influential. Moreover, at different stages of societal development, one of the factor will have greater effect than other factors.

REFERENCES

1. Ali Shariati, On the sociology of Islam, tr., Hamid Algar, (Lectures by Ali Shariati), Berkeley, 1979.
2. A H H Abidi, "Dr. Ali Shariati: The man and his ideals," Islam and the Modern Age, May 1982, p. 95.
3. See my article, "Sociology of Islam: Shariati's viewpoints," Islamic Culture, October 1983.

(Edited; originally published in Islamic Culture, Jan-April 1989.

8

Al-Farabi and His Theory of Dreams

MU'TAZID WALI UR-RAHMAN

(Abstract: Before embarking upon the task of uncritically exposing Al-Farabi's theory of dreams a preamble outlining his psychological doctrines will not be amiss, for it will show the ground on which this theory stands and thus facilitate understanding of his thesis. Here no attempt can obviously be made to dive deep into these doctrines. Only so much of his psychological teachings will receive attention as will help to clarify the basic conceptions).

Al-Farabi's style consists of a series of contentious expressions, which always appear to be profound and scholarly; but sometimes the absence of methodical sequence makes them rather obscure. Being a difficult and an obscure author, it is a mistake to interpret him dogmatically.

In his psychological teaching Al-Farabi shows himself a very faithful disciple of Aristotle. Like his master, he is a staunch upholder and a forceful advocate of the faculty psychology that it was the fashion in those days to present to the thoughtful public. He differs from his master only in minor points. Leaving aside these differences, there is not much to demarcate the one from the other. Aristotle endows the human soul with five principal faculties: Vegetative power, on which the maintenance of the corporeal organism depends; Appetitive power, which is exerted in striving after what is agreeable, and repelling what is disagreeable; the faculty of Sensuous Perception, by which objects perceptible by the senses are represented in our cognitions; the Locomotive faculty, by which we are enabled to move the body and its members, and make use of them in external action; and lastly

Reason. The Appetitive power is of two kinds: the Concupiscible and the Irascible according as it merely strives for what is good, or rises in opposition to the hindrances which stand between it and the attainment of the good it is seeking. Under the faculty of Sensuous Perception he subsumes the faculty of Imagination and Memory.

According to Al-Farabi, man comes into this world equipped with certain faculties which help him to lead a peaceful life, and to meet its dangers successfully, First, and of foremost importance, is the Nutritive faculty, which nourishes the somatic self. After it comes the Sensitive faculty with its five external senses. With the help of one of these he senses heat, cold, etc., or the tangible qualities of the objects. This is the sense of Touch. By the help of the second he obtains the gustatory qualities of external things. This is the sense of Taste. By the third he gets at the fragrance of the things. This is the sense of Smell. The fourth helps him in audition. This is the sense of Hearing. By the fifth he sees light. This is the sense of Sight. Along with these senses is created an Inclination towards what he senses—i.e., he either likes it, or dislikes it. This faculty is known as the Appetitive faculty. This faculty is the basis of volition. Volition is the inclination towards, or away from, what a man perceives, either by the senses or by imagination or by reason. Then there is another faculty which enables a man to reproduce the sensuous image of the sensible objects, without the immediate presence of these objects. This is the faculty of Imagination. This faculty joins certain sensible objects and separates others in a variety of ways. Some of these joining and separations are true and some are false. They are true in the sense that there is a like of them among the sensible objects, and false in the sense, that there is nothing like them in the external world. Inclination also accompanies what a man imagines. After this comes the Rational faculty. With the help of this faculty it is possible for a man to conceive of intellectual and intelligible things, to discriminate between the beautiful and the ugly, and to master arts and sciences. Here again inclination accompanies what a man conceives.

Now in every one of these faculties there is a "chief" and several "menials" and "servants." The "menials" and "servants" are dispersed throughout the body, and the "chief", by its very nature, controls and manages them. The liver, for example is an organ, which is a "chief" and a "servant" at the same time. It is mastered by the heart, but in its turn masters the gall-bladder, the spleen and the like. Similarly the bladder serves the heart, and so on. Similar arrangement obtains in the senses. In the Sensuous faculty the well-known five external senses are the "menials' and the "servants," and they are dispersed in the eye, the ear, and so forth. The "chief" over them is that power, which combines what all these "servants" have gathered. This power is known as the Common Sense. This "chief" also dwells in the heart. The faculty of Imagination is, however, an exception. It has no "menials" or "servants." It is unitary, and is also located in the heart. It is, by its very nature, a "chief" over the sensible objects. The Rational faculty is different in this respect from all the other faculties. Its 'menials" and "servants" are not of its own class. It lords it over all the other faculties. The Appetitive faculty has its "servants" also. All the organs of the body, all the nerves, and all the muscles, in short everything and anything which helps in the execution of the bodily movements, are these "servants." This "chief" also has its eat in the heart. This obviously means that heart is the "capital" for all the "chief" faculties.

With the help of this introduction we shall be able to follow Al-Farabi through the exposition of his dream-theory, to which I now proceed.

Even a cursory glance over what Al-Farabi has written about dreams discloses three chief features of his theory:—

(i) Al-Farabi ascribes much importance to the working of Imagination in dream-perception.

(ii) He bases his theory on the doctrine of the temperament in vogue in those days in the realms of Psychology and Medicine.

(iii) He believes that dreams are symbolic, and that we can

dream of anything and everything of which we have had experience during the waking state. So that he has no difficulty in explaining any particular dream.

The faculty of Imagination, he believes, stands somewhere between the Sense and the Reason. When by the faculty of Sensuous Perception we actually sense a thing, and when this faculty functions normally, the faculty of Imagination is absolutely passive, in so far as it is engaged in receiving the impressions from the sensible objects. In addition to this it is in the service of the Rational faculty, and at the same time it helps the Appetitive faculty. Now when the Appetitive, the Rational, and the Sensuous faculties reach their first perfections and cease to perform their respective functions—as happens in sleep— the faculty of Imagination becomes free. It no longer receives the fresh impressions, which sensible objects pour upon it. At the same time it ceases to serve the Rational, and to help the Appetitive faculties. Now it can comfortably work with and on those impressions of sensible objects that it has so far received and retained. This work takes the forms of aggregation and segregation, in so far as it is its nature to join some impressions and to separate others.

So far it has been assumed that the only function of the faculty of Imagination is to preserve and to retain the impressions of the sensible objects, and to join, or to separate them. But in reality it has a third function also. This third function is Representation or Reproduction. This means that it can form as image, or an exact representation of the sensible objects whose impressions it has preserved. This representation generally takes two forms. Sometimes it represents sensible objects with the help of the five senses, by combining those impressions that it has preserved, making a copy, as it were, of those objects. Sometimes it represents intellectual objects, and at other times it represents the Nutritive and the Appetitive faculties. It can also represent the temperament that a body is moist, it represents this moisture combining those sensible objects which can represent moisture, e.g., water. If this temperament happens to be dry, then this dryness is represented by those sensible objects which can adequately represent dryness. Similarly with coldness and heat of the body. We can go even to the extent of saying that this faculty is, as it were, a form in the body, and the body endows it with its own temperament. But we should not lose sight of the fact that the Imagination is a mental faculty. As such it accepts this temperament according as it is in its nature to accept, and not according to what it is in the nature to accept, and not according to what it is in the nature of the bodies to accept. When a wet body, for example, affects another body with its wetness, this second body becomes wet like the first. But such is not the case with the faculty of Imagination. When wetness, this second body becomes wet like the first. But such is not the case with the faculty of Imagination. When wetness affects it, it does not become wet itself, but it accepts this wetness in the shape of those sensible objects which can adequately represent wetness. It is just as it happens in the Rational faculty. In accepting wetness the Rational faculty only accepts its nature, for everybody knows that the concept of wetness is not itself wet. In the same way when anything affects the faculty of Imagination, it accepts from the agent what it is in its nature to accept. Now suppose a thing affects it, and it is in its nature to accept it, and to accept it in the very from in which it is received. In such cases there are two ways in which the faculty of Imagination accepts. It either accepts the thing as it is, and in the very form in which it is offered, or it represents it by the help of sensible objects which can adequately represent it. Any if it is in its nature to accept it as it is, it accepts it simply because it (the faculty of Imagination) can represent that thing by means of those sensible objects which reach it, and which are fit to represent that thing. It cannot accept intellectual objects as they are. Whatever it has to deal with such objects, it does not accept them as they are in the Rational faculty. It represents them by the help of those objects with which it represents sensible objects. In the same way, when body endows it with its own temperament, it accepts that temperament in the shape of the sensible objects which have that temperament and so can adequately represent that temperament. When it is given an object which it is possible to sense, sometimes it accepts it as it is, and sometimes it represents that sensible object by some other sensible object.

From the above it should be clear that the Imagination, working in the service of the Sensuous Perception, produces two different kinds of dreams. Sometimes it is a reproduction of our actual experience during the waking state. We see and do in our dreams what we have actually seen and done in our normal waking life. This is the form that our dream-consciousness usually takes. This sort of revival, or recall, we known, is one of the primary functions of Imagination. So we have little, if any, difficulty in explaining these revival-dreams. In such dreams the Imagination works freely, unaffected by the limitations of space or time, and unbounded by the extremely narrow circle of present interest. In the other form of the dream all these things obtain, save that the things dreamt of are not exactly those of which we have had experience in the waking consciousness. Here the Imagination substitutes other objects of sense for the real ones. But, of course, these substitutes have some kind of relationship with the original objects. In the first case the Imagination substitutes one object of sense for another object of sense. In the second place, the substitute is of a nature that can adequately represent the original. For the table we do not dream of the moon. Here the symbolism of the dream-content comes in. Such dreams, and such only, stand in need of interpretation. This feature of the dream again does not require much explanation, for this substitution is another of the functions of Imaginations.

This is not all. Our dream-content depends upon the condition of the body as well. When there is much of heat in the body we generally dream of hot things. Similarly when coldness preponderates we usually have dreams of things cold in nature—ice, for example.

In short our dream-content, according to Al-Farabi is determined (1) by our actual normal experience, and (2) by the temperament of the body at the time of dreaming.

So far we have taken account of the working of Imagination in connection with the Sensuous Perception, and the consequent cognitive nature of the dream. But dreams are not always cognitive in nature. We dream of movements as well. Sometimes it happens that we make actual movements as we should do in the waking state. Sometimes we get up in our sleep and make actual movements of eating, for example. How does this happen? Now we know that the execution of movements is a function of the Appetitive faculty, all the motor organs of the body being its "servants." When this faculty is prepared for its specific impulses, e.g., for rage, or for passion, or for any other act, it is at once imitated by the faculty of Imagination, and the physical activities through which these impulses satisfy themselves drop out. In such cases the organs serving the lower faculties sometimes become prepared to act in a way exactly similar to the way in which they act when serving the Appetitive faculty. All this activity is taken up by the faculty of Imagination, and thus we get a representation sometimes of one activity, and sometimes of another. Nor is that all. When the temperament of the body is such that it is followed by a passivity in the Appetitive faculty, that temperament is represented by the activity of this faculty. So the organs serving this faculty actually produce those acts. When the body assumes temperament which is followed by a passion for marriage, for example, in the Appetitive faculty, that temperament is represented by the actual acts of marriage. This activity is not due to the actual presence of the sexual impulse. It is due, rather, to the fact, that the faculty of Imagination represents that impulse by the acts, which that impulse leads to. Similarly it frequently happens that a man gets up in his sleep, and begins to walk up and down, or begins to beat some imaginary person, or to flee from him, In all such cases there is no man to beat, or to flee from. What happens is, that the representation of the faculty of Imagination stands for the things represented, and evokes motor responses as if that thing were actually present.

So the manner in which the motor dreams are produced is not a mystery. It is exactly similar to the manner in which the cognitive dreams are produced. Here again the faculty of Imagination reigns supreme. The dream-movements, in other words, are excited, not peripherally, but centrally. They are of the class of ideo-motor actions. Then again we see that the dream-content is determined by the temperament that the body assumes at the time of dreaming.

There remains a third type of dreams—dreams of intellectual objects. So far we have seen the change that objects of sense and movements undergo under the influence of the faculty of Imagination. It must have been noted that Al-Farabi's conception of the nature and functions of the Imagination is absolutely sufficient to explain the dreams we have taken account of so far. This same conception serves as the day for the solution of dreams of rational and intellectual objects, because the Rational faculty also undergoes a similar change in the faculty of Imagination. Rational and the intellectual things are represented by adequate things. Thus a rational thing of extreme perfection, the first cause for example, is represented by the best and the most perfect of sensible objects,objects of extreme beauty and attraction. A defective rational thing, on the other hand, is represented by the lowest and the most defective of sensible objects—objects of extreme ugliness. In other words, the perfection and the beauty of the sensible objects is directly proportional to the perfection and the beauty of the rational objects. Thus all the objects of sense can be used to represent rational and intellectual objects.

The Active Intellect is the agency through which potential rational things become actual, and the Potential Reason is transformed into the Actual Reason. This latter change takes place through the instrumentality of the Rational faculty. Reason is of two kinds: theoretical and practical. The latter kind has to do with present the future particular objects. The former, on the other hand, conceives knowable rational and intellectual things. The faculty of Imagination is a *via media* between these two forms of Reason. Now whatever the Rational faculty receives from the Active Intellect is like the light that the eye gets in vision. This light emanates from the Active Intellect, and shines upon the faculty of Imagination. Thus an activity is started in the Active Intellect for the sake of the faculty of Imagination. This activity sometimes gives to the Imagination those rational things which are fit for the theoretical reason, and sometimes those sensible particulars which it is the business of the practical reason to receive. The faculty of Imagination represents the former by the sensible objects which compose them, and the later it accepts in the very form in which they are represented, and sometimes it represents them by other sensible objects. It is characteristic of the practical reason that it works its material (the sensible particulars) without deliberation. Of these some are actually present, and others are to make their appearance in the future. But whatever the faculty of Imagination gets is untouched by deliberation. The Active Intellect endows the faculty of Imagination with the particulars in dreams and "true visions" and it (the Active Intellect) endows the faculty of Imagination with rational objects as well. But the Imagination uses copies instead of the originals. All this happens in sleep. In happens in the waking state also, but very seldom, and with a very few people. It is a curious fact, however, that we dream more of particular, than of rational, objects.

To be brief, we dream of rational objects just as well as we dream of objects of sense, or of movements. But, sticking as Al-Farabi does to the old notion of the higher faculties ceasing to function in sleep, he has difficulty in explaining such dreams. His ingenuity, however, carves out a way for him. The Rational faculty, he asserts, does not work in dreams as it works in the waking state. It transforms its objects into objects of sense and then does its work. In other words, in dreams all intellection is carried on in terms of sensible objects. It looks difficult to explain how this happens. But here again his conception of the nature and functions of Imagination comes to his rescue. The action of the Imagination, he thinks, is necessary for intellectual cognition, inasmuch as we must keep the object of Intelligence before us under the form of a sensuous image, and this image is represented by the Imagination. From this it may be interred that Al-Farabi does not deny the recurrence, or occurrence, of logical concepts, and therefore of logical ratiocination, in dreams, as his predecessors, and some of his modern co-workers were, or are, in the habit of doing. This misleading notion has lately been corrected by Bergson in his admirable lecture on dreams. In fact Bergson goes to the paradoxical extent of saying that it is the excess of logical explanation that is responsible for all the inconsistencies of frequent in dreams. Al-Farabi does not go so far. As a matter of fact he is not explicit on this point. This much, however, is clear that many dreams to explain which so many quaint, and in some cases barbarous, theories have been put forward, can be very easily and readily explained by this extremely simple and straight-forward theory. Even the wish-fulfilling nature of dreams, which was the cause of so much botheration for Freud, and which brought down so much criticism on him, is easily understood, and explained with the help of this theory. Al-Farabi's conception of the nature and functions of Imagination is very convenient, and stands him in good stead on many occasions. And who can say that it is unacceptable to the modern thinker? In supporting and advocating this theory of dreams one can very easily be accused of applying the scale of values to determination of the nature of things. It is not the intention of the present writer even to suggest that this theory is good and valid because it is simple. It has to be accepted at its face-value. We must not, however, over-look the point that it is for the last thirty years or so that the dream problem has been able to attract the their serious attention of psychologists and philosophers like Freud and Bergson. The late Prof. Rivers, of revered memory, had to complain about this deplorable—or should we say criminal?—negligence on the part of thinkers in the age of Enlightenment. This accusation does not, however, apply to Muslim thinkers, as almost every Muslim thinkers of not in every age has written treatises on dreams. They did not take dreams to be a negligible bye-product of the waking consciousness, nor the result of some serious mental or cerebral derangement. Naturally their explanations are in terms of the psychological concepts known to them, as are the explanation of the modern thinkers. Some credit must be given for their attempts to understand an important mental phenomenon, even though we may now be in a position to label these attempts, and results, as crude and "unscientific." They were quite "scientific" at the time when they were first put forward and anyhow were much better than the contemptuous attitude even of modern thinkers.

Revised and edited; originally published in Islamic Culture Jan. 1936.

9

Muhammad Ali's Islamic Weltanschauung: An Appraisal

JAMAL KHWAJA

(Abstract: Appraises the Islamic world view of Muhammad Ali, and finds that if he "had combined his intellectual brilliance, prodigious memory, dynamism, colourful personality, oratory, mass appeal and Islamic commitment with philosophical depth, a broad historical perspective and a balanced temperment, the history of the Indian subcontinent might have been different").

A critical analysis of Muhammad Ali's Islamic Weltanschauung is desirable because his memory is still cherished in India and Pakistan, and also because many features of the intellectual and political situation that he faced, still exist despite the tremendous changes that have taken place during the last half a century. Now an average Indian Muslim of the upper middle class receives almost the same kind of education as Muhammad Ali received and thus feel alienated from the Muslim masses and the "ulema". Likewise, the pull of a relatively more educated Hindu urban elite, the pressure of Hindu revivalist forces, movements of Islamic. Reusurgence abroad, the Great Power struggle for domination over the world the figure today as they did during Muhammad Ali's age. That is why Muhammad Ali still has an attraction for numerous Western educated Muslims. A Sympathetic but critical study of Muhammad Ali becomes all the more necessary because our culture woefully lacks in the critical appreciation of our hores and great men, as distinct from their glorification.

Before proceeding to Muhamamad Ali let us first clarify the

notion of Weltanschauung which is a basic way of looking at or viewing the most general nature and significance of the universe with special reference to the status and destiny of man in the total scheme of things. In this sense of Weltanschauung one just cannot live as a human being without accepting one or the other outlook, though he may avoid metaphysics in the sense of a superscientific description of Reality, as it is in itself, as distinct from its perceptual appearance, as its scientific conceptualisation according to the scientific method. Thus even declared positivists, agnostics, scientists and laymen, who for some reason or other, shun metaphysis altogether cannot avoid having a Weltanschauung i.e., relate themselves to the universe and have a more or less static attitudinal orientation to life as a whole.

A Weltanshauung is *sui generis* rather than a pre-scientific or pseudo-scientific theory. Nor is it disguised poetry or religion, though it is similar to them in having a broadly 'expressive' rather than a factual function in man's life.

Granting this much and assuming that several types of world views are possible and that they find actual acceptance by different persons, why should we accept one rather than the other? Everyone knows that scientific theories are accepted on the basis of empircal evidence alone. A Weltanschauung, however, cannot be so tested as it is primarily a way of relating ourselves to the universe rather than a description of the universe. However, one can make a free and authentic choice of a Weltanschauung instead of rigidly adhering or unconsciously defending or rationalising the Weltanschaung assimilated as part of one's cultural conditioning. This is the philosophical attitude which yields best results when (a) one makes a sympathetic survery of all the different interpretations of the universe, (b) analyses the implications and entailments of each interpretation, (c) checks each interpretation, for its internal consistency, and (d) checks all relevant putative facts for their accuracy and selectivity. After one satisfies the above conditions, to the best of one's ability, one can justifiably claim that that interpretation or Weltanschaung which authentically gripe one's existential depths is valid and may justly be recommended to others for their consideration and inner acceptance, without claiming any coercive proof that one's own interpretation is true.

Let us now briefly describe some of the salient features of Muhammad Ali's Islamic Weltanschauung before examining it in some depth. It should suffice to say that God is the one only self-existent supreme Being and Creator, loves and guides His creatures suiting their created natures, governs the ongoing course of creation, rewards the good and punishes the evil. God guides man through His messenger, the last and greatest being Muhammad, to whom God revealed the Qur'an, the final and infallible word of God, and the ultimate sovereign authority. The sovereignty of God and the authority of Muhammad, as his Prophet, are one and the same and cover every aspect of life without any distinction between the sacred and the secular. Man's real freedom, welfare and salvation lies in his willing surrender to God and His prophet. This surrender makes him free from bondage to all false gods and enables him to fully develop his God—gives faculties of reason and perception, subject to the final authority of God and the Prophet.

Divine revelation to prophets before Muhammad had a limited spatio-temporal jurisdication, whereas in Qur'an has a universal and eternal validity. Thus Qur'anic Islam is not merely a religion like others, but the final religion which is divinely ordained to supersede and absorb all other versions of pre-Quranic Islam. Likewise the Muslim community or *ummat* is not one among several others, but is uniquely ordained to prevail over all others and eventually establish the kingdom of God on earth before the final dissolution of the universe, according to the divine Plan of creation, governance and final retribution. The Islamic community has been charged with the obligation of peacefully calling man to Islam. Muslims are one community and the Khalafat is the symbol of their spiritual and potential political unity. Wherever, Muslims form part of a wider multi-religious community, as in India or elsewhere, they should cooperate, as a group, with other groups for promoting common good without, however, giving up their own group and identity inside functionally based secular associations. Any policy which erodes their Islamic identity or autonomy would obstruct their adherence to the *shariat* in every walk of life.

The above beliefs and views of Muhammad Ali can neither be proved or disproved, precisely because they are the elements of a Weltanschauung. We can, however, as already indicated earlier, scrutinise them according to the 4 points methodological programme mentioned earlier. It would also be noted that Muhammad Ali's interpretation of Islam is not the only possible one, to question which would necessarily amount to rejecting Islam as such.

For instance, there is nothing un-Islamic in preferring Sir syed's liberal and proto-Secular approach of Islamic communitarianism, or questioning Muhammad Ali's view that Islam makes no distinction between the spiritual and the secular. Again, we do not give up our Islamic faith if we hold that, though the institution of Khilafat played a vital formative role in the early history of Islam, it is not an article of the Islamic faith. In the final analysis Muhammad Ali' conception of Islam, or for that matter, anybody's conception of any religion is correlated with his basic conceptual framework and his factual knowledge of nature of society. This specially applies to one's conception of God. Thus a person who is well aware of the nature cause of earthquakes would hardly agree with Gandhi's view at one time that the Bihar earthquake in the thirties was a divine punishment for the preceding communal riots. We can thus go ahead with out evaluation of Muhammad Ali's interpretations without fear of necessarily rejecting Islam as such.

Let us first see where Muhammad Ali's factual information when relevant to his argument, is not correct or is incomplete and selective. While trying to caution Muslims against the dangers of philosophy and of a liberal approach to religion, Muhammad Ali says that Paul hellenised the simple Semitic concept of God by assimilating it to the concept of Logos, thereby introducing the evil germ of theological speculation and hair-splitting controversies that eventually turned Christians away from serving God and living the good life. The same type of error was committed by the Mutazalite theologians during the Abbaside period, but the results were not so disastrous. Muhammad Ali goes on to record that a much greater Hellenic transformation in Christainity took place due to the impact of the Renaissance. Christianity which was an institutional religion (even though not a complete code of conduct in the unique Islamic sense) retreated into the sphere of the transcendental spirituality away from man's collective life. Ever since this fatal rapture between religion and man's collective life western man has lost God and his own soul though he may have conquered nature. Let us see where Muhammad Ali goes factually wrong. First, Paul's conception of Christianity was, after all, not so radically different from Peter's. Western Christianity inspired by Paul continued to be a total way of life as developed in Christian causistry even though he detailed regulations are absent from the Bible and the Gospels. Nor did the Renaissance of Reformation, as such, transform Christianity from an institutional religion into a pure transcendental spirituality. This transformation, for better or for worse (depending upon one's conception of the proper function or jurisdiction of religion in the total economy of life) came much later in the 18th century due to the social—cultural effects of the growth of science and technology and even more so due to the increasing scientific temper of life. It one ignores the above facts it becomes easy for him to hold (as Muhammad Ali, Iqbal and Maududi and many others infact do) that Islam alone provides us with a complete code of conduct, with no distinction between the spiritual and the secular and that this unique character of Islam must be preserved against the onslaughts of modernism, secularism and liberal Christianity or Hinduism. Both Iqbal and Maududi oppose secularism, though it does not quarrel with religion, but only restricts religion to what is deemed to be its proper sphere.

Muhammad Ali shows on awareness of the concrete ways through which science and technology influence our beliefs, attitudes and moral ideas. He could not understand that the new style of Christianity which gradually emerged after Industrial Revolution in Western Europe was not due to man's defiance of God, but due to his greater insight into the facts of nature, on the one hand, and into the nature and function of religions faith and morality on the other. This clarity of vision was the gift of the Enlightenment in the 18th century and was the fruit of the cumulative wisdom of great minds—Locke, Hume, Kant, Schleiermacher and others. Neither Muhammad Ali not Iqbal could take these facts into account. However, Sir Syed did implicitly, if not explicitly, grasp this new concept or theory of religion in the 18th century. This is why he does not emphasis the institutional aspect of religion but rather the personal I-Thou relationship between man and God. He makes a distinction between the spiritual and the mundane, and stands for regulating mundane matters in a democratic manner, in the light of the cumulative wisdom of human family as a whole, rather than adhere to any particular school of Islamic law or particular period of Islamic history. Though Sir Syed had arrived at this position in his late mature phase, this was his genuine conviction and he sincerely admired English culture and civilisation at its Victorian best.

Muhammad Ali committed a mistake when he assumed that religious faith has no need whatsoever for theological reasoning or philosophical support. Man must function as an integrated being, free from between his head and heart or between different spheres on his conceptual framework. Thus Paul was justified in mediating between the concept of Logos and Christ. Likewise, the Prophet had to interpret his revelatory experience in the semitic framework of divine revelation through an angel. The Mu'tazalite theologians were also justified in trying to construct a systematic theology even though they made many mistakes. Indeed no attempt at theological synthesis can claim to be final.

Muhammad Ali either ignored or was unaware of the role of economic factors and group interests in shaping man's Political, moral and religious ideas, i.e. ideological systems in the Marxist sense. One need not be a historical materialist to realise the crucial truth in the penetrating insight of Marx that there is a close correlation between our ideals and our interests as a general rule.

Our moral ideas cannot help being essentially incomplete, relative and fluid due to the even changing power relationships, group interests and growth in our factual knowledge. When, for example, mechanisation and automation lead to the devaluation of sheer muscle power, this more or less inevitable leads to a levelling up of the status of man and woman. Under these circumstances any system of ethics or law that fails to concede complete equality of the sexes is most likely to strike half the human race as unjust, provided, of course, there is liberty of conscience and freedom of expression. Likewise, the ideal of private charity to help the needy will no longer have the old appeal and social relevance in an age where industrial progress makes it possible to abolish poverty and create mass graded affluence on the basis of equal opportunity for all, provided, of course, our population remains under control. In short, the intimate interplay of ideals and interests, and the crucial role of economic factors in history do not find due recognition in Islamic Weltanschauung and political orientation of Muhammad Ali. This is amply reflected in his rather lopsided passionate concern for preserving the Khilafat, or, more exactly, the Turkish empire before the during the First World War, and also in his romantic hope that a handful of delegated from India at the Islamic Conference in Saudi Arabia would succeed in instituting an Islamic Republic. His sentimental and romantic approach stands in sharp contrast with the political maturity and realism of Sir Syed and also of Jinnah.

Let us now see if and to what extent Muhammad Ali remains unsware of some of the implications of his Islamic Weltanschauung. First, if the *Sunnat* has the same binding authority as the Qur'an, nor merely in purely theological or spiritual matters, but in life as a whole, this entails a very drastic curtailment of human freedom, since the putative authentic sayings of the Prophet contain very specific detailed injunctions, quite unlike the highly general principles enuciated in the Qur'an, with a few exceptions. It seems Muhammad Ali had not adequately recognised this implication.

Secondly, Muhammed Ali also did not realise that his Islamic communitarianism, with its correlated politics of separate elecorates in India and of pan-Islamism in the world, was totally opposed to the logic of the Indian national situation as well as the human situation in general. Under the impact of British political domination and its scientific and democratic culture and due to the vision and reformative genius of enlightened Indian souls our society was slowly but surely moving towards liberal religion and secular democracy. The fateful concept of separate electorates and the romantic politics of Pan-Islamism were completely out of tune with the humanist and secular temper of the age. It is significant that Muhammad Ali's advocacy of separate electorates was not the reaction of a disillusioned politician against alleged or real Hindu chauvinism, as in the case of Jinnah. He became the champion of the demand for separate electorates and also of pan-Islamism from the very beginning as a matter of principle rather than of policy. His emphasis on Muslim solidarity and Islamic resurgence under Khilafat suspices, was not rooted in a broad critical historical perspective which is necessary for appreciating that the ideal of a multi-religious humanism (more concerned with the inner quality of man's life rather than with his nationality or religious denomination) is a higher and move valid ideal than his or Iqbal's non-religious pan-Islamism. Neither of them could view Islam as a great world religion among other. Both stood for displacing all other religions by Islam, the one and the only universal religion. They were unable to see that all great religions in the world have the potentiality of a universal rational appeal, provided they are renewed from within on the basis of creative fidelity to the tradition and a critical receptivity to ever growing factual knowledge. Indeed, self-renewal, in this sense, is actually taking place in all enduring world religions, whose most perceptive believers are steadily moving in the direction of a functional humanism and religious pluralism instead of clinging to traditional denominationalism. The polemical temper of Muhammad Ali together with his unfortunate neglect of sociology and philosophy conspired to keep him tied down to the level of Islamic apologetics and topical journalism and prevented him from growing into a statesman committed to a really mature Islamic Weltanschauung. In this respect both Sir Syed and Azad tower above him.

As mentioned earlier, Muhammad Ali holds that modern liberal Christianity is a degnerative version rather than an evolutionary development due the impact of the scientific temper of the modern mind. Since Muhammad Ali does not like Islam to meet the same fate he stresses the organic unity of the spiritual and secular and criticises the modern concept of religion as spiritual experience or existential response without institutional forms and constraints. While Aurobindo, Tagore, Radhakrishanan and many other Hindu thinkers freely accept the modern approach to religion together with its political corollary of secularism, the Muslim mind has been very reluctant to do so. Muslims tend either to turn away from religion, so do Marx and Russell, or to accept religion in its monolithic sense, as do Muhammad Ali and Iqbal. Educated Muslims in all Asian countries have been used to thinking in terms of superficial Islamic modernism without reconstructing religious thought, as Iqbal tried to do. Recently orthodox has taken a new shape which may be termed as 'neo-orthodoxy'.

It is high time when Muslim intellectuals in India and elsewhere should critically reflect on the nature and function of religion in a human situation dominated by science and technology, the ethics of egalitarianism and humanism, on the one hand, and torn asunder by the conflict of ideologies on the other. I am convinced that it is not Muhammad Ali's or Iqbal's approach to Islam, but the approach of Sir Syed (minus, of course, his obvious limitations and errors of judgements) and also the approach of Azad (who is his early phase thought exactly like Muhamad Ali) which will satisfy the modern Muslim mind. Iqbal's Islamic existentialism fully in tune with the contemporary protest against the cultural hegemony of science immediately and powerfully grips the Muslim mind to its depth partly due to Iqbal's poetic genius and partly because of the sweet echoes of familiar concepts. At the same time Iqbal's monolithic conception of religion weakens his rational appeal to those modern Muslims who have outgrown the medieval concept of religion as a total code of conduct, but who value religion greatly as man's deep response to the mystery of Being. Such Muslims are agreed that man cannot live either by Science, morality, or an art alone, and that religion, in some from or other, is an indispensable aspect of man's life.

Muhammad Ali did not or rather could not begin from where Sir Syed had left, because Muhammad Ali was not as philosophically and temperamentally gifted and fitted for the job as was Iqbal, who, in fact, did begin where Sir Syed had left. But the mature fruit of Iqbal's endeavours brought him closer to the Pan-Islamic politics of Jamaluddin Afghani rather then to the nascent secularism and religious pluralism of Sir Syed and Hali. This vital thread in Sir Syed's thought was taken up only by Azad, despite has topical differences with the Aligarh School. Muhammad Ali on the other hand, deviated from Sir Syed both in the interpretation of religion as also in political orientation. If Muhammad Ali had combined his intellectual brilliance, prodigious memory, dynamism, colourful personality, oratory, mass appeal and Islamic commitment with philosophical depth, a broad historical perspective and a balanced temperament, the history of the Indian subcontinent might have been different.

Revised and edited; originally published in Islam and the Modern Age, Nov. 1979.

10

The Predicament of the Muslim Intelligentsia

SYED ALI ASHRAF

(Abstract: The foremost predicament that the Muslim elite is faced with is of finding a new rational basis for their faith… Far more challenging are the indirect attacks on Islam by the West…I have highlighted four problems as these are concerned with basic principles, and once we tackle them the other problems will get solved automatically).

The word 'Intelligentsia' was first used by a Russian novelist, Boborykin, in the 1860's for a group of intellectuals who were thinking independent or who were the thinkers of the revolution. Since then the term has been used to mean various classes of people. But it is extremely difficult to identify this group with any social class. Therefore, some use the term intelligentsia to refer to anyone engaged in non-physical labour, whether a lyric poet or a veterinarian (such, for example, is the Soviet definition); others apply it to a person with a liberal education regardless of the nature of employment; yet others confine it to persons critically disposed to the existing economic and political order, and ready to sacrifice themselves in order to change it fundamentally in accord with some higher (but secular) ideal. 'Ultimately', concludes Richard Pipes in his forward to the Russian intelligentsia number of *Daedalus*, 'the criterion turns out to be a subjective one, and to define the term 'intelligentsia' with any degree of accuracy it would be necessary to have free access to all the groups which could possibly come within the meaning of the term. Then, Muslim intelligentsia are that group of educated *umma* who are thinking critically about their present life, traditions, conventions, ideals and faith. They might have had modern western education or, like Abduh and Afghani, they might have had traditional education in madrassahs. Their basic qualification is that they are educated and that they are trying to think for themselves and are not satisfied with the existing order of things. This does not mean that they owe allegiance to any secular ideal. On the other hand they may be intensely religious and still dissatisfied with the existing order of things. They are held together by the simple but deeprooted bond of belonging to one large Muslim community which is basically supra-national in character. They may be Turks, Arabs, Kurds, Iranians of Pakistanis, but they have strong cultural affinities and deep bonds of emotional kinship which supersede their consciousness of belonging exclusively to one particular nation. But they are aware of disintegration or disturbing inroads by new force into their age-old concepts and conventions and are trying hard to find some solution to their manifold problems. One section of this intelligentsia gives precedence to nationalism. They are ready to undermine their Muslim consciousness and propagate their Turkishness or Arabism or Bengalism as superior to or more relevant than their consciousness of being Muslims. It is this class which is organising the destinies of the Muslim nations of the world sometimes by getting power and sometimes by opposition. But the basic characteristic of both the sections is their dissatisfaction with things, events, methods, processes of political and economic growth.

The foremost predicament that the intelligentsia is involved in is the predicament of finding a new rational basis for their faith. Christians and Jews always considered Islam a heresy. There have been resurgences of direct and indirect attacks on Islam since the beginning of the nineteenth century, that is, since the time the first Christian missionaries went out to preach in countries such as India and North Africa and since the beginning of the Industrial Revolution. The direct attacks are not so dangerous as the indirect attacks or, rather inroads. It is the direct attacks that I shall deal with first.

In the nineteenth century these attacks were normally directed against the Messenger of God (Peace be upon him) and it is but natural that it should be so. As our awareness of the revelation which we get in the Holy Quran is derived from our implicit faith in the truthfulness and indeal nature of the Prophet (peace be upon him), the attack by non-believers naturally has to be directed against him first. This kind of attack we have seen in Sales's introduction to his translation of the Quran and can still be seen in the distorted interpretation of facts in Levy's *Sociology of Islam.* I need not discuss this because this was not a serious problem for the Muslim thinkers to solve. They replied to the charges brought against the Prophet (peace be upon him) and some of the replies, for example the one by Syed Ameer Ali, are convincing. They may be termed apologists by Smith, nevertheless they have tried to reply as best as they could. What is basically wrong in the approach of a large number of our thinkers who meet this type of challenge is that they try to conceive of the western moral and ethical values to be in some ways superior to their own, and therefore try to fit in their replies to this framework. This may be seen, for example, in some of the replies to the charges against the marriages of the Prophet (peace be on him) or against the charge of inequality between man and woman in Islam.

Far more challenging are the indirect attacks. Some of them of them are attacks directed not against any particular religion: they are the attacks on religion and on the interpretation of religion by modern sociological or anthropological formulae. When in 1960 the Soviet government started to attack Islam while courting the Muslim countries in the Middle East, We were not astonished. The picture that Walter Kolarz, for example, has portrayed of Islam in the Soviet Union proved that it is part of their athesitic campaign against Islam. What is more disturbing is when we see the same attitude in western orientalists such as Smith or Grunebaum. Grunebaum, while speaking in the seminar on Islam and the modern world in Karachi, presented the thesis that Islam is what the people make it to be; that is, Islam must be judged by the practice of those who profess it. Smith in his book entitled *Islam in Modern History* has tried in his own way to prove the same theory. Both of these are the two aspects of the same sociological approach to religion that we notice among the anthropologists. They only reply that we may give to this question is by asking another question — will what the people who profess to be Muslims practise be called Islam when they happen to throw all the fundamental precepts of islam to the winds and practice something which is forbidden in the *Qu'ran* and the *Sunnah?* We have always made a distinction between principles and practice. But these gentlemen seem to confuse the two. The logical conclusion that they, or anyone, can draw from such arguments as their, is the familiar one that we notice in Soviet propaganda against islam, that is, it arose at a particular time and place and tried to meet the demands of the day. Here we notice a conflict between two approaches: one, which believes in the existence of man in time and space and the other which considers man as living both in time and eternity, both in a place and in the infinity which is the infinity of God. The problem therefore cannot be solved just by making a compromise between the sociological and religious approaches to life. It is a much deeper problem and can only be solved by taking an entirely different stand to the very idea of knowledge. Iqbal realised this problem and tried to solve it by providing a rational basis for 'revelation. The challenge ultimately is to the nature and validity of revelation; therefore, he started by showing how revelation is by far the most valid source of human knowledge. Iqbal's work needs further elaboration and modification; it also needs further revision and refinement. But it must be said that it is by far the best approach to this problem. More metaphysical is the approach of Frithjof Schuon. The other approaches such as Sir Syed Ahmad's or Khalifa Abdul Hakim's who tried to do the same thing for Islam that the Christian theologists had tried to do for Christianity in England in the nineteenth century, that is, to prove that Islam is scientific, that the *Qur'an* contains all the things that modern science is trying to discover, seems to be childish in the face of the basic question which is not solved, the question about the validity of revelation and the tentativeness of scientific generalisations. Moreover, an intellectual formulation of arguments alone will not be a sufficient justification of faith. Faith has its own form of rationality. The rationality of faith lies in a deeper experience of reality. not simply in an intellectual analysis. Intellectual analyses must follow, and not procede the experience of reality. They only difficulty about this experience lies in its subjectivity and limited nature. The experience of the Prophet (peace be upon him) and my experience may not coincide. I may have a partial view of reality and I may consider this experience as the experience of total reality. How do I judge myself? How do I know whether my experience is partial or complete? I may do so only by referring my experience to experience of someone whom I may accept as the person who has acquired that ultimate experience. That is why it is necessary to posit the experience of the Holy Prophet (peace be upon him) as the ultimate criterion of judging the truth or falsity of my experience. Unless the experience of the Prophet (peace be upon him) is disproved we have no right to state that all that Islam stands for is temporary, meaningful only for a time and for a place. Science cannot be considered to be the criterion of judging the truth or otherwise of such experience, because Science does not claim finality or truth. It is tentative; its premises may be challenged and disproved by new theories. Therefore, all scientific knowledge or all knowledge based on scientific methods may be considered as tentatively true. Anthropological or sociological findings are valid within the limits of their being tentatively true with reference to the limited knowledge available to mankind. The human species has lived in this world for many millions of years. Our historical knowledge is limited to only five thousand years. Most of our early reconstruction is guesswork based on limited discoveries. There is no reason why new discoveries should not disprove our theories. We should look at what theories are propounded about the origin of civilisations and what is happening to our theories because of new archaeological surveys of the Indus valley. We cannot therefore, judge that which is based on an inner experience of some reality by applying a standard which we have evolved in order to judge external phenomena.

Our faith, however, is not always shaken by what science teaches us or by our unconscious acceptance of the scientific approach. It is shaken by our lack of Knowledge of science and it limitations. Ortega and Whitehead have already shown how science and the scientific approach fails to explain the greatness of human emotions and feelings, how it is basically inhuman because it deals with atoms, energies, chemical substances and not with human personalities and the total man. It is, therefore, necessary for our intellectuals to get a clear idea about science, its premises, its achievements and its limitations. The greatness of our religion cannot be appreciated by a superficial compromise or by an attempt to show how 'scientific' our religion is, but by an understanding of all that science stands for and all that our religion stands for.

Though the attacks on faith present some of the acutest challenges to Muslim intelligentsia, generally these challenges take the form of attacks on law and the traditions based on law. As the Muslim law (*Shariah*) is all embracing, as this law was designed to interpret and support the entire socio-cultural structure of the Muslim *ummah,* a challenge to *Shariah* (Muslim law) means a challenge to our traditional way of life. The question that is today agitating the minds of the Muslims may be briefly stated thus: Is Muslim law flexible enough to meet the situations that we are facing because of our contact with the West?

Before we try to assess the implications of this question and estimate the worth of the replies we should take note of an attitude which is implied in this question. This question never arose in the pre-modern period (i.e. the period before the advent of Renaissance in Europe) because Muslim culture was the dominant culture of the day. It arises today because the culture of the West is dominating the modern world. With the acceptance of modern technology we also implicitly indicate our acceptance of western civilisation and all that it implies. Here we face a fundamental problem. Technology by itself is without any human culture, but because it has been bread in a civilisation whose standard of living has been raised by it, we are lured by it. The basic characteristic of this civilisation is its secular liberalism. It encourages unlimited free thinking and unbridled rationalism. But the final outcome is more negative than positive. It has demolished old gods but it has not been able to give any suitable substitute. It has encouraged individualism at the cost of social solidarity. It is true that probably from a more technical point of view modern men may be considered collectively better organised, more thoughtful than their forefathers. But they have achieved this better standard of living and better social ethics at the cost of personal ethics and family solidarity. They think more of the entire society than of the next-door neighbour. They do not known what values are because they want to free themselves from the authority of eternal values. Therefore, all that we find in the West is a poor substitute, an evolutionary concept of the nature of values. This concept is hopelessly inadequate because the evolutionary nature Does not correspond to any evolution in the moral and intellectual capabilities of man. Moreover it has made everything uncertain, fluid because it has taken away from those who believe in it any standard of reference. We cannot judge ourselves with reference to the past because according to this principle, we have evolved out of the past, hence we should be morally, intellectually, biologically superior to or different from what our forefathers were. In other words we can only judge ourselves with reference to the present because we do not know the future. But we know that we are not perfect. We are what our past has made us. Therefore, we move in a vicious circle. Unguarded free thinking has only created a large number of problems for us.

By referring, therefore, to this liberalism we in Islam are courting the same fickle and uncertain mistress. Because of the prestige that we attach to liberalism, we ask the question which I posited earlier, the question regarding the flexibility of Muslim law. It is necessary for us to be absolutely clear about the relationship between liberalism and Islam before we undertake the task of providing an answer to this question. Islam does not encourage unbridled freethinking and chaotic experiments with life whereas liberalism and rationalism do. Islam lays down the basic laws of self-discipline and establishes a scheme of values which we see in the ultimate criteria of absolute mercy, benevolence, justice, truth and honesty. Liberalism destroys this scheme and makes society and its values relative. Islam demands that man should submit his will to the demands of this higher law. It is not the law of nature; it is the law of higher nature, the law of perfection. The *Qur'an* lays down these principles and the *Sunnah* exemplifies them. The validity of the *Qur'an* and the *Sunnah* lies in their efficiency in organising good life, in making us feel an inner satisfaction and peace which no amount of freethinking and rational disquisition can bring. Therefore, we should not try to judge the *Qur'an* and the *Sunnah* with reference to liberalism as it is interpreted today in the West.

This, of course, does not mean that freedom of thought is banned in Islam and that we live within closed doors. It is permitted within the limits imposed by the *Qur'an* and *Sunnah.* If one wants to remain a Muslim and at the same time be liberal, he must accept those limitations. The fact is, that a modern Muslim intellectual cannot deny the gains of sa liberal outlook and is attracted by its positive results. But he confuses liberalism, western civilisation and technology. Moreover, as he finds that at the apex of the modern education system in his country is a modern university with its scientific 'liberal' outlook, he attaches more and more importance to everything that speaks of scientific liberalism. That is why he wants a western type of equality between man an woman, he wants the marriage laws to be changed and monogamy to be supported. The western system of education which has become the state-supported and state-propelled system in the Muslim world has encouraged us further by making us aware of our own values. Only a few of the Muslim families can claim to have had education for several generations. Therefore, when a modern Muslim looks at his home, he finds himself better educated than his parents. Hence he cannot easily be governed by his parents' view or the education in religious lore which his parents might have given him in early days. Therefore most of our intellectuals are strengthened in their belief that a change is necessary if we are to make headway in the world.

But law cannot be so easily changed. One way out was found by Kamal Ataturk who abandoned all Islamic laws in order to modernise his country and free it from the control of the custodians of Muslim law, who, during his time, were also the custodians of economic, political and moral orthodoxy. Egypt had tried to solve it by maintaining two systems of law and by integrating the the old maktabs and the modern primary schools. Nasser abolished the duality by modernising law. Pakistan is trying to solve some of these problems by changing some of the personal laws and by introducing religious instruction in its schools. But Throughout the Muslim world there are now two systems of education, the old madrassa system with old madrassahs like Al-Azhar, Deoband and Nadwa at its apex and the western system with the modern university, with its liberalism and secularism, at its apex. Thus, there is an orthodox class of people in each Muslim country which is mostly unaware of other schemes of values. This has made the problem acute because most of our intellectuals tend to confuse the conflict of ideas with the conflicting groups of people. Orthodoxy is condemned by some not because orthodoxy is bad in principle, but because, they say, the orthodox groups are too authoritarian, are not generally capable of thinking clearly, and with all their limitations, try to brand any progress as anti-Islamic.

It is better for Muslim intellectuals to look at the Problem from the point of view of principles and their results, rather than from the point of view of a partisan in the social struggle for supremacy. It is also necessary to be dispassionate in their approach. Passionate partisanship will lead to political upheavals and turn each Muslim country into a battlefield. Already we have seen violence and bloodshed in Egypt, Turkey, Indonesia and Iran. Already each Muslim country is deeply divided into the more religious-minded masses and the avant-garde groups of educated young men and women. We should also look to the West and learn a lesson from what is happening in the moth-eaten liberalism of the West and be aware of the deep social and psychological problems that they are facing.

The problem is basically an academic one. There are ample signs of new and healthy developments which we should not overlook. When we take these developments into account and try to find solutions we may be able to find certain general principles which may be applied to all future situations and save the *ummah* from breaking into irreconcilable camps.

The most important sign of this new development is in the rediscovery of the principole of *ijtihad.* It was first used by Hadrat Mudah ibn Jabal when the Prophet (peace be on him) sent him as a judge to Yemen. On the eve of his departure to assume his office over there, the Prophet (peace be on him) asked him 'According to what will you judge? He replied, 'According to the book of God.' 'And if you do not find it in it?' 'According to the Sunnah of the Prophet of God' 'And if you do not find it in that ! 'Then I will exert myself to form my own judgment.' Jamaluddin Afghani, Abduh and Iqbal are the most successful exponents of this movement in recent years. The important thing to take note of is that *ijtihad* should not overstep the *Qur'an* and the *Sunnah.* And only the person who has moulded his life and thought according to the *Qur'an* and the *Sunnah* has the right to exert himself in that manner because only such a person has the inner light and conviction and sufficient spiritual maturity to find out the true solution. Moreover, the other principle that each Muslim ought to remember is that *ijtihad* should not mean just an escape into a realm of freethinking. It must always imply thinking freely within the limits imposed by the *Qur'an* and the *Sunnah.* Time and place, society and races, personal, communal or national interest should not make us forget that the fundamental laws are unchangeable because they are God-given; certain modes of application may change.

I believe once these ideas crystallize and take a proper shape, the Muslims will be in a better position to meet the demands of the day. I should, however, like to point out a gaping pit into which some of us might stumble. We should not judge Islam with reference to Western standards of life and thought as we sometimes tend to do. Take for example the question of the equality of men and women. The *Qur'an* explicitly indicates that man has some rights over the woman, divorce right, for example. The *Sunnah* indicates that the woman is second in command in the family. On the other hand the woman has some rights over man. she has the right to have alimony, right to be looked after even after divorce, right to get complete protection from all difficulties and inconveniences. But men and women have the same political and economic rights. Just because the West speaks of equality, we should not lose sight of the excellence of Islamic law based as it is on certain fundamental aspects of human nature. The bugbear of equality should, again, be judged not with reference to a theory of nature whatever it be, but with reference to the authority of the *Qur'an,* and the resultant efficacy of such a system. If men and women are to be considered entirely equal men should have the same right as the woman are to be considered entirely equal men should have the same right as the woman to get money for his consent to live as husband, women should not demand any protection from men, and a husband should not be responsible for his wife for any period after divorce. Think what will happen to a pregnant woman if she is divorced and if she has to fall back upon her own resources. By all this I want to emphasise the attitude that one should take to the clear-cut injunctions of the Qur'an and the Sunnah.

The next major problem that the Muslim intellectual has to face is the problem of Islam in modern history. By this phrase I mean such questions as nationalism, geographic and racial loyalties, minorities in a Muslim state and the relationship between the *ummah* and the national group. Here I would like to state a general principle which might be of some help in disentangling some confusion in which we find ourselves. It is obvious that our states are independent. Why should we talk of nation-states? Can we not talk of one nation divided up into several states? Is it necessary for us to bring about geographical, linguistic or racial unity in order to have one nation? Pakistan was divided into two wings which are linguistically, ethnologically, historically different. They had religious and cultural unity. This was one of the greatest experiments in history. The unity faile only because material interests superceded all spiritual needs and values. We may be Pakistanis, Iranians, Egyptians or Turks, but we are Muslims first and foremost. The drift in the present-day world is towards more and more unification.

A Muslim nation can live in a commonwealth of states and pull their resources together. I believe that if we can solve the problem of Islamic law we shall be able to solve this problem too.

The fourth major predicament that the Muslim intelligentsia is confronted with is the problem of finding in Islam some basic principles for the economic development of the Muslim countries. This problem would not have arisen had not capitalism-with-interest become the prevailing economic system of these countries and had not interestless economy been evolved by godless socialism. A Muslim can accept neither. But he finds the world divided into two camps and he also finds some elements in both compatible with his faith, attitudes and approach to life. He has not evolved a third economic system which can combine the virtues of both and vices of neither. A Muslim hates interest and the sharp difference between the rich and the poor bred by capitalism. His society is not as yet affluent enough to make ineffective the lure of socialism of the type produced in Russia and China. His society at the same time cannot accept godlessness and regimentation. He also finds it extremely difficult to evolve a third system because both capitalism and socialism are the products of industrialisation. As he has also accepted industrialisation without previously thinking out a different economic system, he finds his choice extremely limited. As a result his economy is not interestless and there is every fear that he may be rapidly proceeding towards a socialist system. It is the lack of social justic in the capitalist system as evolved in his own country that makes him think of socialism as a possible panacea. Our learned people did not wake up to this social injustice till the people reacted violently to it. That is why the intelligentsia is suspicious of the traditionally learned Muslims and their ability to solve the economic problem with the help of Islam. The 'ulema' have talked of interestless economy, but they had not studied deeply the economic prolems. As a result their protest against our existing economic system or capitalism has been a protest only from the point of view of the dogma. They have failed to master modern thought and evolve in practice an interestless economic system that brings social justice and equity. Attempts are now being made by

Muslim intellectuals to evolve such a system.

The basic approach, I think, should be governed by principles of social justice, equity, freedom and an interest-free economy. From the Qur'an and the example set by the Prophet (peace be upon him) and the first four caliphs the principles and practice can easily be drawn. One has to apply them to a modern context and evolve a third system governed by a basic human sympathy that governed the systems evolved by the Prophet (peace be on him). Islam provides us not only with the ideals of social justice, but also with the fundamental principles of production and distribution of wealth. At the same time it allows sufficient scope for the evolution of a system that meets the demands of time and place. These principles may be summed up as follows:

(1) Individual ownership is not forbidden;
(2) Exploitation of this principle of ownership cannot be permitted if this leads to imbalance and the suffering of many for the gains of a few;
(3) The principle of social welfare should govern both the production and the distribution of wealth;
(4) Equal opportunity must be given to each individual to have shelter, food, clothing and education.

On those basic principles the economic system of the state can be planned. It is for the Muslim intelligentsia to work out this plan. It may be said that Islam need not be thought of while drawing up this plan. But without a philosophy or an ideology no system can work mechanically. Human beings need an impetus to sacrifice their private interest in favour of some greater return. Islam provides this motivation. It is the moral purpose of Marxism that provides that impetus to communists. But the objective provided by Islam is formulated on some universal and eternal concepts of truth and justice. Hence while the Marxist concept can become outdated, the Islamic concept cannot.

I have taken these four problems because they appear to me to be concerned with basic principles. Once we are able to tackle them, the other problems will get solved almost automatically. Let us not forget however that in the welter of our problems we must not overlook the fact that Islam has not come for us, the Muslims, alone, it has come for entire humanity.

These problems are intrinsically related to the education that produces modern intelligentsia. We have two education systems which create conflicting groups. We cannot just modernise the traditional by introducing modern subjects as Mufti Abduh tried to do at Al-Azhar. Nor can we make the modern system Islamic and its products Islamic-minded just by teaching and preaching Islam to students. Modern education which the Muslim countries have borrowed from the West gives preference to intellect over the spirit, teaches social and natural sciences and even humanities from a secular point of view and on the basis of secularist philosophies which are at the root of those subjects. That is why the root cause of all predicaments lies in the secularisation of society and the educated community through the secular system of education at present dominant in all Muslim countries. The Muslim intelligentsia have become aware of this root cause of all evils. That is why they met in Holy Mecca in 1977 at the First World Conference on Muslim Education, redefined education, reclassified knowledge and suggested that a new curriculum should be formed and new research undertaken to formulate Islamic concepts for arts and science subjects. It is not an easy task. Along with the attempt to solve the predicaments mentioned earlier, it is necessary to reform education, redesign the curriculum, rewrite text books and retrain the teachers. Broad redesigning was done last March at the Second World Conference on Muslim Education but the root problem has not been solved. The conflict generated in the souls of young Muslims needs to be removed in order that they may tackle the other predicaments with greater success.

(Revised and edited; originally published in Islamic Quarterly).

11

Developments of the Thought

MOHD. NOOR NABI

(Abstract: Traces the impact of Greek philosophy on Islamic thought and development both by way of absorption and reaction. Provides overall conclusions of philosophical doctrines which, so far as the Islamic creed is concerned, are generally uniform, and came to fruition in the comprehensive system of Ibn Sina).

The Philosophical Movement

Early scholastic theology, under the influence of 2nd/8th century translations of works of Greek philosophy and science, emerged as a vigorous and brilliant movement of scientific and philosophical thought which produced works of great value and originality from the 3rd/9th to the 6th/12th centuries.

The materials with which this philosopical system was constructed were Greek ideas; in its material or content aspect, therefore, it is Hellenistic throughout. But the actual construction, the system itself, has an indubitably Islamic stamp: all along its metaphysical frontiers it reckons with the corresponding religious metaphysics of Islam and consciously tries to create points not only of contact but of coincidence with the latter. But this it does only in so far as the rational Greek character of the material would allow. Herein lies both its brilliant originality and its tragic fate in Islamic history; for, having failed to satisfy orthodox requirements, it was denied the passport to survival.

Over against the orthodox dogma of creation, it upheld the doctrine of the eternity of the world. But in order to do justice to religious consciousness, it affirmed that the world was an eternal effect of God *vis-a-vis* whom it had a unilateral relationship of absolute dependence. In the making of this doctrine, it sought the help of the monistic Neo-platonic doctrine of emanation and discarded the Aristotelian theory of the dualism between God and Matter. Matter, therefore, instead of being an existent *per se* independently of God, was derived ultimately from God at the end of an emanation process. It further sought to draw a fundamental distinction between God and the World, to soften even the rigours of emanation, with the categories of necessity and contingence: God is the Necessary Being, this world is contingent. Orthodox theology accepted this distinction and built upon it its other doctrines but rejected the doctrine of the eternity of the world.

On the basis of the Plotinian idea of the ultimate ground of Reality, the One of Plotinus, as interpreted by his followers and endowed with a mind that contained the essences of all things, the philosophers reinterpreted and elaborated the Mu'tazilite doctrine of the Unity of God. According to the new doctrine, God was represented as Pure Being without essence or attributes, His only attribute being necessary existence. The attributes of the Deity were declared to be either negations or purely external relations, not affecting His Being and reducible to His necessary existence. God's knowledge was thus defined as 'non-absence of knowable things from Him'; His Will as 'impossibility of constraint upon His Being'; His creative activity as 'emanation of things from Him,' etc. In the framework of the Greek theories of Aristotle and Plotinus, it was impossible that God should know particulars: He could cognize only universals since a cognition of the particular would introduce change in the Divine Mind both in the sense of a temporal succession and a change of different objects. But this theory could hardly be accepted by any religion for which a direct relationship between the individual and the Deity forms the core of interest. Accordingly, Avicenna devised a clever theory which would do justice both to the demands of religion and the requisites of his philosophy. God, according to this theory, knew all the particulars since He, being the ultimate cause of all things, necessarily knew the whole causal process. Thus, God knew from eternity that, for example, a solar eclipse would occur, with all its particular characteristics, at a particular point of the causal process. This type of knowledge would require no change in the Divine knowledge since it removes the necessity of perceptual knowledge which occurs at a definite time and place.

From Greek epistemological and metaphysical theories, again, the Muslim philosophers acquired the idea of a radical dualism between body and mind, which under Greco-Christian influences had also developed into an out-and-out ethical dualism between the material and the spiritual. This affected the Muslim philosophers' eschatological teaching very fundamentally. The philosopher al-Farabi (d. 339/950) held that only the soul survived in an individual and, further, that only the souls of thinkers survived, 'undeveloped' minds being destroyed at death. Ibn Sina held that all human souls survived, body being unresurrectible, although he allowed that souls, after being separated from their bodies, especially those that are 'undeveloped' but morally virtuous, felt a kind of 'physical' pleasure since they were incapable of experiencing purely mental states. But in general he taught that the resurrection of the body was an imaginative myth with which the minds of the Prophets were inspired in order to influence the moral character of the unthinking masses. Ibn Rushd (Averroes, d. 594/1198), the Spanish Arab philosopher who introduced medieval Europe to Aristotle in his own interpretation, came nearer to orthodox Islam with his doctrine that although the same body could not be identically resurrected, a numerically different but qualitatively identical body, a *simulacrum,* would be supplied.

Having thus reached a stage of consciousness where the entire philosophical metaphysic seemed to correspond, point by point, to theological beliefs of religion but never exactly tallied with the latter, a general problem was raised before the philosophers about the nature of religion and philosophy and their mutual relationship. Either there was a double truth, one apprehended by philosophy, the other by religion, or the truth was unitary but appeared now in rational, and again in a metaphorical, imaginative form. The first alternative, that of two truth, did not seem possible rationally and so the philosophers decided to pursue the latter line of thought. Religious truth is but rational truth, but instead of being expressed in nakedly rational formulas, manifested itself in imaginative symbols—a fact which was responsible for its widespread acceptance by, and effectiveness among, the masses. Thus, religion is but philosophy for the masses, and, once accepted, is philosophy *of* the masses, having as its primary function their moral education and purification.

In order to make this view possible, an intricate and brilliant theory of Prophetic Revelation was constructed to do justice to the Islamic phenomenon as the philosopher saw it. Basically, nothing new was imposed on the Greek system of thought: the materials were those of late Hellenism, but these were pressed into a new direction so that a novel, original pattern emerged from them. The Greek theory and psychology of cognition were internally manipulated to yield the idea of a unique type of human intellect which intuitively apprehended the Reality in a total sweep and then clothed this truth, through an inner impulsion, into figurative symbols to make them accessible to the common man. Thus, instead of saying, 'If you pursue moral good, your mind shall attain the real spiritual freedom which is bliss,' the prophet said, 'If you are virtuous and perform these *specific acts,* you shall enter Paradise and will be saved from the flames of Hell,' etc.

The philosophical system, thus constructed, was a magnificent creation of the Islamic civilization. In itself it was an impressive achievement, and both in the those of its *Weltanschauung* and in its actual structure it represents a genuine landmark in human thought as it stands on the threshold between antiquity and the Modern Age. But *vis-a-vis* the religion of Islam it created a perilous situation for itself. It was not so much in the actual doctrines professed by it taken severally that the danger lay, but in its overall judgment on the nature of religion and its implications for the Shari'a. For its individual doctrins—the eternity of the world, the nature of eschatology, the nature of God, etc. — could be controverted or modified by criticism, but the status that it assigned to religion and to the Shari'a could not fail to be rejected if religion was not to be reduced to a kind of spiritual mockery.

Orthodoxy and Philosophy

The natural theology of the philosophers, then posed a patent threat to the revealed content of Islam. The very points of its original achievement in religious thought became the target for orthodoxy's suspicion and attack, i.e. the points where it had sought deliberately and consciously a liaison with orthodox dogma and had hoped for acceptance as a valid interpretation of Islam.

The orthodox refutation, formulated by al-Ghazali in his classic work 'The Incoherence of the Philosophers' (*Tahafut al-Falasifa*), argued against the philosophers' position with regard to religious doctrine point by point and revealed both its self-contradictions and its insufficiency from the religious point of view. The doctrine of the eternity of the world was shown to be impossible even rationally apart from the fact that it denied the God of creative activity in the real sense of the word. For the philosophical doctrine of the necessary emanation of the world from God was substituted God's voluntary activity. The rational constitution of God, operating by an inherent rational necessity, was replaced by the Ash'arite concept of the Will of God. similarly, the purely spiritual character of the philosophers' eschatology was rejected.

But the most crucial basis of the orthodox dissatisfaction with the philosophers' religion concerned the nature of religion itself. It was here that the most sensitive nerve of Islam was to be located. The philosophical theory of the Prophetic Revelation, which saw in the Prophet an immensely endowed intellect and spirit, capable of coming into contact with the Universal Intellect or the Archangel, was not completely rejected; on the contrary, some of its new elements, especially the intellectual perfectionism of the Prophet, were incorporated into the *kalam* doctrine. But the character of the Revelation, as being essentially intellectual, was rejected and especially the idea that religion is but a symbolic form of this intellectual truth. The nature of the ultimate Reality for orthodox Islam could not be solely intellectualized, but directly inspired moral activism. The net result of this was a revindication of the primordial and absolute status of the Shari'a which the philosophers had declared to be mere symbolism adequate only for the masses. But the most important legacy which this philosophical teaching left for Islam and which the orthodoxy unhesitatingly adopted was the division of Being into necessary and contingent. Henceforward, this constituted the burden of the *kalam* proofs for the existence of God: the created world as contingent effect requires the existence of God, the Necessary Being, as its cause.

Henceforth, two ways were left open in which philosophy could operate, and it pressed itself through both these channels. One was that philosophical speculation should continue despite the strictures of orthodoxy and should seek for itself a heterodox medium. This medium was found in philosophical Sufi thought, a fact which was undoubtedly facilitated by the mystical tendencies in the thought of the Muslim philosophers themselves, especially in that of Ibn Sina. We shall describe this important career of philosophical thought in Islam below. The other alternative was to give up the idea of producing a rival system to theology as far as religious dogma was concerned and rather to work within the orthodox system. This is what made possible the expansion of the *kalam* into a systematic body of thought comprising epistemology and metaphysics, an expansion which first appears in the work of the theologian-philosopher Fakhr al-Din al-Razi (d. 606/1209). Within this system, however, an astonishingly wide scope was offered for the exercise of speculative reason, an activity which had a very lively and rich career for several centuries but which has been little studied by modern scholarship which seems so far to stop at al-Ghazali's refutation of philosophy.

The orthodox *kalam* had accepted the philosophical doctrine of the necessary and the contingent but, as we pointed out above, they rejected an objective distinction between essence and existence.

Ibn Sina had taught that God gave existence to essences which were in themselves non-existent. God bestowed existence thanks to the fact that He is pure Existence, possessing no other nature than Necessary Being. On this view, existence was 'added to' essences in some sense. The orthodox rejected this doctrine because of the fear that if Being was regarded as univocal, i.e. had the same meaning when applied to God as when applied to the world—then this would result in pantheism and that despite the fact that God's Being was thought to be necessary whereas the Being of the world was considered to be contingent. Accordingly, the orthodox *kalam* declared Being to be equivocal, i.e. it had different meanings when applied to God and the world.

The protagonists of the philosophical tradition developed their doctrine by introducing further distinctions and held that 'being' had two different applications. In one sense, it denoted the particular being of a thing (the 'haecceity' of Duns Scotus in Western scholasticism), and in this sense the term was equivocal because everything is unique in this respect. And, consequently, God's peculiar Being, far from flowing into other existents, was unknowable. But in another sense, being is an abstract idea, generalized from actual existents. This abstract concept must be univocal if it is to be applied to God and to creatures. Being in this latter sense, it was argued, is the proper object of metaphysical inquiry which should deal with its general properties (*umur 'mma*). Indeed,a group, notably among them the philosopher-theologian Qadi Abu'l Thana' al-Urmawi (d. 684/1285), contended that the doctrine of God should be separated from this doctrine of Being which should constitute the proper domain of *kalam*-metaphysics. This was, however, rejected by the theologians, jealous of their preserves, on the ground that this would create a super-science over *kalam*.

Thus the tension between philosophical thought and dogmatic theology continued down the centuries even within orthodox islam which had transported within its own theological systems a great mass of philosophical and metaphysical ideas. The protagonists of philosophy within this liquid atmosphere gave up certain of the more extreme of the anti-dogmatic conclusions of the classical philosophers. This neo-philosophical activity came to life especially since the 7th/13th century when the *rapproachement* between philosophy and theology had been on a definite footing and had recovered a certain balance, after al-Ghazali's total rejection of philosophy, though the work particularly of al-Razi, which henceforth becomes the centre of controversy. In the 7th/13th century itself there arose a number of eminent philosophical writers and critics who, while defending philosophy in general, nevertheless accepted orthodox positions on the most critical and sensitive points of the dogma. For example, Nasir al-Din al-Tusi (d. 672/1273), an acute and clear thinker, rejects the doctrine of the eternity of the world and defends Islam on this point.

But the tension between the traditionists — the Ahl al-Hadith - and the philosophers remained more basic and permanent. From time to time it erupted into fierce outbursts of the traditionist attacks on intellectualism. To the right wing traditionists, *kalam*-theology itself had become suspect because of its very *rapproachement* to philosophy. This traditionism found its monumental expression in the 8th/14th century in the prolific work of Ibn Taymiya, which wa destined to be of lasting import. Especially in his important work 'The Harmony between the True Tradition and evidence of Reason,' he severely criticized the thesis both of the philosophers and the theologians. But the struggle continued. In al-Azhar, in Egypt, philosophy was extradited from the syllabus later centuries and was restored after the dawn of Muslim Modernism towards the end of the nineteenth century by the efforts of Jamal al-Din al-Afghani and his disciple Muhammad 'Abduh. A 13th/19th century author of note in India, 'Abd al-'Aziz Pahrarawi (Pahrara is a village near Multan, where he died before the age of forty in 1239/1824), from the circle of the Ahl al-Hadith, wrote a bitter satire on philosophy. It begins :

> 'O 'Ulama' of India!...you hope to attain bliss by the cultivation of rational sciences, but I fear lest your hopes should be frustrated.'

The satirist goes on:

> 'You have adopted the sciences of the infidels as your Shari'a as though the philosophers of Greece were your Prophets.' And ends with an appeal for the study of the Hadith.

Philosophic Religion

While the purely intellectual philosophical tradition survived in the form of commentaries or handbooks with different rhythms either as an instrument of theology or as its critic, philosophy after al-Ghazali developed in a new and important direction which may be called a purely religious philosophy or philosophical religion. This development, although profoundly influenced in its course by Sufism and its modes of thought, is, nevertheless, to be distinguished from the latter. For, the phenomenon we have termed philosophical religion, although it often identifies its doctrines with those of the Sufis, especially of speculative Sufism, is characterized by rational argumentation and purely intellectual and logical thought-processes while Sufism relies exclusively on gnostic experience or intuition and uses poetic imagination rather than purely rational processes.

In assuming a religio-centric character, this new movement was helped by the philosophy proper, described earlier on, had itself a strong religious nature in that, on the basis of purely naturalistic and rational principles and using these as its point of departure, it had built up and culminated in a world-view which is undeniably religious. But the new philosophy was also under the spell of Sufi spiritualism which diverted its interest from the field of natural philosophy except in so far as it could use the general concepts of natural philosophy for its own religious ends.

This new philosophical tradition begins with the work of Shihab al-din al-Suhrawardi, the 'martyr' (executed at Aleppo in 587/1197) founder of the 'philosophy of illumination,' and reaches its final formulation, deeply influenced by the Sufi thought of Ibn al-'Arabi, in the monumental work of Sadr al-Din al-Shirazi (d. 1050/1640), entitled 'The Four Journeys,' which has not yet been properly studied. The fundamental doctrine of this tradition is the principle of the 'grades of Being,' i.e. a doctrine of pantheism built and elaborated on the basis of the Neoplatonic theory of emanation (the most important single source used by them is the so-called 'theology of Aristotle' consisting of passages from the *Enneads* of Plotinus with a Neoplatonist commentary). Another grand theory, closely allied to the principle of the 'grades of Being,' is that of cognition which asserts the identity of thought and being. From these two arose the third important doctrine which came to play a central role in its religious world-view, the essential contribution to the development of which was made by Sufi thought, is the doctrine that affirms a 'Realm of Similitudes (*'Alam al-Mithal'*), i.e. an ontological world of images where the spiritual reality from above assumes the form of concrete images and where the gross bodies from the material realm from below change into subtle bodies and images.

The first two doctrines were developed by al-Suhrawardi. He criticized the Avicennian thesis of the distinction between essence and existence and removed the basis of the philosophers' distinction between God and man. Correspondingly, he negated the distinction between possibility and necessity and declared these distinctions to be purely mental and subjective. Further, he attacked the idea of duality between matter and form and formulated a doctrine of pure existence which tolerated the only distinction within itself of 'more or less' or 'more perfect and less perfect.' Indeed, al-Suhrawardi denounced all Aristotelian categories as pure subjective myths. His whole trend of thought led to the impossibility of any definition whatsoever, for definitions presuppose absolute distinctions in reality, and it was on this function of definitions that the Aristotelian-Avicennian system was built. Consequently, for al-Suhrawardi, reality was one, homogeneous continuum punctuated only by 'more or less' or 'grades of Being': 'the whole of God is Being and the whole of Being is God.'

Beside this monistic picture of reality, al-Suhrawardi developed a theory of knowledge according to which cognition came about not through the 'abstraction' of forms as the philosopher had taught, but by a direct awareness or immediate presence of the object. He upheld the phenomenon of self-awareness as the primordial characteristic of all knowledge and declared, resurrecting the old Zoroastrian concept of 'Light,' this awareness to be the fundamental self-luminosity of Being. Thus, as the stream of Being processes from the ultimate Reality by emanation, so does the stream of Light or immediate consciousness from its ultimate source. Consciousness itself is, therefore, a continuum differentiated at various points by the only category of 'more or less.'

This trend of thought profoundly influenced the whole subsequent development of metaphysical thought in Islam, both Sufic and philosophical: its importance and depth cannot be over-estimated. It produced in Islamic speculative thought a characteristic quality of what might be termed a subjective humanism with regard to the universe and its constitution. The human cognitive faculties are projected into the ontological structure of the Reality which appears as a person. Just as man has sense-perception, imagination, rational thought and spiritual intuition, so is the universe objectively invested with these faculties. Especially favourably was this line of thought cultivated by the Sufis whose methods of personal experience of reality peculiarly predisposed them towards it. Thus, the mystic Ibn al-'Arabi (560-638/1165-1240) was the first to develop the idea of the universe as the 'macro-anthropos (*al-insan al-akbar*)' or 'macro-persona (*al-shakhs al akbar*).' Man is called 'micro-anthropos (*al-insan al-saghir*).' This doctrine is the reverse of the idea of the macrocosm and microcosm. Where the former patterns of Universe on man, the latter patterns man on the Universe.

In this many-tiered homocentric structure of Ibn al-'Arabi's reality, a very prominent role was played by the 'realm of similitudes' which is the ontological counterpart of the human faculty of creative imagination. It is a vast, unlimited realm indeed — quite as infinite as the human imagination which, in fact, does nothing but reflect the Images in the 'realm of similitudes,' just as the faculty of sense-perception only represents perceptual images of the material world, or the intellect only mirrors the ideas objectively existent in the Intelligible World. This world of similitudes or images was specially invoked to explain the living symbols, neither purely spiritual nor purely material, which were the objects of mystic and religious visions and experiences. In these experiences, the purely spiritual reality, the object of spiritual experience, also clothed itself in the quasi-material form of an image directly apprehended by the faculty of imagination. This is the realm wherein the Prophets saw angels in human form; and, finally, this is the place where the events so vividly portrayed in religion concerning the Day of Judgment do occur.

This doctrine of the multi-level reality with the world of imagination in the middle is a peculiar development in the medieval Islam and was accepted by a majority of the orthodox Sufis. It gave to much of Islamic mysticism its characteristic ethos. Finally, it reacted back on philosophy and found its rational grounding and philosophical formulation in the 11th/17th century in the work of Sadr al-Din al-Shirazi, alias Mulla Sadra, the architect of the last great philosophical system in Islam.

Mulla Sadra having accepted from al-Suhrawardi the monistic doctrine of the grades of Being in terms of 'more or less,' develops a doctrine of cognition and the nature of the human soul. The human soul is not a single-level entity having different faculties of cognition, but is of different levels (*nasha'at*) corresponding to those of the ontological reality. The powers of the mind are not mere powers but are literally constituents of reality. The soul, therefore, not merely 'knows' reality but participates in it and is identified with it: it is not merely receptive but creative. It follows that at higher levels of experience, the mind experiences and becomes whatever it wills and thus attains absolute freedom from the finite existence of the material world.

This doctrine of phenomenological idealism asserts a complete identity of thought and being, of mind and reality. Knowing is the ultimate and primordial form of being and, therefore, that theory of knowledge is completely rejected which declares that cognition is a process whereby the mind *conforms* itself to reality. Originally a form of Neoplatonism, this philosophy takes on a new character through the phenomenology of Sufi intuitionism as developed by Ibn al-'Arabi and his followers. Based on spiritual empiricism, it is essentially personal. The truth is that its theoreticism is only apparent and formal. At bottom it sought to cater for the religious need of refined minds in the later Muslim Middle Ages: the need on the part of the individual to live in peace with the universe in a society that was fast becoming subject to internal decline and disintegration.

Thus, philosophy in Islam did not die with the orthodox attack of al-Ghazali as is commonly supposed by modern scholarship. It had, on the contrary, a vibrating life down to the 11th/17th and 12th/18th centuries. But it character was radically changed through the influence of mysticism. From a rational endeavour to understand the nature of the objective reality, it became transformed into a spiritual endeavour to live in harmony with that reality. This is achieved through an intellectual romanticism by an identification of the human mind with reality, of thought with being. This was an easier task than solving thc difficult questions that reality imposed on the mind if the two *confronted* one another. It gave comfort at a time when the external situation was far from comfortable. At a popular mass level the same need was being answered by a total spread of Sufism in Muslim society, a subject to which we must now turn.

Revised and edited; originally published as chapter seven, The Philosophical Movement in Islam.

12

Development of Dogma

M Z SIDDIQI

(Abstract: Traces the origins of various theological schools, like Murjia, Mu'tazila, Maturidi, ahl al-Hadith, etc. as well as the development of philosophy and kalam in Islamic thought.)

Introduction

The Qur'an is essentially a religious and ethical document aiming at the practical goal of creating a morally good and just society composed of religiously righteous men with a keen and vivid awareness of a God who enjoins good and forbids evil. Consequently, pure theory is minimal. Perhaps the nearest it comes to speculation is in its exhortations to contemplate the vastness and regularity of the universe, but even this argument from design is used not to establish the theoretical existence of God but to depict His living majesty and full-blooded purposive beauty. The emphasis is on faith-in-action. For this, the necessary moral and psychological factors and tensions were supplied. Human pride was emphatically humbled beside God's majesty and omnipotence. On the other hand, those who sought to escape action, taking refuge in divine omnipotence, were repudiated, and the essential freedom and responsibility of human action was vividly portrayed. Together with the repeated condemnation of human arrogance and conceit, despondency was categorically rejected as being characteristic of the devil and his followers, the infidels. Human nature was criticized as weak and fallible but the sense of urgency of human initiative was patently maintained.

This simple but effective and practical attitude inculcated by the Qur'an and the Prophet was first shocked into reflection by the upheavals during the Caliphates of 'Uthman and 'Ali. But when, under the Umayyads, the unity of religion and state was disturbed, it led to widespread and deep heart-searching.

The Murjites and Kharijites:

The first question that was raised in Islam was: does a Muslim remain a Muslim after a grave sin? Or, is faith alone sufficient or must it express itself in works as well? The extreme sect of the Kharijites (the 'Seceders') maintained that a grave sinner no longer remains a Muslim and turned the fury of their *jihad* against the established rule and the Community in general in the name of a transcendent the extreme idealism which they combined with uncommpromising fanaticism. 'Decision (rule) belongs to God alone' was the watchword of these tribesmen, who were strong in Iraq and Persia. The pious leaders of the Community in Medina were largely dissatisfied with the Umayyads; but a major part of religious opinion, in its powerlessness, slowly acquiesced in the regime of the Umayyads and declared that the possession of faith alone was sufficient for a person to be defined as a Muslim and that works were not essential. For them 'Decision belongs to God alone' come to mean that political power, seen as having been established by God's will, ought not to be disobeyed. These people, called the Murjites (*Murji'a,* i.e. those who 'postponed' judgment on people until the Last Day) recommended that one should desist from passing judgment on a grave sinner whose fate will be decided by God.

In their first appearance during the time of 'Uthman and 'Ali, the Murji'a represented the mild and moderate opinion against the strong factions for and against 'Uthman and 'Ali. During the Umayyad period, however, this moderate attitude slowly sank to the level of pure determinism, thus falling in line with the popular moral laxity and becoming an instrument in the defence of the Umayyad regime which, in turn, encouraged the dissemination of their views. Thus the Murji'a of the early period of 'Ali, who took a neutralist position in the political quarrel between 'Ali and his opponents and were therefore also called Mu'tazila (the 'neutralists'), came to be called Jabriya, 'pre-determinists'.

The true tradition of these early political neutralists and religious moderates, who comprised the majority of the Companions and the Medinese in general, was during the Umayyad ascendancy located in Medina. The religious leadership at Medina, although shocked at the violent jolt that the Islamic state had received at the hands of the Umayyads, and generally dissatisfied with the latter, nevertheless refrained from active rebellion and concentrated instead on the elaboration of the religious sciences of law and Hadith. The ethos of piety, practicalism and moderation of Medina—which, being the true home of the religious development of Islam in the early centuries, occupied a central and paramount place — set the tone for all subsequent development of Islamic orthodoxy whose central character, as we shall presently see, is the gradual assimilation of extremism into moderation. It was to win the day, and came to full fruition in the 'Abbasid Caliphate.

The Mu'tazila

Outside the Hijaz, however, and especially in Iraq, this attitude of practical religiosity was soon to be subjected to stormy philosophical speculations by outside influences. Iraq was already, before Islam, a battle-ground of ideas and theories which came from different directions. Hellenism, Hellenized Christianity, Gnosticism, Manichaean dualism and Buddhistic elements provided the stock ideas for philosophical, religious and moral speculation. And although, as said above, the initial reflexive impulse to moral issues was generated by events within Islam, these were soon to be transformed in the great cities of Iraq into speculative issues.

The first tangible figure that we meet in Basra in the 1st/7th and early 2nd/8th century is that of the famous Hasan al-Basri (d. 110/728), who is to be regarded as representative of Medinese piety. He strongly rejected the deterministic interpretation of Islam, and regarded man as responsible for his actions. But it is abundantly clear from his writing that he was motivated by pietistic morality rather than speculative curiosity. For we do not find in him a purely philosophical discernment of the issues. He sometimes argues (on the basis of Kur'an) that *all* actions emanate from man who is responsible for them; at other times that all good is to be attributed to God while all evil is to be referred to the devil and to man (again on the basis of the Kur'an). Thus, two different motives are in play here: to save the goodness of God and to make man responsible *especially for evil deeds*. The purely philosophical question of whether God or man is the productive agent of *all* acts does not concern him at all.

But the more systematically thinking minds could not accept this pietistic rejection of determination and voiced their opinion in favour of an unequivocal authorship of man of his own acts: only thus could praise and blame, reward and punishment for man and the justice of God become intelligible. This thesis they pushed to its logical conclusions with regard to the nature of God and the destiny of man. Similarly, on the question of the relationship of faith to deeds, whereas the Kharijites regarded a grave sinner as an outright infidel and the main body of Muslims considered him a 'sinner-Muslim' the Mu'tazila held that he was neither as Muslim nor a non-Muslim. This doctrine is known as that of the 'intermediate state'.

It is probably this doctrine of the 'intermediate state' of a grave sinner that gave the new movement its technical name of Mu'tazila, 'neutralists', and which distinguished them from the old political neutralists. It is not, however, certain when this name was given to them. According to the generally accepted Sunni tradition, they were given the name when their founder, Wasil ibn 'Ata' (80-131/699-749) 'broke off' (*i'tazala*) from the circle of al-Hasan al-Basri. Many orientalists have, however, denied this and attempted different surmises. Goldziher thought that the name (the Arabic root means 'to abstain from', 'to be neutralist', 'to be aside from') refers to their abstemiousness and piety. But although the pious character of the early Mu'tazila cannot be doubted, they were not more pious or abstemious than al-Hasan or many other people. Nor can they be regarded as a continuation of the old political neutralism, as H.S. Nyberg holds. On the contrary, while the bulk of the thinking elements of the Community were political neutralists, the Mu'tazila were by the large (including their leaders) pro-'Ali although some of them did not declare for either party in the earliest civil wars. In any case, their break with al-Hasan and the practical piety of the Medinese branch was of far greater consequence for the future development of Islam.

Thus, in their origins, the Mu'tazila were not 'free-thinkers' as they have been sometimes called. They were not pure 'rationalists' (despite their claim that reason is an equal sources, with Revelation, of moral truth), although the impulse to a *systematic thinking out* of dogma, unlike traditional Islam, was certainly an activity which made them pursue their ratiocination further and further as time went on. Indeed, the deterministic doctrine which the Mu'tazila were fighting at home was also shaped early into a systematic doctrine at the hands of such men as Jahm ibn Safwan (put to death in 128/746) who advocated, in all probability under foreign influences, an uncompromising and absolute determinism. But, above all, as newer researches have shown, they waged a relentless and successful struggle in defence of Islam against outside attacks of Manichaeism, Gnosticism and Materialism. In doing so, they perforce produced the first systematically thought-out creed for Islam, but, inside Islam, they had gone too far beyond the limits which traditional Islam could recognize as valid. The outside dangers having been quelled, they struggled inside Islam on the twin platforms of the 'justice and unity of God' wherein they increasingly showed themselves as rigid and intolerant advocates of Hellenistic rationalism, and were finally defeated with their own weapons.

The doctrine of the freedom of the human will as advocated by the Mu'tazila came soon to be a part of the wider theological concept of the 'Justice of God' and overshadowed its original aspect, the freedom and responsibility of man. From among the various constituents of the Kur'anic concept of God, power, mercy, will and justice, they isolated this last one and carried it to its logical conclusions that God *cannot* do the unreasonable and the unjust. In this connection they developed their doctrine of the 'Promise and Threat' according to which God can neither pardon the evil-doer (and therefore violate His Threat) nor punish the good-doer (and violate His Promise). Taking the Kur'anic statements about the promise of reward and threat of punishment as categorical statements of future *facts,* they deduced that God would not only be unjust if He did not carry out His promised and threats, He would be a liar. Consequently, the Qur'anic dicta concerning the mercy and grace of God were interpreted by them in terms of necessity and duty: God *must* do the best for man; He *must* send Prophets and Revelations to mankind. If He did not do the best for man He would neither be just nor God. These doctrines were developed patently under Hellenistic influence and more especially under the influence of Stoicism, as indeed Stoical influences have been established beyond doubt in other doctrines of later *kalam.* In the eyes of the orthodox, this freedom for man was bondage for God. They accused Mu'tazilism of extreme humanism and they insisted that God is above the human concepts of justice: that it is not just for God what man considers as such for Him, but that which He does for man appears at the human level as just and rational. Thus, whereas the Mu'tazila subsumed the idea of God under that of human justice, the orthodox subsumed the idea of justice under that of God.

As with the problem of justice, with that of the Divine Attributes, the Mu'tazila went to extreme limits. Starting with a genuine anxiety to safeguard the idea of Divine transcendence, they explained away all expressions of Scripture and the Hadith that contained anthropomorphism in a rational spirit and ended up by negating all the Divine Attributes. God is pure Essence having no eternal names and qualities, affirmation of which, according to them, was tantamount to a form of polytheism. This was their version of *tanzih,* 'divine transcendence' which according to the orthodoxy rather consisted in the absoluteness of His attributes, Power, Knowledge, Will, etc. Consequently, the Mu'tazila were branded as *mu'attila,* i.e., those who denuded God of all content and rendered Him unsatisfactory for religion consciousness.

And although the Mu'tazila, in their turn, accused orthodoxy of *tashbih*, i.e. 'likening God to man', so far as religion was concerned, there could be hardly any doubt about the final issue. As Professor Gibb has put it: 'The orthodox rightly rejected these pretensions (of the Mu'tazila) for in religion anthroposophy is a more insidious solvent than anthropomorphism.'

Indeed, the Mu'tazila carried their rationalism so far as to claim parity for reason with revelation in the discovery of religious truth. They were not content only with a declaration of the superiority of reason over tradition, but put it on an equal footing with the Word of God as religious guide. The implications of this went even further: since they could not accept the Speech of God as an Attribute of God, they declared the Kur'an to be created word. On the subject of the Attributes and especially with regard to the Word, they were undoubtedly influenced by Hellenistic ideas especially in their Christian formulations about the Logos. But since they held reason to be the essential constitution of God, a purely Greek idea, the net result was to put reason above revelation. The orthodox held the Kur'an to be the eternal Word of God, and the Mu'tazila, when their doctrine temporarily became the state-creed in the Caliphate of al-Ma'mun and his successors, persecuted their representatives, especially Ahmad ibn Hanbal (d. 241/855), who was flogged and imprisoned for resolutely refusing to believe in the Mu'tazila dogma.

It is, however, undeniable that the Mu'tazila movement did a great internal service to Islam not only by attempting to erect an edifying picture of God for refined minds but, above all, by insisting on the claims of reasoning theology. This attempt, as we shall presently see, did leave a legacy which was, to some extent, taken up in subsequent developments. But while the Mu'tazila movement itself lasted, its excessive emphasis on formal rationality, indeed on an apotheosis of reason (in its later development), created a severe reaction in the orthodoxy. Orthodoxy, while maintaining in spirit its original ethics of integrative, broad and stabilising catholicity, was nevertheless, in its actual formulas, pressed into a reaction under the aggressive attitude of this proud and hollow rationalism. While the Mu'tazila stuck rigidly to 'Reason and Justice of God' and the freedom of the human will, traditionalist orthodoxy, in order to save vital elements in religion, put almost exclusive strees on the formulations of Divine Power, Will, Grace and determinism. In its definitions, therefore, orthodoxy fell in danger of losing the comprehensiveness of the original simple faith. Henceforth Islam was launched on a career where its dynamic formulations had only a partial and indirect relationship to the living realities of the faith.

Ash'arism and Maturidism

The right wing of orthodox traditionalism was represented by Ibn Hanbal and his school. But the truly broad catholic spirit of Islam was crystallized by the compilers of that unique phenomenon in Islam. By a fairly broad-minded exercise of their 'orthodox' insight, these men allowed to fall within the scope of the acceptable Hadith a body of authoritative material that allowed for latitude and integration of points of view and opinions that could not be fitted into one mould. It exhibits no external or supcrficial wisdom but an impeccable scrupulousness and an inner and genuine insight into the spirit of the Prophet's teaching and the early Community's understanding of it. The Hadith was opposed by the Mu'tazila who nevertheless slowly lost ground by the latter half of the 3rd/9th century; on no other hypothesis than this can we really understand the absolute success of the Hadith in that century.

Yet, the success of the Hadith was not due to the fact that it was, in its formulations and content, a possibly valuable amorphous mass, but because at bottom it expressed a definite spirit of religious realism that had characterised both the Kur'an and the early Community. It brought under the aegis of the Sunna all the necessary religious elements that were implicit or explicit in the Kur'an. Side by side with the coming to fruition of the Hadith, a widespread movement of dissatisfaction had started with the *cliches* of the rationalist school. Their newer views began to shape on the basis of their acquaintance with tradition and their gradual acceptance of it.

The most celebrated name in this newer movement, which turned the tables on the Mu'tazila by their own dialectic, is that of Abu'l-Hasan al-Ash'ari (d. 330/442) who broke from his Mu'tazilite master al-Jubba'i in maintaining that Divine Justice could not be defined in human terms. The following oft-quoted passage celebrated this *coup de bouleversement:*

'Let us imagine a child and a grown-up person in Heaven who both died in the True Faith. The grown-up one, however, has a higher place in Heaven than the child. The child shall ask God: "Why did you give that man a higher place?" "He has done may good works", God shall reply. Then the child shall say, "Why did you let me die so soon so that I was prevented from doing good?" God will answer, "I knew that you would grow up into a sinner; therefore, it was better that you should die a child." Thereupon a cry shall rise from those condemned to the depth of the Hell. "Why, O Lord! did You not let us die before we became sinners?"

Al-Ash'ari's formulation of dogma essentially represents an attempt at a synthesis of the hitherto largely unformulated orthodox position and that of the Mu'tazila. This is, as we have pointed out before, the very ethos of orthodoxy. But his actual formulas unmistakably show the character of a reaction of orthodoxy to the Mu'tazilite doctrine, a reaction from which he was unable to escape completely. The net result is therefore a partial synthesis and a partial reaction. On the question of human free will he erected, on the basis of certain Qur'anic texts, his doctrine of 'acquisition'. According to this doctrine, all acts are created and produced by God but attach themselves to the will of man who thus 'acquires' them. D.B. Macdonald has seen in this formula an attempt to do justice to the psychological fact that man has the consciousness of owning his voluntary acts. But, to begin with, man has the consciousness not merely of owning his deliberate acts but also of producing them; and both the Mu'tazila and their opponents were aware of the argument from direct consciousness. Secondly, the problem that al-Ash'ari set out to resolve was not so much a psychological as a moral one: how to reconcile Divine Omnipotence with human responsibility. And if man's consciousness of owning his acts is itself created by god, as al-Ash'ari believes, then man 'acquires' neither the one nor the other. The principle that seems to be at work here is that all power is referred to God while responsibility must remain with man. The principle itself, although it has a metaphysical form, is religious and moral in its essential character.

Similarly, on the problem of the Unity of God, al-Ash'ari taught that God has real, Eternal Attributes, but attempted to safeguard against anthropomorphism. God knows by virtue of His Attribute of Knowledge, wills by virtue of His attribute of Will, etc. These are neither identical with His Essence nor different from it. They are real although we do not know their 'how', and in this connection al-Ash'ari makes use of the negative dialectic of the Mu'tazilites which ultimately comes from Neoplatonism. As to rewards and punishments, he emphasizes both the absolute Power of God and His absolute Mercy and Grace: He may punish or reward as He will. This is done not to uphold any caprice and arbitrariness on the part of God but again in order to express the religious attitude of humility and fear. Like all Attributes, God's Speech is eternal and uncreated. But the Kur'an as we know it, a definite text of a certain length, etc., is only *an expression although an expression par excellence* of the Eternal Speech of God which in itself is a 'Mental Word.'

Thus, al-Ash'ari confirmed the absolute Power and Grace of God was orthodoxy had maintained it. All acts take place by the Will and 'Good Pleasure' of God, whether good or evil. As said before, al-Ash'ari was strongly under the influence of the orthodox reaction against the Mu'tazilite doctrine which seemed to restrict God's power. And, indeed, he made no secret of the fact that he did not want to deviate from the teaching of Ahmad ibn Hanbal. This absolute Power of God was further supported by an atomistic theory of nature denying causation and potentialities in natural bodies and providing for the direct efficacy of god for the production of events, whether physical or mental.

Another theological system which grew up almost contemporaneously with that of al-Ash'ari is that of Abu Mansur al-Maturidi (d. 333/945) of Samarqand in Transoxiana. Maturidism is very similar to Ash'arism in basic outlook, but differs from it in certain important points. Al-Maturide, like al-Ash'ari, holds that all acts are willed by God, but unlike him, maintains that evil acts do not occur 'with the good pleasure of God'. More important, Maturidism, while emphasising the Omnipotence of God, allows the efficacy of the human will and, in some of its later development, the absolutely free human production of acts was unequivocally stated. In these later developments, indeed, there is agree interaction between the two systems, and the doctrine of the absolute inefficacy of the human will generally lost its force although the Ash'arite dogma, backed by some important Hadith, still retained it.

An important problem discussed widely by Muslim dogmatists and theologians was that of the 'degrees of faith'. This was connected with the question of faith and works, and subsequently came to be connected with the idea of the Omnipotence and Grace of God under the influence of speculative theology. Those who held, like the Mu'tazila and the Kharijites, that acts were an essential part of the faith, also held that faith increases and decreases, is quantitative — and could reach a zero degree, despite the profession of the faith by the agent. The Murjites, on the other hand, believed that faith was something qualitatively unanalysable and simple, not admitting either degree or measurement. The Sunni *kalam*, as expected, was between the two in principle, but on the whole inclined to the tenets of the Murjites. This was undoubtedly in order to check fanaticism and persecution, and the Sunnis, accordingly, maintained that, with a genuine profession of faith, an irreducible amount of faith came into existence which was incapable of being eliminated by almost any external behaviour, although it could increase or decrease beyond that point. The Kur'an repeatedly affirsm the encrease of faith (e.g. III, 167, and elsewhere) and incessantly urges acts born of genuine faith; and the Hadith speaks of intimate connection between acts and intentions, although certain Hadith, which apparently counselled moderation and were to the effect that none shall be eternally damned with a 'grain of faith', were seized upon by theologians in this connection. Indeed, the 'Ulama' henceforth limited their function of the 'tendence of the soul' to the formulas of belief and issuing *fatwas* (authoritative legal opinions) on external legal matters. This fundamentally explains the subsequent tide of the largely anti-orthodox Sufi movement which claimed exclusive right to cater for the inner, spiritual welfare of individuals. But in the meanwhile, a split occurred within orthodoxy itself. The main continuation of the old traditional school of Medina, the 'People of the Hadith', not only opposed Ash'arite solutions of dialectical theology but rejected the dialectical theology itself. The Kur'an and the Sunna, they contended, must no be defended by a 'reason' that lies outside these, but the true 'reason' is to be found rather within them. They accused the Mu'tazila, in effect, of betraying the true spirit of the Kur'an and the Sunna in the process of defending them by rational formulas. Nevertheless, Ash'arism, as a system of dogma, slowly overcame opposition and finally won recognition in the East in the 11th/17the century through the efforts of the great Seljuq wazir Nizam al-Mulk and the brilliant theologian and religious reformer al-Ghazali. But the friction between the religious spirit of the Ahl al-Hadith and the rationalizing tendencies of the Ahl al-Kalam continued and culminated in the 7th/13th and 8th/14th centuries in a vigorous reassertion of puritanical activism in Ibn Taymiya and his school. But before that the *kalam* had to face a more thorough-going rational movement of the Muslim philosophers.

Philosophy and Kalam

The Islamic philosophical movement, from the point of view of its amplification of Islamic doctrine, was an outgrowth of the Mu'tazila *kalam*. Against the rationalsit system of the philosophers, al-Ghazali (d. 505/1111) represented the first great reaction, monumental in the depth and durability of its influence. A truly searching religious spirit (he has often, with justice, been compared to Augustine), he went through a series of spiritual crises. Early in life he became disillusioned with the traditional *kalam* theology because of its formalism and externality. In his search for truth, he studied philosophy but found it not only far from orthodox Islam in its teachings but above all lacking in certainty in its proofs. In religious convictions he searched for a type of mathematical certainty. This, as the balance of religious forces in the structure of Islam stood at that time, he found only in sufism (Muslim mysticism).

This explains why, after refuting the philosophers' theses in his famous work, the *Tahafut al-Falasifa,* al-Ghazali did not attempt an alternative philosophical system. The answer is that no metaphysic, purely rationally constructed, would satisfy the religious need of certainty. Nevertheless, despite his rejection of Greco Islamic philosophy in general, he adopted certain beliefs from it. Thus he finally adopted from the philosophers the views, which was in harmony with the Sufi ethics, that man is soul alone to the exclusion of the body.

But if the need for religious certainty impelled al-Ghazali to mysticism, his mysticism led him back to a rediscovery of the Qur'anic conception of God as formulated in the Ash'arite *kalam.* He was thus destined to prove the first and greatest reformer of Sufism for which at the same time he secured a place in the structure of Islamic orthodoxy. And, what is even more important, he brought the formal, dogmatic formulation of the orthodox *kalam* into contact with the living religion, thereby revitalising them and infusing into them the original spirit of the Revelation. He thus dealt a powerful blow to pure scholasticism, softened the dogmatic character of the creed and established a vital nerve between the inner and the exterior aspects of religion. Armed with this, he wrote his great work *The Revivification of the Sciences of the Faith.*

Al-Ghazali has puzzled many a modern writer. Some have wondered whether he was essentially a mystic or a theologian, although he is described as both. In some quarters, which have dared to be more decisive on the matter, his mysticism has been rejected with the thesis that he is really a *mutakallim* ('declaimer') who devised a purely *psychological* method of concentration on the dogma, the two being linked purely mechanically. To us it appears a capital misunderstanding of al-Ghazali. Fundamentally, al-Ghazali affirmed an agnosticism about the ultimate and absolute nature of God and maintained that He was knowable only in so far as He was related to and revealed Himself to man. This revealed and relational nature of God is constituted by the Divine Names and Attributes. Mysticism reveals these to man in their true nature. He, therefore, rejected the extreme Sufi claims of absorption, union and incarnation. He was in pursuit not of religious aesthetics and artistry but of religious *morality.* The religious certainty he sought did not consist of security, safety and calm repose, but of moral purification and the war against vice that degraded man. Thus it was that he came to substitute for the 'Prime Mover' of the philosophers and the 'Essence of Essences' of the Sufes, the ultimate 'Commander' of the Qur'an. The *kalam* formulates that Command: mysticism reveals it to man in a way that his whole being is transformed into its receptacle and organ. And although there may be found unconcealed contradictions in al-Ghazali's intellectual aspect, the spiritual integrity and organic unity of his personality is beyond a shadow of doubt.

The synthesis thus achieved by al-Ghazali between Sufism and *kalam* was largely adopted by orthodoxy and confirmed by Ijma'. Its strength lay in the fact that it gave a spiritual basis for the moral practical *elan* of Islam and thus brought it back to its original religious dimensions. But the balance was delicate and could be maintained only within the limits of a strictly moral ethos. Within orthodoxy, there were two groups which did not adopt al-Ghazali's synthesis. One of these, which actually opposed al-Ghazali, was the right-wing Ahl al-Hadith, the traditionalists who considered both parts of the synthesis, the *kalam* and Sufism, as foreign and therefore suspect elements, and actually attacked al-Ghazali for using weak and even forged traditions to support his Sufic interpretations. The other, the more intellectualist Mutakallims, could not accept the plea for a reduced and purely practical *kalam* which did not satisfy demands of formal intellectualism. They thus expanded the theses of the traditional *kalam* to reckon with the new philosophical challenge and reinforce the Islamic creed. Their main doctrines we shall study presently.

But unexpected developments took place about a century after al-Ghazali, which used the *kalam* in quite a new direction with a purpose wholly alien to it. Sufism, when developed into a speculative system, turned the moral doctrine of the Unity and Omnipotence of God of the *kalam* into a monistic pantheism of mystic philosophy on the basis of the philosophical doctrine of emanation. In this theory, the scholastic-Ghazalian Names of God are transformed into a network of hietrarchical manifestations or epiphanies of the Divine Essence through which the mystic progressed to be united with the Being of God.

The main stream of *kalam*-theology, however, could not reject reason in favour either of pure mysticism as al-Ghazali had done, or of simple traditionalism like the majority of the Ahl al-Hadith. The rationalist challenge, whose first phase began with the Mu'tazila, became far more systematic and formidable with the advent of the philosophical movement, and left a permanent legacy. The Islamic dogma, therefore, had to be restated equally systematically and with a corresponding vigour with the same logic as the philosophers had used. The greatest and most incisive formulator of the new systematic theology is Muhammad ibn 'Umar, known as Fakhr al-Din al-Razi (d. 606/1209). At first a pure rationalist and almost indistinguishable from the philosophers in his theses, even a vindicator of certain philosophical doctrines (e.g. that of the eternity of the world) against al-Ghazali, he gradually embraced the Ash'arite creed and undertook to defend its tenets. Later, the results of this systematic theology were set forth by al-lji (d. 756/1355) in a work entitled *al-Mawaqif* which attracted commentators for several centuries.

All the relevant philosophical discipline were studied and elaborated by the new systematic theology. Greek logic, especially its theory of knowledge, was assiduously cultivated. This together with physics (theories of nature) and metaphysics, formed the basis for theology. In each of these fields, the theories of the philosophers were elaborated, modified or rejected according to what was seen as implicit in the dogma. In the theory of knowledge, congnition was declared to be a non-essential, external relation between the knowing mind and the known object. This was the Islamic answer to the philosophical epistemology which, at the level of pure cognition, declared the identity of the subject and the object in the act of cognition and which, despite the efforts of Ibn Sina (Avicenna) to safeguard it against any pantheistic suggestion, or incarnationism, was, nevertheless, being manipulated by many Sufi theorists in terms of a final identity between God and man.

In the field of natural philosophy, controversies continued between the atomism of the *kalam* and the Aristotelian, philosophical theory of matter and form, which was the basis of the philosophers' theory of causation. The Mutakallims rejected and Aristotelian doctrine of matter and form as a prerequisite for rejecting natural causation and restated the early Ash'arite atomism with fresh arguments until affirmation of atomism and denial of natural causation came to be looked upon as almost a cardinal religious dogma regarded as a necessary step to prove the temporal creation of the world and the Islamic eschatology.

The most patent and cherished subject for systematic theology, however, was the most widely discussed problem of Being which had started with early *kalam* but which was erected into the most fundamental theological doctrine of his system by the philosopher Ibn Sina. The philosophers had attempted to draw a distinction between God and the world, a distinction which was to be adopted by St. Thomas Aquinas in the West as the foundation of his theology, on the basis of a theory of essence and existence. All created things, according to this theory, were composed of an essence and a fact of existence or actual being which was conferred upon them by God who is simple Being without any essence and whose only real attribute is being: God is existent *per se*; everything else exists through God. Hence God is the Necessary Being while all created things are contingent *per se* and necessary-by-God.

The philosophers had, by this doctrine, sought to distinguish fundamentally between God and the world: at no point can a created being *become* Necessary Being. But by allowing existence to be a common attribute of all created things, bestowed by God, it was tempting to argue that all things 'shared' in the Being of God, especially in view of the fact that the philosophers' God had no essence. This was, in fact, argued vigorously by thinkers such as Shihab al-Din al-Suhrawardi (put to death in 587/1191) and by the great Sufi thinker Ibn al-'Arabi (d. 638/1240). The systematic theology emphatically rejects the distinction between essence and existence, affirms that essences are created at the time of their existence, attributes an essence to God, which, as in the case of created beings, is indistinguishable from Divine Existence. Thus, by making existence unique in the case of each being, it eradicates even the slightest tendency to pantheism and develops into a form of existentialism.

The systematic theology of Islam, as it developed after al-Ghazali, has not been adequately studied by modern scholarship. But an extreme doctrine wherein systematic theology corroborated the philosophers' teaching was that of an uncompromising determinism and a flat rejection of human freedom. Fresh arguments were put forward, with the help of the philosophical stock of ideas, to strengthen determinism. In the doctrine of Fakhr al-Din al-Razi, there appears no scope even for al-Ash'ari's doctrine of the 'acquisition' of the act by the human agent. The Mu'tazila, in their attempt to establish human freedom, had appealed to direct consciousness of freedom on the part of the agent. This psychological approach was now resumed, deepened and turned the other way round. A theory of human motivation was developed to show, on the one hand, that while a specific motive holds sway, action (or non-action) becomes absolutely necessary, and, on the other, that we are not the authors of our acts but God is, on the ground that we are never fully aware of the details and consequences of our actions. for an agent to own an act properly it is necessary for him to know exactly and completely the empirical conditions and consequences of the action. This principle of quantitative correspondence between knowledge and action led to the conclusion that only an omniscient being can, strictly speaking, act.

This limpidly systematic and excessively logical body of doctrine imposed itself henceforth on the educational institutions of Islam throughout the Middle Ages. It undoubtedly touched in its subtleties and logical *finesse* the lofty pinnacles of reasoning. But it is truly scholastic both in its spirit and its content: with all its subtle reasoning, it expressly formulated and, in the very process of this formulation, exhibited a fundamental lack of confidence in human reason. While nobody need quarrel on grounds of religion with its doctrine of Being and its theory of knowledge, where it performed a real service for Islam, it is difficult to defend its solution of the problem of freewill on religious grounds. On this central problem of religious consciousness, with which the very history of religious thought started in Islam, it had moved far beyond any reasonable distance from the spirit of the Kur'an and the ethos of the early Community. Even with al-Ash'ari and his early followers, the problem had retained its original moral urgency, but in the hands of the systematic theologian it became a purely doctrinaire pedantry.

There is a fairly common view among modern scholars, according to which this uncompromisingly transcendentalist picture of God, entailing a denial of trust in natural properties and the immanent processes of nature, and freedom of the human will, is to be based squarely on the Kur'an or is, at least, the most logical development of its teaching. This judgment, examined in the light of the Qur'an itself, seems considerable less than a half-truth. In the religious history of Islam, however, there were genuine factors for concern over the transcendence of God being compromised. In particular, the Dualist challenge seems to have been persistent in one form or another. Manichaean Dualism was combated and overcome in the early centuries, but was not destroyed. Then came the philosophical doctrine of the eternity of matter, which the Iranian Manichaean thinkers, like al-Suhrawardi, were not slow in interpreting in the spirit of their own ancient doctrine. But even after this challenge was no longer a living danger, the new challenge of pantheistic Sufism prevented the *kalam*-orthodoxy from re-thinking its formulation of the dogma. The result was that on the question of freewill, the balance of forces was over-whelmingly weighted in favour of determinism in the Middle Ages. The philosophers argued for a pure rational determinism; Sufism, on the basis of both the philosophical teaching and a peculiar interpretation of the theological doctrine of the Unity of God, advocated a monistic determinism, and *kalam* itself began to teach a complete theistic determinism. Together, these forces constitute the giant theoretical wheel of Medieval Islam revolving around the axis of Determinism. Further, for this theoretical conspiracy, a strong enough basis was provided in the concrete realities of life by the political situation where increasing despotism both sustained and was sustained by this theoretical attitude.

The Ahl al-Hadith, suspicious both of Sufism and *kalam*, were the only group that remained outside this great wheel of Determinism. The vicissitudinous and multilateral relationship between this group, the *kalam* and Sufism, with their uneasy alliances and tensions is what henceforth gave vitality to Islam as a religion and constitutes its story until the modern period. Before describing this interplay, however, we must study the development of the most central religious concept of Islam, that of the Shari'a, which will put the developments we have examined so far into perspective and render subsequent history more intelligible.

Revised and edited; originally published as chapter five, in Islam.

13

The Future of Islamic Studies

ZIAUDDIN SARDAR

(Abstract: The picture of Islamic studies as arigid discipline with sub-discipline s must be abandoned. If it has to evolve as a multi- and inter-disciplinary subject then Islam cannot be taught as a religion or culture or even a civilization. Conceptual analysis will give Islamic studies a meaning…).

Introduction

Muhammad Iqbal, an outstanding Muslim philosopher of the century, argued that Islamic Studies had four basic objectives. In a letter written in June, 1925, to the Secretary of "All India Muhammadan Educational Conference", which was then developing a curriculum for the Islamic Studies course at the Aligarh Muslim University, he wrote that the purpose of Islamic Studies is "to educate and train well-qualified theologians"; "to produce scholars who may, by their researches in the various branches of Muslim literature and thought, be able to trace genetically the continuity of intellectual life between Muslim culture and modern knowledge"; "to turn out Muslim scholars well-versed in the various aspects of Muslim history, art, general culture and civilisation"; and "to produce scholars who may be fitted to carry on researches in the legal literature of Islam". Iqbal had obviously given the matter some thought, and he elaborates each objective.

The training of well-qualified theologians, he argues, is necessary to satisfy the spiritual needs of the community. "But the spiritual needs of a community change with the expansion of that community's outlook on life. The change in the position of the individual, his intellectual liberation and infinite advance in natural sciences have entirely changed the substance of modern life so that the kind of scholasticism or theological thought which satisfied a Muslim in the Middle Ages would not satisfy him today." Therefore Iqbal was looking for a new and more innovative way of teaching Islam. He dismissed the syllabus suggested by the Conference: "it is perfectly useless to institute a school of Muslim Theology on older lines unless it is your objective to satisfy the more conservative portion of our community", he wrote. What is needed, he argued, "is intellectual activity in fresh channels and the building of a new theology and *kalam"*. Iqbal was too far ahead of his time. In the event, the "conservative" forces had their way.

However, the move to reform the syllabus of Islamic Studies at the Aligarh Muslim University was not without significance. It was the academic expression of a growing concern amongst Indian Muslim scholars that Islamic Studies needed a fresh breath of life. In the same letter Iqbal suggests that students of Islam should be persuaded to study science and mathematics, economics and sociology, while students of natural sciences should attend such courses as "Science in the Muslim World". He and other intellectuals of his time were firm, on the one hand, that Islamic Studies should not be the sole preserve of "Muslim theologians" and, on the other, that Muslim students of natural and social sciences should be exposed to Islamic studies.

The idea that modern Muslim universities should have departments, schools or institutes of Islamic Studies has its roots in the revivalist movements of India and in the thoughts of such reformers as Iqbal. Indian universities such as Aligarh, Osmania and Allahabad established departments of Islamic and Arabic Studies which awarded graduate and postgraduate degrees early in the twentieth century. Thus "Islamic Studies" as a discipline received its first, to use Mohamed Mackeen's words, "academic, though somewhat inarticulate, formulation as a university grouping" in India. This "formulation" has had considerable impact on the evolution of the discipline.

Islamic Studies in the Muslim World

In the 1950s when some Muslim countries obtained their independence, old universities were expanded and a number of new universities were established. Islamic Studies received a new impetus: the departments were broadened and somewhat "modernised". Along with the traditional subjects of *tafsir, fiqh,* Arabic, etc., new courses such as "Islam in the Modern World" and "Contemporary Revivalist Movements" began to be taught. A great deal of emphasis was beginning to be laid on the traditional/modern dichotomy and issues such as birth control, "Islam and science", Islam and modern ideologies, came into the syllabus. The universities of Cairo, Decca, Karachi and the Punjab and the 'Universited Islam' in Djakarta all updated their Islamic Studies courses in this way. The new universities of Malaya, Ibadan and King Saud in Riyadh adopted the more up-to-date version of the discipline.

However, not all universities acquired separate departments for Islamic Studies. In some universities like those of Alexandria, Damascus, Rabat and Baghdad, Islamic Studies was integrated within the departments of faculties of Art or Humanities and disciplines such as literature, languages, history, law and so on, and had various courses dealing with Islamic aspects. For example, the Department of Law would offer a course on Islamic law. In certain other universities, like those of Ankara and Tehran, "Islamic studies were incorporated within the university structure under a more specific classification as faculties or department of theology based on the Western models of the faculties of divinity and theology". Thus the Istanbul University established a School of Divinity in 1949 "to study religious principles in the light of scholarly principles."

Only at the University of Cairo did Islamic Studies have a unique status: the discipline had a whole faculty to itself. The *Dar al-'Ulum* was named after an institute founded in 1871 for studies on religion, language, literature and engineering. In 1946 this institute was brought within the university and given the status of a faculty which ran courses on a whole range of Islamic topics.

While the discipline of Islamic Studies was going through these changes, the old established Islamic universities of al-Azhar in Cairo. Qarawiyyin in Fez, and Zaytunah in Tunis, with their roots going back to over a thousand years of history and tradition, continued to teach Islam in the traditional manner. Only al-Azhar went through a radical change. In 1961 it was transformed into a "modern university" with constituent colleges for Islamic Studies, Arabic Studies, management and administration, engineering and industry, agriculture and medicine. However, the traditional al-Azhar became the prototype of the Islamic University of Medina which was founded in 1960.

The emergence of the more modern courses of Islamic Studies, however, has not radically changed the contents of the discipline. Both in the traditional institutions of Islamic learning such as al-Azhar, Deoband and Medina universities, and the modern universities, Islamic studies are essentially theological studies of defined purpose and content. The objective, as Iqbal pointed out, is still to produce well trained scholars of Islam. The syllabus in both types of institutions is based on the classical Muslim tradition which has evolved through centuries of growth and reform. It consists of the Qur'an and Hadith which occupy a central position, while Shari'ah, scholastic theology and Arabic grammar, rhetoric and logic play a supporting role. Modern universities would, of course, add courses which would touch on contemporary issues and controversies.

There are strong reasons why the classical approach to Islamic studies is concentrated on this framework. Mackeen, for example, argues that this framework "owes its origin and structure to the political, social and intellectual patterns in the expansion of Islam and, above everything, to orthodoxy, the master criterion of Muslim thought and practice. But this range of studies is not totally different from that which obtained in medieval Europe, where the trivium—namely, grammar, logic and rhetoric—formed the basis of a system in which Biblical studies, scholasticism, theology and law figured prominently. The grammar was Latin, the universal language of the all-powerful Church. Logic furnished the weapon for argument as well as a convinient method of escape to erudite obscurities.

Rhetoric provided the foundation necessary for disputation and oratory in an era of the spoken word. A fact which is not often realised even by the Muslims themselves is that the major disciplines like scholastic theology and law were the ultimate outcome of a genuine urge to pin down with precision the terms of a civilisation and were not in themselves wanting in intellectual content and value. There were centuries of hard thinking and application behind them. Scholastic theology (*`ilm al-kalam*), for example, is an independent scientific discipline based on rational concepts and the use of scientific tools, namely, logic and physics."

While the critics of the classical methods of teaching Islamic Studies are right in pointing out that this curriculum is somewhat out of touch with contemporary reality, the reforms they have introduced have been hardly innovative. Modern universities may not teach rhetoric and logic, but they retain the bulk of the classical syllabus. Moreover, the new courses that have been introduced do not form an integrated part of the whole syllabus, but are always an appendage to the classical syllabus. Mackeen himself has nothing to add to the classical contents. He suggests that Islamic Studies should 'spread over' to the following fields: religion, philosophy and ethics, sufism and music, literature, art, archaeology and history. While these subjects may expose the students of Islamic Studies to topics that are outside the classical syllabus, the discipline itself benefits little. Adding such subjects to the periphery of Islamic Studies would hardly give the discipline an integrated, coherent and contemporary structure. The modernist criticism of the syllabus and contents of classical Islamic Studies is devoid of philosophical content and systematic analysis of contemporary reality.

Both the classical and modern approaches to Islamic Studies concentrate on Islam as a religion and culture. Whether, it is memorising the Kuran or Hadith, mastering the opinions of the classical jurists or learning Islamic history, the emphasis is on rote learning and collecting facts. Islamic Studies essentially amounts to a vast storehouse of facts and opinions which the student accumulates during the course of his or her study. No wonder then that the contemporary *'Ulama'* and scholars of Islam are noted for a conspicuous absence of the ability to analyse, argue and appreciate contemporary issues.

Islamic Studies in the West

In the West Islamic studies followed a somewhat different course. The roots of Islamic studies in the West lie deep in the colonial history. Marshall Hodgson argues that Western scholarship came to Islamic studies through three paths. "First, there were those who studied the Ottoman empire, which played so major a role in modern Europe. They came to it usually in the first instance from the viewpoint of the European diplomatic history. Such scholars tended to see the whole of Islamdom from the political perspective of Istanbul, the Ottoman capital. Second, there were those, normally British, who entered Islamic studies in India so as to master Persian as good civil servants, or at least they were inspired by Indian interests. For them, the imperial transition of Delhi tended to be culmination of Islamicate history. Third, there were the Semitists, often interested primarily in Hebrew studies, who were lured into Arabic. For them, headquarters tended to be Cairo, the most vital of Arabic-using cities in the nineteenth century, though some turned to Syria or the Maghrib. They were commonly philologians rather than historians and they learned to see Islamicate culture through the eyes of the late Egyptian and Syrian writers most in vogue in Cairo." Hodgson considers other western paths to Islamic studies—the Spanish and some Frenchmen who were interested in studying Muslim Spain and the Russians who were preoccupied with studying northern Muslims—as less important.

Whatever the path, the objectives of Islamic studies in the West were simple and direct: to understand the Muslim mind and culture so as to facilitate colonisation and to meet the demands of the growing colonial civil service. These objectives ensured that Islamic Studies in the West was a problem-oriented discipline—how could Islam be shown to be inferior? How could Muslims be persuaded to accept their fate as subject people? How could they be made intellectually and hence physically insular? etc.—that was pursued within the framework of Western values and cultural systems. It was this framework that produced orientalism, to approach and methodology of studying Islam that has been analysed so penetratingly by, amongst others, Edward Said. The major function of the centres of Islamic Studies at Cambridge, Oxford, Leiden, Sarbonne and Berlin Universities was to produce civil servants trained in the art of colonial administration, to arm Christian missionaries with arguments for conversion, and to produce a body of scholarship that justified European domination of Muslim lands.

The colonial legacy is evident in most current Islamic Studies courses in Western universities. They are taught with a blend of zealous philanthropy and latent self-interest. The links with foreign policy are never far away. However, Islamic Studies in the West do have a distinct advantage: because Islam is studied as a "problem", albeit from the perspective of Western values and culture, there is a strong emphasis on analysis. Best works of oriental scholars, for example, Hodgson's *The Venture of Islam* and D.M. Dunlop's *Arab Civilisation to A.D. 1500,* are works of analysis.

Moreover, with the partial shift in the global power structure and the newly acquired economic wealth of certain Muslim countries, Islamic Studies has received a more sympathetic attention. What that actually means is that in their analysis orientalist scholars now tend to treat the values and culture of Islam on their own terms. Islamic Studies courses now include works by Muslim scholars and Islam is studied as a civilisation.

Perhaps no one has done more in presenting Islam as a civilisation than Hodgson. His work entitled *The venture of Islam,* a systematic and penetrating three-volume study of the civilisation of Islam from its beginning to the twentieth century, is now used as a standard text in most Islamic Studies courses in Western universities. Hodgson has even developed his own terminology of analysis: "Istamdon and Islam" are two of many important terms in his work. "Islamdom", by analogy with Christiandom, is used to describe the society in which Muslims and their faith are predominant—it does not refer to an area as such but to "a complex of social relations" which are territorially reasonably well defined. While "Islamdom" does not describe a civilisation or a specific culture, "Islamicate" is used to describe just such a culture, historically distinct from Islamdom, the society which has been shaped both by Muslims and non-Muslims. Using such distinctions, Hodgson wants Islam to be studied and taught from the perspective of "exceptionalising" historians. That is to say he wants to highlight, emphasise and analyse what is unique in "Islamdom" and "Islamicate" system. Only by concentrating on what is exceptional in the totality of experience that is Islam Hodgson maintains, can we increase our understanding of "Islamdom" and provide an objective framework for Islamic studies. In Hodgson's own words: "for an 'exceptionalising' historian... it is Islamdom as a morally, humanly relevant complex of traditions, unique and irreversible, that can form his canvas. Whether it 'led to' anything evident in modern times must be less important than the quality of its excellence as a vital human response and an irreplaceable human endeavour. In this capacity, it would challenge our human respect and recognition even if it had played a far less great role than, in fact, it did play in articulating the human cultural nexus in time and space and in producing the world as we find it now."

The notion that Islam should be studied and taught from the perspective of an "exceptionalizing" historian is a powerful one. Hodgson is concerned primarily with the exceptional character of Islamic society, culture and civilisation. But what is really unique and exceptional about Islam is not just the society and civilisation that it has produced, which have reached the zenith of human achievements and declined, but its world-view. And it is this world-view that should be the prime focus of Islamic Studies, both in the Muslim world and the West.

Islamic Studies: A Futuristic Perspective

Despite the fact that Muslim scholars unanimously agree that Islam is not just a religion, but a complete way of life as well as a sophisticated culture and civilization, Islam, as we have been seen is never actually studied or taught in its totality. In Muslim universities, Islamic Studies seldom transcends the boundaries of religion and culture. In the Western academia, as indeed in the occident civilisation itself, there is a pathological obsession for treating "religion", "philosophy' and "science" as three different realms of the mind, each with its own methods, laws and truths. In such a mileu, Islamic studies, whether studied within the perspective of an exceptionalising historian or simply as an exotic discipline, can never really acquire a status greater than that of religious studies. Yet, there are obvious insights to be had if the method of Islamic studies was tackled with the methods of "philosophy" and "science."

Let us make the naive assumption that the purpose of Islamic studies in the West is to increase the *understanding* of Islam, its people, culture, society and civilisation in the developed world. Taking cue from Iqbal, the objective of Islamic studies in the Muslim world is to produce well-versed scholars who can tackle, and perhaps solve, some of the formidable problems that face the Muslim societies. Can one suggest a new, radically different, approach to Islamic studies that takes full account of contemporary technological and political realities and serves both objectives? What factors and trends should such an approach take into consideration?

To a very large extent universities in the West and the Muslim world have, up to now, sheltered themselves from the vast complex web of social and cultural problems in the real world outside. However, it is no longer possible to ignore these problems simply because they have acquired a momentum of their own and now threaten to engulf the entire planet. We all recognise these problems and we all know that somehow they are inter-linked and cannot be separated from each other. Each one of them-nuclear ware, demographic trends, depletion of resources, energy problems, global unemployment, environment problems and problems of Third World development—is linked to every other problem and the whole set together forms what the Club of Rome has called the world *problematique.* In this vast complex of problems, any single problem is itself complex. One may think, for example, that the population problem is very simple. A closer look, however, will reveal that the issues go much beyond birth control to age structure of a population, how fast it is growing, the rate of material progress, the availability of food and so on. All these problems are not just technical problems but they also have important ethical components: and their ultimate individual, social and societical solutions must be based on ethical criteria.

Furthermore, these problems are changing and becoming more and more complex day by day. What is more, the *rate of change* itself is changing. Society, therefore, is constantly adjusting and readjusting to change. Developments in microtechnology and genetic engineering now threaten to introduce fundamental changes in society. Cybernetics and artificial intelligence are poised to introduce even more basic changes in our lives. And the process continues.

With such a futuristic backdrop, we cannot afford to pretend further that what we learn at university has no bearing on our personal and societical environment and its future. We cannot now easily assume that our problems can be solved in isolated linear cause-effect sequences. We need to deal with the world in a more profound manner, going much deeper, where all our actions could have serious side-effects and produce a whole lot of interactions and non-linear effects. Thinking in terms of the old fashion logic of cause and effect is totally inadequate to our present situation. Most young people, both in the West and the Muslim world, realise that what they are being taught does not prepare them for the complex decisions and ethical choices they have to make in their daily lives. They require newer methods of dealing with these problems but these methods do not fit any standard syllabus or curriculum.

The future scholars of Islam face a formidable responsibility. If they are to play an active role in raising the consciousness of the *ummah,* in solving some of its most pressing problems, in helping it to adjust to change, then they have to be trained by newer methods that are radically different from the classical approach.

There are two sharp breaks from the conventional approach to Islamic Studies that we need to make. First, the picture of Islamic Studies as a rigid discipline with sub-disciplines in neat little boxes marked "the Kur'an", "Hadith", Islamic law", "Islamic history", etc., must be abandoned. Let the author hasten to add that this does not mean that the traditional content of Islamic Studies should be dropped; rather it should not be taught as isolated components divorced from reality. Moreover, the traditional emphasis is no longer necessary: for example, it is not necessary to memorise all the authentic traditions and the opinions of the classical jurists on which the students spend much time and energy. For even in the poorer Muslim countries, scholars would be able to obtain these, at the touch of a button, from their personal micro-computers. The emphasis on memory and learning facts is now dangerously obsolete. The new emphasis has to be on analysis, solving ethical and moral problems—in short, thinking within Islamic paradigms. Islamic Studies, therefore, must touch all contemporary problems, no matter how irrelevant and remote they may seem in the classical framework. The growing understanding of the linkages and interactions between diverse fields of learning and approaches to discovery of new knowledge that we have acquired suggests the need to adopt a devoted and dynamic approach: in some sense a return to the reality of the unity of all knowledge which was the foundation stone of the classical theory of Islamic education. This then is our link with tradition.

Islamic Studies, therefore, must be taught and researched from multi-disciplinary and interdisciplinary perspectives. Multi-disciplinary approach uses various disciplines to study a particular subject and attempts to create an overall comprehensive picture. For example, studying the Medina State of Prophet Muhammad using the theories and tools of social anthropology, political science and history of technology would yield much greater insights than one would find in a standard book of *Sirah.* The inter-disciplinary approach uses a number of disciplines to explain particular events and situations and attempts to produce a synthesized perspective.

The Hijra, for example, could be studied by examining the historical processes of social change, by a sociological and psychological analysis of Meccan society and of the specific reasons that persuaded Prophet Muhammad to migrate to Medina. Once more the end result would be far more penetrating than one is likely to find in the works of modern scholars. Only students trained in the multi-and inter-disciplinary approach to Islamic Studies can tackle and study the complex, multi-dimensional contemporary and future problems of Muslim societies.

If Islamic Studies is to evolve as a multi- and inter-disciplinary subject, then Islam cannot be taught as a religion or culture or even a civilisation. And this is the second sharp break with the conventional approach. Islam must be presented as a world-view—only as a world-view it solves the problems of its adherents and only as a world-view does it provide a unique, 'exceptionalising' perspective on the political, economic, scientific, technological, social, cultural and spiritual problems of man. And as a world-view it is open to examination by tools and methods of any discipline that can increase our understanding of the problems of mankind. Moreover, as a world-view it is as relevant for Muslims as it is for the West which is crying out for alternative ways and means for solving its problems of alienation.

The basic components of world-views are concepts. It is concepts that shape society, culture and civilisations. The framework of concepts on which the world-view of Islam depends provides the civilisation of Islam with its bearings as well as its methods for solving ethical, moral, social and practical problems. It is these concepts that provide the Islamic society with policy guidelines and make sense of its actions. The successes and failures of particular Muslim societies in a given space-time location have depended on their abilities to operationalise and understand these concepts a new in the face of historical events, new social situations and new discoveries and innovations. It is these concepts that make Islam both universal and eternal.

Islamic Studies then should essentially expose the student to a core of Kur'anic concepts—such as tawhid, risalah, din, akhirah, 'ibadah, 'ilm, jihad, ijtihad, istihsan, shura, brotherhood, ummah, muhasabah, hudud, hisbah, islah, hikmah, haya, tazkiyah, waqf—that are studied from multi and inter-disciplinary perspectives. The world-view of Islam is presented as a country to be mapped. Kur'anic concepts form the basic grid of the map, and the Kur'an, the *Sirah, Shari'ah* and Islamic history, the tools of understanding that are essential for mapping this country. Making a map of a country, like learning to deal with concepts, is essentially a process of becoming more self-conscious of one's environment. We may live in a country and know the mountains and rivers and our way around it. But we may not be objectively conscious of it in the way that one needs to if one is going to make a map of it. We can find our way from one town to another and know the green areas and the desert patches, but we cannot sketch it out on paper with any accuracy, because we do not know the country in *that particular way.* The student is asked to become self-conscious of concepts he may have taken for granted in multi- and inter-disciplinary frameworks. He learns to relate these concepts not just to history but to contemporary reality. He learns to deal with concepts and think within the world-view of Islam. He begins to shape Islamic perspectives on the issues of development, food problems, technological adjustment and other contemporary problems.

As an example consider the concepts Din, Mu'min, Ummah, Khalifah, Shura, Ita'at, shari'ah, Jihad and Amwal which must form the basis of any creditable Islamic political theory. The student first discovers what the Qur'an has to say about these concept and how Prophet Muhammad materialised them in the Medina State. He then discovers what the imaginative and thinking men of Islam have said about these concepts and how they were operationalised by other Islamic societies in history. He finally studies how the tools and methodologies of contemporary political science and other disciplines can be used to gain a fresh understanding of these concepts and how they can form the basis of a contemporary theory of Islam. Thus the student learns the Kur'an by becoming familiar with its basic concepts, he learns the *Sirah* by discovering the role these concepts played in the life of the Prophet, and he learns Islamic history not as a collection of dead and distant facts presented in a chronological fashion from pre-Islamic Arabia to the twentieth century but in terms of how these concepts were operationalised by previous Muslim societies. Multi- and inter-disciplinary analysis provides him with a contemporary insight into these concepts that he needs if he is to tackle the problems of his society. He feels the whole force of Islamic history as a living, dynamic reality. The process forced him to think and seek solution from within the world-view of Islam.

It is clear that such an approach to Islamic Studies cannot be divorced from research. The totalistic and dynamic approach of conceptual and multi- and inter-disciplinary analysis demands continuous research. In this framework learning is no longer a one-way traffic between authoritarian teachers and the taught. Teachers have to learn from learners. And research is the only criterion for teaching. The ideal place for Islamic Studies in a university, therefore, is in an independent institute where research and teaching go hand in hand.

Theories, models, analysis—the characteristics that give a living form to a discipline—are conspicuous by their absence in contemporary Islamic Studies. Concepts are the smallest units of theories and models. As terms combine to form sentences so concepts combine to form theories. To acquire a concept is primarily to learn, and to possess a concept is primarily to know. Moreover, to learn and possess a concept is to be able to *do* something—to develop a theory, devise a model, solve a problem. Both study and research are therefore important for conceptual analysis. By rooting Islamic studies firmly in multi- and inter-disciplinary conceptual analysis we can provide the future scholars of Islam with the essential mental furniture they need to serve the *Ummah*. The challenges that await them cannot be underestimated. Conceptual analysis will give Islamic studies a meaning and provide it with a framework for thinking that might otherwise get lost under the weight of dead facts and meander indefinitely and purposelessly among the vast marshes of theological disputes.

REFERENCES

1. Muhammad Iqbal, "Some Thoughts on Islamic Studies," in Thought and reflection of Iqbal, ed. Syed Abdul Vahid Ashraf, Lahore, 1964.
2. A M Mohammed Mackeen, "Islamic Studies as a University Discipline," Islamic Review, 57:5, May 1969, 13-18; and 57:6, June 1969, 36-38.
3. M M Ahsan, "Orientalism and the Study of Islam in the West: A Select Bibliography," Muslim World Book Review, 1:4, Sum. 1981, 51-60.
4. See my book, The future of Muslim civilisation, London, 1979.

Revised and edited; originally published in Islamic Culture, July 1983.

14

Iqbal's Religious Thought

ANNEMARIE SCHIMMEL

(Abstract: Iqbal's contribution is viewed here by a Western historian, who also is a leading scholar of sufism and Muslim phislosophy. 'I think that just the fact of... internal harmony, and the very logical development of certain ideas from both classical Muslim and modern Western thought, prove the greatness of this thinker'. Concerns specifically with relationship of human being with Lord).

Muhammad Iqbal is such a many-sided personality that since his death the different aspects of his work have been treated again and again by Eastern and Western scholars: his poetical art, his philosophy and its back round, the political importance of his ideas, his theological viewpoint, etc.

As a historian of religion, I can here concentrate on one or two points only which are, however, in my opinion the most important ones in Iqbal's writings, and which show with sufficient lucidity that the great poet-philosopher was perfectly in tune with the great currents of thought visible in Europe during his very lifetime, though he had no access to most of the standard works on religious philosophy. I think that just the fact of this internal harmony, and the very logical development of certain ideas from both classical Muslim and modern Western thought, prove the greatness of this thinker. Let us therefore try to elucidate his main ideas of *tauhid* (God's unity) and of the relation of man, the vicegerent of God, to his Lord as it is expressed in prayer.

Phenomenology of religion acknowledges different types of

monotheism and accepts that the confession of Divine Unity rests on different propositions. There is, for instance, the secondary monotheism in which, starting from polytheistic tendencies, theological speculation comes at last to the realisation that one single reality underlies all the varied manifestations which are called deities, and the manifold gods and goddesses are only functions of the One Divine Being. This type of monotheism may also result from mystic experiences in which the seeker finds himself united with the profoundest depths of the Divine, and regards, thus, the deities only as emanations of the most high indivisible Essence. Or in prayer man chooses one out of the great number of gods and turns towards him in faith and trust as if only He is effective. Or different deities become united for purposes of cult and rite or as a result of the political unification of two peoples with different objects of worship. But this kind of monotheism, which is characteristic of the ancient religions of Egypt, Babylon, India, etc., is always deductive; it does not make a clear-cut distinction between the One and the many, and admits the existence of deities besides the Highest Being. It was only the prophetical experience in Israel (plus Christianity) and in Islam which realized the overwhelming uniqueness of God besides whom all those whom man might have adored until then were non-entities, and which cannot tolerate the worship of anyone other than that God who reveals Himself in the individual life and in history. Mystical monotheism may include all forms of reality because there is nothing existent but God and everything is a part of His life; but prophetical monotheism is always exclusive—that explains the majestic Thou shall not..., and that is why there is the negation in the beginning of the Muslim creed: *la ilaha illa Allah*—there is no God but God.

This formula of the creed forms a favourite pattern in Iqbal's poetical works. It becomes the symbol of the strength and power of Islam; it is indeed, with him, Islam in a nutshell. Starting from the *Asrar,* where the poet announces.

We have honour from the la ilah (AK 1607)

he continues throughout his life singing the glory of these words which are

> *The turning point of the world, and the end of the work of the world* (R 161),

thanks to which the heaven marches more quickly and the sun is sound on his way (alluding, here, to God in his aspect as creator and Sustainer of the visible world).

But Iqbal complains—addressing the ritualists and scholastic theologians—that the word *tauhid* has become eventually a question of mere scholastic hairsplitting (ZK 18). The meticulous disputations about the essence or the attributes of God which fill voluminous books have turned away the interest from 'practical Islam' and are, according to the poet, one of the causes of the deplorable stagnation of Islam—Muslims are no longer alive to the simple fact that bare 'unity of thinking' without 'unity of action' is immature and useless (ZK 18). Against these theoretical applications of the word Unity he protests, and calls to the living experience of Divine Unity which will beget practical Unity too :

> *Whosoever knotted the la ilah illa Allah into his mind,*
> *Has left the fetters of school and Mulla. (AH 143)*

Or, in a more satirical strain, Iqbal says :

> *The free man does not possess anything except the two words la ilah,*
> *But the jurist of the town is (as rich as) a Karun in Arabic Dictionaries. (BJ 50)*

Karun, the Biblical Korah, is famous for his wealth of which he had made no practical use: in his likeness is the learned scholar who is in possession of a large library on Arabic topics and yet does not grasp the inner meaning of the confession of faith (cf. also Mus. 17). But whosoever has understood the inner meaning of this confession of Divine Unity, "sun and moon will move according to his wish" (Pas 15), i.e., he will attain the spiritual stage of complete freedom from everything but God and look upon the world from quite a different angle; since he is obedient to God all things will be obedient to him.

Besides its purely religious significance, the credo *la ilaha illa Allah* has an importance in the realms of art and also of mystic poetry which can scarcely be overestimated. In the Arabic script its alternating letters *alif* and *lam*—two letters with vertical stems—form a wonderful basic pattern for every kind of decorative ornamentation of the formula which is, of course, found wherever Muslims have reached, and in both minor arts and architectural inscriptions these weighty words have been so intricately and bewilderingly interlaced to make them ornate that an uninitiated would scarcely imagine that the essence of Muslim faith is concealed behind them. On the other hand, the rhythmical wording of the formula has made it the typical *dhikr* of mystic circles which can be repeated hundreds of times, either in solitude or in congregation, often accompanied with breath control or rhythmical movement.

The contrast between the two parts of the sentence 'There is no God—but God' has, from early times, often attracted speculative minds who discovered not only a strictly dogmatic meaning but also a deeper mystical truth in the confrontation of the *la* and the *illa.* The great Persian mystics like Sana'i and 'Attar have made use of these contrast-pairs, and Maulana Rumi apologizes in one line for his way of using symbols and allusions reflecting to the creed :

> *When I say 'lip' then I intend the lip of the sea—*
> *When I say 'No' the intention is 'but' (Mathnavi I : 1759)*

And al-Jili writes a variation of the creed in his verse :

> *When they say No, I say But her beauty;*
> *When they say But, I say Her loveliness is radiant!*

Indian Islam inherited this poetical and mystical use of the formula from its Persian masters. Under Aurangzeb, the heretic

Jewish convert to Islam, and a bold poet, Sarmad, was accused of reciting only the first part of the creed, *la ilah;* he replied that he would be a sheer hypocrite if he pronounced the positive as long as he had not freed himself from the state of negation.

Iqbal is an advocate not of the mystical but of the prophetic No of which *soderblom,* the Swedish theologian, has said in his book *The Living God:*

> But No is also needed. Without No there will be no proper Yes. For then all that denies and destroys, degrades and delays what is right and good would be allowed to remain unattacked and unabolished. That is why a No is necessary in the moral warfare of the individual, in the evolution of religion and in the history of the race.

This is the situation in which Iqbal felt himself embedded:

> *To say No in front of everything besides God is life,*
> *From this strife creation is made fresh. (Pas 19)*

It is (as he says in the same poem which can be called the most lucid exposition of the theory of *la* and *illa*) 'the sword of No' which makes the faithful who wields it ruler of the world (Pas 22), a sword, with which the Prophet takes the blood off the veins of the idle whereas the word 'But God'

> *written on the desert became the title-line of our salvation.*
> (R 128, cf. AK 1645 f.)

It is the greatest fault of the men of the present age that they do no longer use this dagger of *la* (Pas 27) which would enable them to resist the temptations of modern civilisation, with its numerous idols. This negation is, of course, only the first stage:

> *In the world the beginning is from the word No,*
> *This is the first station of the man of God. (Pas 19)*

Life does not rest in this place, since creation runs towards the But God (Pas 22). Yet negation is the condition of true life:

Both of them are the destiny of the created world,
Movement is born from negation, quietude from affirmation.

The same idea was expressed by *Attar* eight centuries ago admonishing the faithful:

Become la if thou art going upwards (bala),
For only through la one can move.

It is the dialectical tension of negation and affirmation of the negative and the positive pole that enables life to subsist in every grade, from the basic electric and magnetic current to the highest stages of spirituality.

But who is this God whose unity is to be confessed? How is He to be thought though thoughts cannot reach Him? The later definitions of the catechism teach the pupils that one is obliged to know what is necessary, what is impossible, and what is possible regarding God our Lord...and inform him about the 20 attributes, one of them being essential (His existence), five exclusive (like His unity); seven are called accident-attributes (like His power, His hearing), and seven accidental attributes (like His being hearing etc.). These definitions have framed God into an exactly limited system of rational thought, and have done the same with all parts of the Muslim Creed. But this rational argumentation is rather far from the lively descriptions the *Kur'an* itself gives of God the Creator whose grandeur is attested to by everything created, from the atom to the movement of stars, who is the Judge on the Doomsday, the Merciful to those who repent. From whatever angle we may approach God, He remains a most active and living Being. It is God who have put signs in the world, on earth and in the heavens with the purpose that man may understand who has created him and has breathed His breath into his form of dust, and who has ordered that everything created should obey His commandments and worship Him, who has sent Prophets to all peoples for warning and advising them, and who will summon once more all created beings before His throne to judge them according to their deeds. Modern research has tried to prove that the prevalent attribute of the *Qur'anic* God is His justice; but the theological difficulty is always the tension between absolute justice and absolute power. In the course of time, the living God of the *Qur'anic* revelation has become the rationally described God of the catechism; philosophy and neoplatonic thought had helped in transmuting the active Semitic God of early Islam into a *prima causa, a motor immobilis,* or a merely neutral essence, so that some foreign observers have been misled to the conclusion that Islam is a deistic system.

Iqbal goes back behind the rationalistic commentaries and the mystic speculations to the original *Qura'nic* teachings and describes God first and last as an Ego: His name Allah, as He calls Himself in the *Kur'an,* manifests His personal character (L 72), and the *sura* 112, the short confession of God's unity which is of paramount importance for Islamic thought, theology and spiritual life, is again a proof of God's being an Ego. In the introduction to the *Secrets of the Self,* the first work where Iqbal has laid down his philosophy of the Self, he writes:

> God Himself is an individual, He is the most unique individual.

It is astonishing that R.A. Nicholson has written in his fine studies on the 'idea of Personality in Sufism' which were published only shortly after he himself had translated Iqbal's *Secrets of the Self* into English, that

> We must define, at least in general terms, what we mean when we ascribe personality to God—a question of prime importance for Christians, but on which Moslem theologians have never asked themselves, much less attempted to answer. I would remark, in the first place, that the expression "Divine Personality" cannot be translated adequately into any Mohammadan language....

Iqbal has, however, tried to answer the question, and more than that, he has built his whole system upon this very idea that God is the most perfect personality which he was to prove from the *Kur'an*.

The problem before Iqbal is this: How can the Divine Ego, this "stupendously rich reality" (F. von Hugel) which cannot be described adequately by human words, who is *Ghani,* the most rich who has no need—how can this infinite and overwhelming Being be compatible with personality? Iqbal has been accused of having developed an illogical concept of an `infinite personality' since these two conceptions are contradictory and exclusive. It is of interest to compare his views in this respect with that of modern European thinkers who have, as he had, tried to revaluate the God of the prophetic (i.e., for them Christian) experience. Friedrich von Hugel, the profound English Catholic thinker writes:

> Indeed we can safely hold with Lotze not only that Personality is compatible with Infinitude, but that the personality of all finite beings can be shown to be imperfect precisely because of their finitude and hence that 6 perfect 'Personality' is compatible only with the conception of an Infinite Being; finite beings can only achieve an approximation to it.

Besides the name Allah, and the *Sura* 112 Iqbal has found another proof of God's Egohood in the *Qur'anic* assertion "Call upon Me, and I will answer"— that means the experience of prayer becomes the proof of God's personality. Iqbal shares here the view of one of the leading philosophers of modern Germany, Heinrich Scholz (*d.* 1950), who writes :

> It belongs to the character of the Divine that it is given as a Thou. Thus the content of the religious consciousness of God can never be the same entity that metaphysics calls 'the Absolute.' For it is clearly an absurdity to contact the Absolute in the form of a Thou, indeed even to come into touch at all.

Contact with the Absolute, as sought by many of the most

influential mystics, is only possible on quite other levels of consciousness and ultimately involves a passing away from all qualities of thought and from life in the normal sense of the word. That is also the conviction of C.C.J. Webb whom R.A. Nicholson quotes in his above-mentioned book:

> Only so far as personal relations are allowed to exist between the worshipper and his God, can that God properly be described as personal...

Paul Tillich, too, has stated the importance of a God with whom I have a person-to-person encounter. He is the subject of all the symbolic statements in which I express my ultimate concern.

The emphasis Iqbal laid on the personality of God—which, of course, transcends every imaginable personality—is one of his greatest contributions to the reconstruction of Islamic thought, and is completely in tune with the contemporary interest which concentrates again on the Divine personality and can be marked not only in Christian theology and science of religion, but also in other religions, like Sikhism (according to the interpretation given by Dr. Mohan Singh).

Classical Islamic mysticism had held that real personality belongs to God alone, that 'nobody can say I but God.' In Iqbal's philosophy and theology, however, there are other egos besides God or rather inside the all-embracing Divine Ego. The world itself is conceived as an Ego, and everything created is nothing but an Ego; the unimaginable varieties of them are sustained by that comprehensive Divine Ego who holds them in His own Being—not in His imagination. The existance of those numberless egos on different stages of development—from atom to man—whose existence is not obliterated by the greatest Ego, seems to be self-contradictory, for either the smaller egos have no existence of their own but are organic parts of the Greatest Ego, or they exist in a sphere outside that Ego and cannot come into living and life-giving contact with Him. We may guess that Iqbal's ideas of the relation between the Ultimate Ego and the created egos in something similar to Rudolf

Eucken's nation that

> the singular existences must as a matter of course belong to a universal personal life in order to be or to be able to become that what the striving of their nature aims at; the particular beings will get a character of personality only from a universal personality-life.

One has seen in Iqbal's thought the influence of the spiritual pluralism of J. Ward—to whom he refers also as a parallel to the Ash'arite concept of world and God (L 72)—but the affinity to R. Eucken, whose *Collected Essays* were found in the Thinkers Library, is as great, and is visible in many other concerns too.

Iqbal's idea that God is both immanent and transcendent—immanent as the nature of the self (*cf.* L 62, 73) but transcendent as not being within the grasps of our experience—can be again illustrated by a statement of von Hugel :

> But there is nothing intrinsically unreasonable in thinking of ultimate Cause, Ground and End of the world as certainly not less than, as somehow not all unlike, what we know our own self-consciousness, mind, feeling and will to be, provided we keep the sense that God is certainly not just One Object amongst other objects, or even simply one Subject amongst other subjects, He is not only more perfect than, but distinct and different from, them all...

God, the ultimate Ego, takes in Himself the infinite fulness of life, but His

> infinity is intensive, not extensive. It involves an infinite series, but is not that series. (L64)

The Divine Personality as absolute power who is able to create spontaneously and whose life is creativeness, realizing His infinite energies in nature and history, that is the God of the prophetical religion, and also the God whom the vitalist philosophers had postulated—

> for the comprehension of Reality, Being, under the symbol of purpose, creation realisation, insistence, progress, power, energy, life, has its origin in prophetic teaching,

says N. Soderblom with regard to Bergson's "Semitic" philosophy which has again, influenced Iqbal's thought.

The proposition that God is conceived as an Ego whose Egohood is realized in full in man's contact with Him in prayer leads to the logical conclusion of man's egohood. As Tillich has pointed out:

> Man becomes man in personal encounters. Only by meeting a thou does man realize that he is an ego.

This self-realization of the human ego is the central theme of Iqbal's philosophy and theology not only in the first *mathnawi* which bears the significant title *The Secrets of the Self* but during his whole life. The human ego may be understood as

> higher than everything you see (AZ GR 327; *cf.* the whole question VI)

and may be compared, to a certain extent, to Eucken's concept of the Self which is

> in one meaning the proposition, in the other one the perfection of striving, there as self-being, here as self-becoming, there as a fact, here as a task.

That means, the Self is both existent and still to be perfected, it is a given thing and yet a task before man.

Man, not only from the biological but from the spiritual point of view as well, is the result of immense periods of development (J.v. 23). He should not—as the evolutionists did—inquire too much about the previous states of his biological life but rather ponder upon his future:

> *Why should I ask the wise men: Whence is my beginning?*
> *I am busy with the thought: What will be my end? BJ 81).*

That is Iqbal's reply to the pessimism he saw in the Western world which seemed to be robbed of faith in man's future, whereas he regarded the idea of evolution that he witnessed in classical Islam as a most effective means of giving life a new direction (L 186); he underlines this evolutionary concept by inserting the famous verses from Maulana Rumi's *Mathnawi* which point to the growing possibilities which extend from stone to heavenly beings—lines that have even been read by other commentators as an indication of transmigration of souls.

For Iqbal, there is no doubt that

> throughout the entire gamut of being runs the gradually rising note of Egohood till it reaches its perfection in man, (L72)

that the *dhauq-i numud,* the joy of manifestation (BJ 79), the wish of becoming more and more individual, is the leading force in life. If is the same idea which has been explained by R. Pannwitz in many of his recent philosophical books (and it is interesting to note that both the German and the Sub-Himalayan Muslim philosopher have been influenced to a certain extent by some Nietzschean concepts) :

> As in every life the rising tendency is preponderating—for otherwise there would be no life at all—so every development aspires to a higher step, and on the highest rank to the greatest consciousness, individuation and freedom.

Man constitutes the highest rank in his world because he contains the greatest possible number of ranks in his being, and is, as such, "the first and last cosmic constant," says Pannwitz, whilst the lower potencies—that which Nietzsche had called so acutely "the matter which has learned nothing"—are always in danger of being destroyed (Iqbal would remind here the reader of the example of the drop which has not consolidated its Self and is therefore swallowed by somebody else) and must start again and again to rise gradually on the gamut of individuation; man differs from this matter which forms simply a colony of egos of a lower order, thanks to his striving for perfection.

"Only the individual can reach perfection," avers R. Pannwitz who has drawn as indefatigably as Iqbal the attention of the modern age to the fact that the entelechy is the real meaning of life : translated into Iqbal's poetry that would correspond to the "Address to the New Moon' :

> *Look upon thyself and do not be anxious because of thy void shirt,*
> *For in thy breast a full moon is concealed. (PM 96)*

Man is called to be the *khalifat Allah,* created in God's image like Him an undivisible unity (there is no dualism of soul and body), like Him a creator called to become endowed with the highest qualities as the Prophet had said : *"Takhallaqu bi-akhlaq Allah."*

The most famous expression of man's work as cooperator with God, and as Creator of the sketchy world, is found in the dialogue between man and God in the *Payam-i mashriq,* where man boasts :

> *Thou didst create night and I made the lamp,*
> *Thou didst create clay and I made the cup,*
> *Thou didst create the deserts, mountains and forests,*
> *I produced the orchards, gardens and groves,*
> *It is I who turn stone into a mirror,*
> *And it is I who turn poison into an antidote!* (PM 132)

Man has to give the potentially existing universe its shape and to form out of the given raw-material the best possible world. Thus, creating always new values as a co-worker with God, man is not a superman but more humble than ever, devoted to what is not only he himself but the God in him and he himself as His legate and minister.

This Pannwitzian formulation expresses exactly Iqbal's ideal man. Iqbal has repeated this message of man's work and worth in the present age because his correligionists seemed to have forgotten the *Quranic* phrase of man's destination as divine vicegerent on earth which implies further that this world is not given as property to him but that he is to take it only as a trust from God to Whom he has to give it back at the moment of his death (*cf.* J. Marssphere). This feeling of being only the legate and trustee, not owner, of the created world should prevent the faithful from transgressions in the political and social realm, and be an antidote against both nationalism, land-lordism, and imperialism.

This idea of the Perfect Man (derived from Islamic *sufism* more than from Nietzche's Superman who replaces a God "Who has died") is, in Iqbal's social philosophy, also applied to the Muslim nation.

Iqbal thinks that in this ideal nation which is organised according to the eternal rules of the *Quran,* the individual proper will have space enough for unfolding its powers as widely as possible and realize the *Qur'anic* order to be God's vicegerent, because in this community the most pious one will be dearest to God (*Sura* 49 : 13, R. 120). Both individual and nation are called to this vicegerency, and it is therefore surprising only to those who are not acquainted with Iqbal's way of arguing that he applies Divine qualities to the wakeful nation which is both the realization of the mystical experience uttered by Hallaj : *Ana'l-haqq,* I am the creative truth (AH 98), and of the Throne-verse, "No slumber takes Him nor sleep." (*Sura* 2: 256)

Among the nations that one is of high rank
Which is the Imam of the two worlds—
It does not abstain from its creative work,
For 'sleep and slumber' are forbidden to it. (AH 98)

The ideal individual and the ideal nation are involved every moment in a new work, like God who unfolds fresh creative energies without interruption.

Thus the essential word of Muslim creed—that God is One, who is interpreted as the greatest personality with intensively infinite possibilities of creation—forms likewise the basis of Iqbal's representation of man as real personality, endowed with possibilities for development, the highest being in the pyramid of creatures, nearest to God and yet most endangered by his growing individualisation, but formed, in any case, "After the form of God," and also of his picture of the ideal Muslim nation in which Divine Vicegerency and harmonious development of the faculties of the individual in accordance with the requirements of the community are warranted through a fresh interpretation of the Divine Law, thanks not to bookish learning but to the contact of the faithful with the Living God and their daily experience of His presence, which makes them "say No to all idolatry and polytheism and let the one true God alone be the ruler in the hearts and lives of men."

The cooperation between man—and also the nation which is united in worship—and God finds its expression in prayer. The old sentence *lex credendi lex orandi* holds true also in Islam where the manifold sides of religious life are reflected in the bewildering variety of devotional types, from the merely magical use of certain formulas up to the summits of mystical union with God or the creative dialogue between man and his Lord.

On a smaller scale, the maxim holds good also for Iqbal, in whose work the mystery of prayer is always emphasized : one of the most touching scenes of the *Javidnamah* is the moment, when the poet and his spiritual guide Rumi perform their prayer behind the great reformer, Jamal al-Din Afghani, and the Turkish Prince Sa'id Halim Pasha.

We know from his old servant that Iqbal was keen on morning prayer, that after prayer he used to read the *Qur'an,* and that he did not neglect the *tahajjud* prayers at night.

How great an importance he attributed to prayer and intercession can be appreciated from a pathetic letter to Sir Kishan Prasad, the Hindu Prime Minister of Hyderabad, to whom he wrote in 1918, that, it being the sacred month of Ramadan

> I shall pray after the morning prayer for you... I, the blackfaced slave, sometimes get up for *tahjjud* prayer and sometimes spend the whole night awake. And by the precious grace of God I shall pray for you either before or after *tahajjud*, for at that time a special delight is experienced in the Divine worship—how should it be astonishing if prayer be heard at that time. (M II 193)

Since Iqbal saw in prayer an act not only of obedience but of love which gives man highest spiritual direction, it can be appreciated why, in the *Jawab-i shikwah,* the Muslim community is blamed because they have forsaken this supreme bliss, and are unmindful of its importance for life:

> *Very heavy in your spirits weighs the charge of morning prayer. You would rather love to sleep than rise up to worship Me.*

It is small wonder that some of Iqbal's best poems are either written as lyrical prayers, or inspired by the experience of prayer: it is agreed that one of his masterpieces is the great ode on the mosque of Cordova where he had performed his prayer, and had lived a spiritual upheaval greater than he had experienced elsewhere, and which is echoed in this poem. (BT 133 ff)

Ritual prayer is in Iqbal's interpretation a means to freedom—

> *It come at afternoon—the call for prayer*
> *Which purifies the faithful from the directions (i.e. from this world)*

(Mus 15, description of a prayer led by King Nadir of Afghanistan).

The philosophical explanation of the same fact is contained, already some years earlier, in his Lectures (L 109):

> The timing of the daily prayer which according to the *Qur'an* restores self-possession to the Ego by bringing it to closer contact with the ultimate source of life and freedom, is intended to save the Ego from the mechanizing effect of sleep and business. Prayer in Islam is the Ego's escape from mechanism to freedom.

Daily prayers are thus the most important prescription of the *Qur'an* for the believers, and are their most precious property. They are both jewel and weapon for the Muslim :

> *The profession of faith is the shell, and prayer is the pearl within it.*
>
> *The Muslim's heart deems prayer a lesser pilgrimage.*
>
> *In the Muslim's hand prayer is like a dagger,*
>
> *Killing sins, and forwardness and wrong.* (AK 874 *ff*)

Of the perfect Muslim, one can say :

> *The tremendum of Divine Grandeur is in his standing upright, And the beauty of human worship is in his prostration.* (AH20)

Even the blue sky performs its circumambulation around the free man who prostrates in this sublime way (Pas 50) in which the contact with the Divine has been established and the fate of man in changed (Pas 49), whereas the tasteless and loveless prostration is just like a blur on God's purity (AH 250).

In spite of the paramount importance which Iqbal attribues to the prescribed prayers, he knows that his wishes, his loving and longing words, will break their fixed forms.

> *Wherever I bow my head into the dust, roses rise*
>
> *My asking will not find room in two rak'as of prayer!*

It surely will not. For Iqbal, the whole life must be sublimated to prayer since the greatest prerogative of man is his searching, his ardent pilgrimage towards God. He would not like to be God—

This being God must be a headache—
But this being servant, I swear, that is not headache but heartache! (BJ 30).

This positive evaluation of man's situation as being endowed with the faculty of expressing his longing for God in prayers has guided Iqbal's whole work.

There are poetical prayers of exceeding beauty, especially in the *Zabur-i 'ajam,* in which Iqbal praises the Divine power and fascinating grace in profound verses and tries, as the classical poets had done, to describe the mysterious relation of God and man in rich symbols:

Thou comest to my bosom, in my autumn spring shall glow. (ZA I 55)
Thine is the hawk upon the wing
And Thine the thrush sweet-carolling,
Thine is the light and joy of life,
And Thine its fire and baneful strife. (ZA I 29)
Thou assey of the asseyless,
Ease of the reposeless mind,
Cure of the afflicted spirit,
Save too rare Thou art to find! (ZA I 46)

and with a childlike simplicity he says :

The raw copper which I have, I make it elixir by love—
For tomorrow when I come into Thy presence Thou wilt ask for a gift from me. (ZA I 39)

Presumably the best, the most personal and I dare say the most typical of Iqbal's poems are these prayers. A careful analysis of these prayer-poems would suffice even for the reconstruction of his main religious ideas. In his *Lectures,* too, this problem forms the corner-stone in Chapter III, 'The Conception of God and the Meaning of Prayer,' where he writes :

> ..... The quest after a nameless nothing, as disclosed in neo-Platonic mysticism—be it Christian or Muslim—cannot satisfy the modern mind which, with its habits of concrete thinking, demands a concrete living experience of God. And the history of the race shows that the attitude of the mind embodied in the act of worship is a condition for such an experience. In fact, prayer must be regarded as a necessary complement to the intellectual activity of the observer of Nature... (L 89 *ff*)

From the experience of prayer, Iqbal will prove the fact that God is an Ego, and his proof of God's Egohood is taken—as we have already mentioned—from the *Qur'anic* verse, "Call upon Me and I shall answer you" (*Sura* 40: 62) : only an Ego can address another Ego, and in prayer man both realizes God as the great Thou and himself as a person who is able to speak and to be spoken to. Man who is yearning not as much for perfection as for a direct contact with the Ultimate Reality, tries to pray, asks for a companion, a being to whom he can disclose these inmost mysteries of his heart :

> *Prayer is an expression of man's inner yearning in the awful silence of the Universe.* (L 92)

In many of his poems, Iqbal has expressed what as philosopher he had explained by means of psychology. The longing for the presence of God is one of his favourite subjects and brings him even to the assertion that

> *From longing I sometimes cut his idol from the stone.*
> (ZA GR 221)

To live without this vision, is worse than death :

> *Either open this veil of mysteries,*

Or take away this soul that has no vision! (J 34)
Only this contact with God grants real life :
Who knows the end of the world, the judgement?
As for me, when Thou lookest once, that is resurrection!

Friedrich Heiler has, in his great book on Prayer, distinguished between the 'prophetic' and the 'mystical' as recognisable and sharply contrasted types of religious experience. The goal of mystic prayer, after ascetic preliminaries, is the preparation of the soul for full union with God, the meditation of God's transcendant beauty and the contemplation of His unchanging eternity. A wide variety of religious truths may be the themes of the mystical regulation of meditation; but mystical prayer ends at the moment when union with God is attained, when there remains nothing but the "clear darkness," and the inexhaustible Godhead, a Godhead which can be described either as a Neutrum, as spiritualized force, beyond the personal God, or as the essence of eternal beauty, the eternally Beloved whose decrees are gladly and ungrudgingly accepted.

In prophetic religion, however, God is active, creative personality, the Living God, to Whom men dare come, as they might to a king or a father, with all the tale of their griefs and sorrows. The last goal in the prayer of the prophetic types is not quietude, clamness and detachment of wordly affairs but the realisation of the Kingdom of God on earth. Man's aim is not to be united with God but to unite his will with the Divine will, and work according to His laws.

There is no doubt that Iqbal, in his whole personality, is an excellent exponent of this prophetic type of religion. The poet who had written in the *Asrar* (v. 1629)

Give me the sleepless eye and the passionate heart —

has never ceased asking God for new activities; he wants that God

may quicken the thousand years old dust by my call (ZA I 4), that he, the living Stream, may be granted the deserts and mountains as his proper place so that he can spread out (ZA p. 4).

The Presence of God is, according to Iqbal,

> *a growth undiminishing.* (J. 791)

And when man has reached the climax of prayer, staying eye to eye, brow to brow with the Greatest Ego, he experiences the infinite possibilities in God, and may choose one of them, even asking from God the altering of His will and to grant him a new life, a new destination.

From this keen conviction a question arises that has interested the whole world of Islam (as of other religions) since the beginning of theological thinking and mystical feeling. The question is whether prayer is compatible with the everlasting decree of God, and, if we assume that prayer is allowed — is it efficient? In the *Qur'an,* as is well-known, the ideas of free will and responsibility and of predestination stand side by side. Among the *Sufis,* stern ascetics like Abdallah ibn Mubarak and al-Wasiti, boasted of having never asked God for anything; and when Ibrahim ibn Adham, one of the most outstanding quietists among the earliest generations of Muslim mystics, came into a tempest and his friends asked him urgently to pray for the salvation of the crew, he answered, "This is not the time for praying, this is the moment of surrender." Even among rationalist Muslim modernists there are men who do not attribute any positive value to prayer in the sense of asking a change in the imminent, among them the Indian reformer Sayyid Ahmad Khan.

But most of the theologians and mystics clung to the Divine promise, "Call upon Me, and I will answer you." A prophetic tradition related by Tirmidhi *(qadar,* 6) teaches that "nothing wards off the decree but prayer." The greatest Muslim thinkers, and saints, like Ghazzali and Abd al-Qadir Gilani, were sure that prayer, too, was preordained and belonged to the *qadar,* and that it is not forbidden to use the shield of prayer against the arrows of evil. The famous Persian saint Kaziruni was asked : "When food and sustenance are provided, why does prayer exist, and why do we ask?" And he answered : "In order to show clearly the greatness and high rank of the believer, as God has said: `If I give thee without being asked by thee, the perfection of thy honour would not be revealed! And, therefore, I have ordained prayer, so that thou shalt call to Me and I shall answer thy calling." The idea that God tests man because He longs for hearing his voice in prayer is found as early as in Surraj's *Kitab al-luma* and has been framed in a nice story in Maulana Rumi's *Mathnawi* (VI 4217 *ff*). In all religions, the greatest leaders of the prophetic type have been sure that prayer can change the world, can alter the decrees of God. Luther expressed this idea thus :

> After prayer, God altereth His decree and will, what you may remember well. And here, one must not discuss the secret and veiled change of the Divine will, but learn it, as Psalm CXIX enjoins us : He also will hear their cry, and will help them. He will leave His will and do their will. That is a Christian's greatest dignity and his priesthood that he can come with his prayer into God's presence and prevail upon God.

Notwithstanding this admission of the fact that God's will may change indeed, thanks to the prayer of the faithful, it is agreed that even a greater marvel than the possible change of God's will is the psychological effect of payer. This change of consciousness, which follows real prayer, is its fulfilment:

> *If by thy prayer the wide space cannot be changed,*
> *Perhaps it is possible that thou wilt be changed.*
> *And if in thy self a revolution takes place —*
> *Then it is small wonder when the world changes.* (ZK 167)

With the allusion to the *Qur'anic* verse, "Verily God will not change the condition of men, unless they change what is in themselves" *(Sura* 13 : 12) which is a keyword of Iqbal's thought, the poet stresses the mysterious effects of true prayer as the centre of life.

The extreme nearness to God that man feels in this last experience of prayer leads him sometimes to such a boldness of expression that it comes close to impiety. Iqbal, thus, ventures to utter harsh words that would be unthinkable in the mouth of a contemplating lover, intoxicated by the cup of Eternal Beauty. But this boldness and even harshness is a fact often to be found in very religious people. Even a mystical leader like Junaid al-Baghdadi (*d.* 910) is related to have said : "When love becomes right, the conditions of fine education no longer apply." After and Rumi also tell many stories of people who spoke angrily, even offensively, and without any respect, to God. Turkish mystical poets often criticize God's decrees in their verses, and even today Turkish popular piety knows the saint who has reached the level of *naz,* coquetry, and can scold God without being punished.

As for Iqbal, the revolutionary poetical prayers that he sometimes utters are expressions of his pride of being a human being and, thus, to live on the highest level nature affords. As a strong individuality, he can work, and by his own work better nature, which is, after the first act of creation, still incomplete, and needs man for its perfection, as Iqbal has described it in the Prologue in Heaven in *Javidnamah,* or in the daring Dialogue between God and Man (PM 132).

The Perfect Man, the faithful who talks freely to God, may ask God in the same moment—in a sudden attack on a quietistic conception of God Who is only the beloved but not the lover —

> *What hast thou to do in this world of pain and longing?*
> *Doest Thou have my fire or my restlessness?* (ZA I 6)

and can yet invite Him to come into his loving embrace :

> *Rest for a moment in my lap*
> *From the labour and trouble of this being God!* (ZA I 10)

This last expression leads to the question of the mutual relation between Man and God as expressed in the experience of prayer. In the closing scene of *Javidnamah,* when the poet is standing in God's overwhelming presence, he asks :

> *Life is everywhere searching and seeking —*
> *This delicate question has not yet been solved ; an I the prey or is He?* (JA 1793)

an idea to which he had alluded some years ago :

> *We are gone astray from God,*
> *He is seeking upon the road,*
> *For like us, He is need entire*
> *And the prisoner of desire.* (ZA II 29)

The mutual attraction of man and God, theologically culminating in the idea of the *oratio infusa,* has been felt by all those who have pondered over the problem of prayer, and the problem of grace. Just as the Bible tells that God addressed man first by calling him "Adam, where art thou?" And gave him courage to answer, so the *Qur'an* avers that, before the creation, God spoke to the still uncreated human race: "Am I not your Lord?" to which the generations to come answered, "Yes, we attest it" *(Sura* 7 : 171). These verses point to the fact that the weak creature cannot approach the presence of the Most Holy if he is not called. This mystery, that God seeks man first, has often been expressed in mysticism both Eastern and Western, perhaps in the simplest words by the Persian *sufi* Kharraqani who beheld one night God the Almighty in his dreams, and, overflowing with love and joy, cried out: "O my God, for sixty years have I hoped to win Thy love, and lived in longing for Thee!" And the Lord answered : "Thou has sought Me sixty years? And We have loved thee from the beginning of the world!"

The finest example of the quest of God for man in European literature, that of Francis Thompson's *Hound of Heaven,* is anticipated by Niffari, an 'Iraqi mystic of the middle of the 10th century. And how often do we find the idea that God Himself gives prayer, that He, as Rumi has told us again and again, "causes prayer to grow in us like roses grow from the dust," so that in each "O Lord" of the slave there are a hundred "I am at your service" from God's side; that not only the thirsty are seeking water but also water is seeking the thirsty.

In a *hadith-i qudsi,* God is related to have promised, "When my slave comes nearer to me a span, I will approach him a yard, and when he approaches one yard, I will approach him one fathom; when he comes walking I come running."

That is just what Muhammad Iqbal wants to indicate : the deepest mystery of prayer is the mutual approach of man and God. For the prophetic-minded, the fruit of this mutual approach in prayer will be seen in action—"prayer naturally, spontaneously, issues in action"(Dean Inge). But on the other hand, it is also action that leads man to prayer. The search for truth and knowledge may show itself not only in the accustomed forms of prayer but also in daily life, in scientific explorations and philosophical researches. That is why Iqbal holds that

> ..... prayer must be regarded as a necessary complement to the intellectual activity of the observer of nature. The scientific observation of nature keeps us in close touch with the behaviour of Reality, and thus sharpens our inner perception for a deeper vision of it...

And he continues :

> The truth is, that all search for knowledge is essentially a form of prayer. The scientific observer of Nature is a kind of Mystic seeker in the act of prayer. (L 91)

For scientific research may bring man to a point where he feels the mystery of Creation, where eventually his ardent quest for knowledge approaches adoration. That is the point on which Iqbal's interest is concentrated : the point where *'ishq,* the ardour of love, and *lim,* the ardour of science, may be united, and thus help mankind to reach a higher spiritual level. Since Iqbal includes all kinds of searching in his conception of prayer, it is not astonishing to find the statement that

> ..... in great action alone the self of man becomes united with God without losing his own identity, and transcends the limits of time and space. Action is the highest form of contemplation.

Prayer is the highest form of action, action the highest form of prayer—they complete each other as, to quote Dean Inge once more, "the spiral stair by which man may ascend to heaven." Thus we can summarize Iqbal's view, too. He has expressed this paradox in a key passage of his *Lectures* :

> ...... Prayer .... is a unique process of discovery whereby the searching Ego affirms itself in the very moment of self-negation and thus discovers its own worth and justification as a dynamic factor in the life of the Universe. (L 92)

Iqbal has always seen in prayer, according to the Prophetic tradition, an ascension, a *mi'raj* in which the loving soul breaks the *zunnàr,* the Magic Girdle, of created time, and realizes the word of the Messenger of God, "I have a time with God" *(li ma'a Allah waqt).* He finds himself united with the infinite in midst of finiteness, and eternal in every moment; it is "the hour without hours," which Maulana Rumi has described in beautiful verses *(Mathnnvi* III 2072). This communion with the living source of Time and Eternity makes man himself eternal; he is no longer subject to outward serial time but, as seven centuries ago, *Ibn al-Farid* had said :

> *Though thy intoxication will have but the life of a moment*
> *Thou wilt regard time as a slave to thy command.*

He then sees everything *sub specie aeternitatis,* after having witnessed the 'new birth' (J 142 *ff*) and the spiritual resurrection which is the content of this conscious participation of the Fullness of Divine life. So, he is no longer the vehicle of the day, but the rider of time (ZK 36), and since, according to Iqbal,

> It is time as an organic whole that the Kur'an describes as *Taqdir* or the destiny. (L 49)

man can even deal freely with destiny, can use the possibilities which are hidden in God where there is no net of causal consequence. (L 49)

The poetical connexion between Iqbal's concept of eternal growing and development as well as the never-ending craving for higher spiritual stages and closer connexion with the Divine life on the one hand, and his philosophy of time on the other, is given in the old motive of the Road, the path, and, perfectly true to the tradition of Islamic mysticism, in the motif of Ascension or Heavenly journey. It is not an accident that he has expressed his deepest thoughts in the *Javidnamah,* where all the divergent lines of his thought are brought into one perfect whole.

This symbolisation of man's craving for Divine Presence as a journey, a way, is as old as mankind. Evenly Underhill has devoted a special paragraph to the mystical symbolism in which she contrasts the symbol of love, and that of alchemy—the sublation of the cooper of the human soul into pure spiritual gold—with that of the journey which has been preferred by all those mystics and poets who lay stress on the dynamic character of religious life. The poets of the Hebrew Psalms have expressed their longing for the Holy centre of their religion, for Jerusalem, which has been transformed later on into the symbol of Divine Presence, the everlasting goal of Pilgrim's Progress, who lives in

> *the hope of the City of God at the other end of the road,*

or for Mount Carmel where the difficult steps of renunciation, meditation, and prayer lead. This pilgrimage towards the goal never reached has found its most famous expression in Islamic literature in the works of Farid al-Din Attar, whose *Mantiq al-tair,* the journey of the thirty birds through the seven valleys unto Divine Union, has become, since long, a favourite model in the phenomenology of religions, especially because of its combination of the ancient soul-birdmotif with that of the journey. Attar's *Musibatnamah,* however, which has been examined by H Ritter in his monumental work *Das Meer der Seele,* is the perfect expression of this eternal journey of which everything created partakes; stars and streets and man and animal are moved only by the search for God.

Attar's ideas have been taken over by Maulana Rumi who has praised in hymnical verses the miraculous effects of this spiritual way—

> *If a tree would move with foot and wing,*
> *It would not feel the blows of the axe nor the wound of the saw.*

The Persian epics which deal with the tragical figure of Majnun in search of his beloved Laila, and, in India herself, the story of Sasui wandering through the mountains, seeking her lost beloved — a story which culminates in the words

> *let me run, let me run, and never find....*

and numberless other examples show how familiar the Islamic world was with this motif eternal journey which is a means, as the single one, for unceasing spiritual development—not in vain was the mystical order called *tariqa,* the Path.

For Iqbal, with this strong vitalistic tendency, the unceasing movement was the proper symbol: therefore his *nom de plume Zindahrud,* Living Stream, in the *Javidnamah,* therefore the title *Bell of the Caravan* for his first collection of the Urdu poetry.

I would even assert that the most beautiful verses in Iqbal's poetry are those in which he sings the delight of movement:

> *I do not sit in the nest because of the joy of flight—*
> *Sometimes I am on the rose-twig, sometimes on the bank of the canal.* (PM 174)

This idea of eternal wandering makes him say that

the station is nothing but a milestone of the road. (Lalah 62)

and that even

the crooked road is better than the station. (Lalah 72)

He would surely have agreed with Blake: "Expect poison from the standing water". For every moment of standstill means a drawback, and since man has to unfold his inner possibilities through untiring activity (the word taken in the widest possible meaning), Iqbal says in a Heraclitean strain

Journey is reality, stillness only symbolic,
The secret of life is nothing but taste of flight, (BJ 171)

and he avers, taunting the traditionlist:

They have made me acquainted with the joy of flight—
Thou seekest a nest in the space of the garden. (ZA II 4)

Behind every station new surprises, new possibilities are open (BJ 70), just as the human heart with its unfathomable depth cannot be explored at al (ZA GR 231). Like 'Attar, Iqbal, too, holds that everything is in movement, and that the road is a traveller even as the wayfarer (J 1720); but it is only man who is able to enjoy this wandering and the change and growth of consciousness which is caused by the journey towards God—and into God.

I am as long as I move—not moving, I am not (PM 150)—

that is the Iqbalian—and one may say perhaps vitalist-transformation of the Cartesian *cogito ergo sum.*

The ardent pilgrimage is the privilege of man. The angels are excluded from it, being perfect in their own right; they do not know the never-ending burning with which the human soul is entrusted (AH 16). To the divine bird which human soul is, there is one thing more awful than death: that is the food which ensnares it and hinders it from the flight to heaven (BJ 83)—a sentence which sounds alike to the sighs of mystics who complained of the imprisonment of the poor soul-bird in the cage of the body; but what is intended in Iqbal's verse is the constant call to reach higher levels, which does not include a contempt of the material world, but is rather a refuse to those who are blind to the endless open ways before the personality.

Underhill has pointed out that

> through all these metaphors of pilgrimage to a goal there runs the definite idea that the travelling self in undertaking the journey is fulfilling a destiny, a law of the transcendental life...

and that holds true also for Iqbal, though he probably would not agree with the mystics that this journey must be made "against nature". For him, it is in spite of the struggle which is implied in it, the only true way of nature—towards its most perfect entelechy. The poet has used, though rarely, the old symbol of the way into one's self which is so significant of the mystic interpretation of the road-symbol. This journey into one's own depths means

> *To be born without father and mother,*
> *And to pick the Pleiads from the corner of the roof.*
> (ZA GR 225)

Through this interior journey which brings man into contact with the deeper layer of his own personality which he has to sublimate, he can become the spiritual ruler of the world "from the Fish up to the Moon" (ZA GR 232), and reach new spaces beyond the Galaxy (ZA II 34). This motif of descent into the depths of one's own heart has often been described—in Islamic and non-Islamic literature—as a kind of Heavenly journey, of Ascension; but on the whole the religious types which prefer the one to the other motif can be distinguished rather well. The motif of ascension proper has been preferred by those who wish to stress the personality and transcendence of God Who can be addressed by human words, and can be witnessed through His work in His creation (*via eminentiae*)—whereas the motif of descent has been more frequently used by those mystics who see in God the immanent, impersonal power which cannot be described but by negations and through silence (*via negativa*).

And though Iqbal has never used the ascent motif in its elaborate form—as an ascent in fixed grades and steps (as systematising mystical thought liked to do)—he is, on the whole, a very fine representative of the ascension-type.

The motif of ascension and Heavenly journeys has been treated by specialists so intensely during the last years that it is not necessary to underline the extreme importance which this religious experience—and symbol—has had from times immemorial in both primitive and higher religions. The motif may be interpreted both in a cosmological and psychological sense: it can express the fact that the spirit in the moment of ecstasy can see and understand the different attributes of the created Universe before reaching the Creator beyond the attributes or the psychological truth that man has to pass through different stages of spiritual preparation which may be compared to the seven spheres. In Islamic thought, the ascension gets its special importance due to its connexion with the Prophet's *mi'raj,* his heavenly journey, during which "he stood upright" (*Sura* 53:6) before the Almighty, without mediator angel. This journey has become the prototype of the spiritual journeys of the mystics beginning from Bayazid Bistami (d. 874) to Avicenna and Suhrawardi to *Ibn al-'Arabi,* who describes his autobiography in the form of a *mi'rajnamah,* and 'Abd al-Karim al-Jili: these mystics, whose visionary recitals have been studied most carefully during the last years, particularly by H. Corbin, have systematized the spiritual way, whereas Maulana rumi, far from imprisoning the heavenly experience into the system of reason, has never ceased praising the enrapture of the loving heart which does not care for the difficulties and stations of the road but spreads its wings and sings, animated by longing:

That is love: to fly heavenward,
To rend, every instant, a hundred veils!

Rumi has, however, put his finger on the fact that this ascension is a psychological experience. (*Mathnavi* III 4512 *ff*)—

the nearness of God is beyond reckoning...

and Iqbal is therefore perfectly right in introducing him in the *Javidnamah* as explaining the mystery of *mi'raj* as 'new birth' and 'change of consciousness'. It is exactly what Sarmad has expressed in a quatrain, which was one of the causes of his execution as a heretic:

Not Ahmad went into Heaven, but Heaven came into Ahmad!

Iqbal, though persevering in his spiritual interpretation of the flight towards heaven, has nevertheless made use of a classical motif connected with these Heavenly journeys. Not that he has, in a beautifully arranged epic, dwelt upon the astronomical peculiarities of the single spheres, their colours, their scents, their influences on human mind (as, for instance, nizami did in the *Haft paikar*), but he has taken over the motif of other-worldy discussions, and of a visit to the Other World as a means of political or literary criticism. From the Zoroastrian *Arda-Viraf-Namah* to early Chinese literature this motif is found everywhere, and as Lukian, in the 2nd century A.D., regarded the Other World as a suitable place for learning something about the Homeric question, so in the 11th century the blind Arab poet *al-Ma'arri* made, as his interpreter Prof. Nicholson remarked wittily, "paradise a haunt of immoral but immortal poets", who discuss difficult verses and crucial questions of Arabic grammar: the *Risalat-al-ghufran* is one of the most ingenious travesties ever written, though lacking completely in religious feeling. A year before Iqbal published his *Javidnamah,* in which he has combined the ascension-motif with that of the Heavenly discourses (no doubt under Dante's influence) the Iraqi poet Jamil Sidqi al-Zahawi wrote his satire *Rebellion in Hell* in which he makes the well-bred and highly sophisticated inhabitants of the Hell discuss all the issues of his time at sake, yet, again, without any religious feeling.

It is worth mentioning that even up to the 18th century, great scientists and philosophers like Kepler, Huygens, Kant and Swedenborg were inclined to the hypothesis that the planets may be inhabited by beings of different form, and Kant persumed that the perfection of those heavenly creatures might grow in proportion of their distance from the sun, that, for instance, the inhabitants of Jupiter would live on a very high spiritual level. And the Swedenborgian visions show, in some respect, similarity to Iqbal's qualification of the inhabitants of the spheres: the Poet has shown, in the Heaven of Mercury, a beautiful specimen of "specialization of spiritual energies", as Swedenborg calls the peculiarity of this sphere, and in the Heaven of Mars—in contrast to the traditional, accidental and oriental conception—the "unity of thinking and speaking, of spirity and body" which the Swedish visionary had witnessed in that sphere.

These may by accidents, but, in any case, significant ones: the reader will observe how much Iqbal's description of his way through the spheres diverges from the traditional picture of the other world. In his dealing with this age-old motif his method of working and writing becomes once more visible: interpreting traditional symbols in a new way changing them and transforming them according to his own system, and combining the deepest religious experience—every prayer is an ascension—with the exposition of his socio-political ideals.

The ascension, the never-ending journey during this life and after death, unto God and into God's abysses, the growing without diminishing: that is one of the central notions in Iqbal's poetry. His philosophy of the steadily growing human ego, of the attraction of the all-embracing Divine Ego, of unceasing quest and unsatisfied love as condition for his growth, the importance of prayer in which the prophetical ascension is repeated again and again: all these factors contribute to his predilection for this motif, and the fact that even in his only attempt of leading his readers through different steps of the heavenly regions his description differs notably from those of his predecessors shows that a systematization of the upward movement was not intended, and would have been opposed to his doctrine of free creative possibilities throughout the world. One may be reminded of Rumi's verse:

Love is the ascension towards the roof of the King of Beauty,

Read the story of the ascension from the cheek of the lover!

ABBREVIATIONS

AK *Asrar-i khudi*
R *Rumuz-i bikhudi*
PM *Payam-i mashriq*
ZA *Zabur-i 'ajam*
L *Six Lectures on the Reconstruction of Religious Thought in Islam*
J *Javidnamah*
Mus *Musafir*
Pas *Pas cha bayad kard*
Bj *Bal-i Jibril*
ZK *Darb-i Kalim*
AH *Armaghan-i Hijaz*
GR *Gulshan-i raz-i Jadid*
Lalah *Lalah-i Tur*
M *Maktubat, 2 vols., ed.* 'Ata'allah.

IMPORTANT SOURCES

F. Heiler, Erscheinungsformen und Wesen der Religion. *E.* Stuttgart, 1960.

F. Heiler, Das Gebet, Munchen, 1923.

N. Soderblom, The Living God. London, 1933.

F. Von Hugel, Essays and Addresses. London, 1924/28.

H. Scholz, Religionsphilosophie. Berlin, 1921.

H. Scholz, Der Unsterblichkeitsgedanke als philosophisches Problem. Berlin, 1920.

P. Tillich, Love, Power and Justice. New-York-London, 1954.

T. Andrae, Die letzten Dinge. Deutsch von H.H. Schaeder. Leipzig, 1938.

Benz, Swedenborg. Munchen, 1948.

E. Benz, Der ubermensch. Eine Diskussion. Zurich, 1961.

H. Corbin, Avicenna and the Visionary Recital. London, 1960.

M. Eliade, Le vol magique, NUMEN II. Leiden, 1956.

R. Eucken, Der Sinn und Wert des Lebens. Leipzig, 1918.

K. Goldammer, "Wege aufwarts" and "Wege abwarts." Eine heilige Kirche, 22. Munchen, 1940.

R. Hartmann, Die Himmelsreise Muhammads und ihre Bedeutung in der Religion des Islam. (Vortrage der Bibliothek Warburg, 1928)

R.A. Nicholson, The Idea of Personality in Sufism. Cambridge, *R. Otto,* Das Heilige, 26th ed. Munchen, 1947.

R. Pannwitz, Beitrage zu einer europaischen Kultur. Burnberg, 1951.

R. Pannwitz, Der Nihilismus und die werdende Welt. Nunrberg, 1954.

H. Plessner, Das Verbalntnis der Zeit zum Tode, Eranos-Jb. XX, 1951.

H. Ritter, Das Meer der Scele. Leiden, 1955.

H. Ritter, Muslim Mystics' Strife with God, Oriens V, 1952.

H.H. Schaeder, *Die islamische Lehre vom Vollkommenen Menschen.* ZDMG 79, 1925.

M. Scheler, *Liebe und Erkenntnis.* Munchen, 1955.

E. Underhill, *Mysticism,* 4th ed. New York, 1956.

E. Underhill, *Collected papers,* 3rd ed. London, 1943.

G. Widengren, *The Ascension to Heaven and the Heavenly Book.* Uppsala, 1950.

R.C. Zaehner, *Hindu and Muslim Mysticism.* London, 1960.

Revised and edited; originally published in Studies in Islam, April 1968.

15

Islamization of Knowledge: The General Principles and the Workplan

ISMA'IL RAJI AL-FARUQI

(Abstract: It deals with the present maladies and suggests a method to treat the maladies. "That teacher in the Muslim world universities are not possessed by the vision of Islam and are not driven by its cause is certainly the greatest calamity of Muslim education... It would be a great step forward if Muslim world universities and colleges were to institute compulsory courses in Islamic civilization as part of their basic studies program for all students").

Malaise of the Ummah

The world-*ummah* of Islam stands presently at the lowest rung of the ladder of nations. In this century, no other nation has been subjected to comparable defeat or humiliation. Muslims were defeated, massacred robbed of their land and wealth, of their life and hope. They were colonized and exploited, cheated and fooled, proselitized and forcefully or bribefully converted to other faiths. And they were secularized, Westernized and de-Islamized by internal and external agents of their enemies. All this happened in practically every country and corner of the Muslim World. Victims of injustice and aggression on every count the Muslims were nonetheless vilified and denigrated in the representations of all nations. They enjoy the worst possible "image" in world today. In the mass media of the world the "Muslim" is stereotyped as aggressive destructive, cheating, exploiting, ruthless, savage, lawless, terrorist, uncivilized, fanatic, fundamentalist, archaic and anachronistic. He is the object of hatred and contempt on the part of all non-Muslims, whether developed or under-developed capitalist or Marxist, Eastern or Western, civilized or savage. The Muslim World itself is known only for its inner strife and division, its turbulence and self-contradictions, its threat to world peace, its excessive wealth and excessive poverty, its famine and cholera epidemics. In the minds of people everywhere, the Muslim World is the "sick man" of the world; and the whole world is led to think that at the root of all these evils stands the religion of Islam. The fact that the *ummah* counts over a billion, that its territories are the vastest and the richest that its potential in humans material and geopolitical resources is the greatest, and finally that its faith—Islam, is integral, beneficial, world-affirming and realistic religion, make the defeat the humiliation and the misrepresentation of Muslims all the more intolerable.

Major Effects of the Malaise

1. *On the political Front:* The *Ummah* is divided against itself. The colonial powers have successfully fragmented the *ummah* into some fifty or more nation-state and set them against one another. The boundaries of the Muslim states have been so defined as to create perpetual friction for every state with its neighbours. Political machination by the enemy continually exploits those areas of friction and creates causes for alienation and hostility. Internally every Muslim nation state is in turn divided against itself, its population being heterogenous, and one group being assigned hegemony over the other groups by the colonial masters. No nation-state was given the time and peace, or the resources to integrate its own citizenry so to make them a single entity; and no two states were allowed to unite so as to constitute a greater whole. To make things still worse, the enemy has imported aliens into the Muslim World in order to guarantee perpetual strife between them and the natives; or converted the natives to a Western Christianity which necessarily implies their estrangement from the Muslim brothers or infused into non-Muslim natives a notion of their identity which sets them in conflict with the Muslims. Finally, the enemy has created hostile "foreign" states

within the body of the *ummah* to divert Muslim energy away from reconstruction and to drain it in futile wars, or to serve as base should colonialism decide to reoccupy the land for the colonial powers' economic strategic and political interests. No Muslim state is secure internally; and none is secure exernally. Ivery Muslim government spends the greater part of its resources and energy on securing its own power within, and integrity without.

Throughout the Muslim World except in a few regions where the enemy had found rulers ready to cooperate colonial administration has destroyed all political institutions in the land. When the time came for colonial administrations to withdraw, they entrusted the power to the native elites who had already been subjugated and Westernized. But the real power lay only in the military which was destined to grab it at first opportunity. In the majority of cases, muslims are ruled by the military because they are devoid of political formations capable of operating the government, or of mobilizing the masses for resistance of leading them into constructive political action; or, more simply capable of acting in tandem with one another.

2. *On the Economic Front*: The *ummah* is non-developed and backward. The overwhelming majority of its members everywhere are illiterate. Their production of goods and services is far below the need which is always satisfied by import of finished goods from the colonial powers. Even in the strategic necessities of life the staple foods, clothing, energy and hardware, no Muslim state is self-sufficient. Every state would be exposed to famine if the colonial powers wish for any reason to stop their unfair trade with it. Everywhere, colonial interests have been creating consumerist desires and demands for colonialists' products, while the needs of Muslim for productive hardware goes unheeded. In their competition with local Muslim productivity, the colonialists seek, and they often succeed, to knock it out of the market. When some industry is developed with the colonialists' help, it turns out to be dependent upon colonialist raw materials, or finished components, which they alone supply thus subjecting the industry

to function at their mercy to subserve their colonialists goals. In most cases, the new Muslim industries are not designed to meet the crucial needs, but those tangential needs created by colonialists intensive advertisement. Muslim agricultural self-sufficiency is their first enemy, science at this stage and for a long time to come, that is the necessary pre-requisite of Muslim resistance to any colonialist scheme. Everywhere through false promise of better living in the cities, the lot of temporary jobs in speculative building-construction and consumer-goods industry, and exploitation by landlords and tax collectors, Muslim farmers are uprooted from their villages. They migrate to the cities to live in shanty towns dependent upon imported staple foods and ready to answer the call of any damagogue.

The oil bonanza which Allah ta'ala found fit to grant to some Muslim countries has proven little of the ni'mah it was supposed to be. Found mostly in scarcely populated land the new wealth compelled the governments to follow racist lines to dissipate the wealth in artificial, "cosmetic" development of their lands. Indeed, the new wealth is so abundant that no such pursuits could exhaust it. Hence, it is channelled for "easy and secure" investment in financial markets of the non-Muslim World where it helps the enemies of Islam become stronger. Political instability in every corner of the Muslim World makes long term planning and investment too risky for any careful investor. Thus Muslim World areas endowed with potential for significant agricultural or industrial development remain devoid of funding capital; and the wealth which could develop these potentialities into actual prosperity for the whole *ummah* is channelled elsewhere.

3. *On the Religion-Cultural Front*: The centuries of Muslims decay have caused illiteracy ignorance and superstition to spread among Muslims. These evils have caused the average Muslim to recoil in the bliss of blind faith to lean toward literalism and legalism or to surrender his spirit to his "shakh." All this bred into him no small measure of venerability. When the modern world impinged itself upon him, his military, political and economic

wackiness caused him to panic. He therefore sought half measures of reform which, he thought, would speedily recapture for him, his lost ground. Unwittingly, he took to Westernization, lured by the successful example of the West and prompted by his Western or Westenized advisers. In areas under colonial administration, Westernization was ordered and promoted by every possible means at the rulers, disposal.

Well meaning or otherwise, Westernizing Muslim leaders did not know that their programmes would sooner or later undermine the Islamic religion and culture of their subjects. The connection between the manifestations of Western productivity and power and the Western views of God and man of life, of nature, of the world, of time and history, was too subtle for them to observe; or, in their hurry to mind. A secular system of education was built which taught Western values and methods. Soon, it began to pour into society generations of graduates who were ignorant of their Islamic legacy. Their ignorance combined with suspicion of the guardians of the legacy, namely, the *'ulama'* who were well-meaning despite their conservatism, literalism legalism or mysticism. A gap began to develop within the ranks of the *ummah* dividing it into Westernizing secularizers and opponents of secularization. The colonialist powers saw to it that the former became the decision-makers in society.

By the colonialists directly or by their native stooges everything Islamic fell under attack. The integrity of the Quranic text, the genuineness of the Prophet (SAAS) the veracity of his *sunnah,* the perfection of the *shariah* the glories of Muslim achievements in culture and civilization—none of them was spared. The purpose was to inject doubt in the Muslim's confidence in himself, in his ummah in his faith and ancestors, to undermine his Islamic consciousness to subvert his Islamic personality and thus to make him more subservient, lacking the spiritual stamina necessary for resistance. The colonialists and their stooges filled the Muslim's daily life with effects promoting Western culture, Newspapers, books and magazines, radio and television, cinema and theater, records and tapes street posters and neon signs bombarded him daily with such effects. Muslum governments took pride in a new boulevard they opened in their capitals dotted with Western-style high rise office or apartment building; but they were not shamed by the squalor and degradation of the whole rest of their towns and villages. Westernized elites frequented public halls to watch or hear a movie, an opera a concert or a drama, and their sons and daughters read about them in books in the secular or missionary schools and colleges, without realizing their incongruity with everything else they thought or did. Those of them who completed their self-Westernization stood out more oddly against their Muslim environment and background. The integrity of Islamic culture and the unity of the Islamic style of life shattered in their own persons, in their thought and action, in their homes and families. Western social institutions and customs were introduced with impertinence. Instead of raising themselves from their decay to the hights of virtue and social efficacy envisaged for them by Islam Muslim women began to hanker after the manifestations of Western decay: gradual nudity and tabarruj, economic independence aimed at induvidualist liecence, egotistic pursuit of measure and avoidance of duties imposed by the extended family. In short, despite all claims to the contrary to the extent that he Westernized himself, the Muslim has in fact barbarized himself. His life has become a hotch-potch of more than one style discontinuous with his past. He has made of himself something neither Islamic nor Western, a cultural mostrosity or modern times.

The Self-Perpetuating Core of the Malaise

There can be no doubt that the main locus and core of the malaise of the *ummah* is the prevalent educational system. It is the breeding ground of the disease. It is in schools and colleges that self-estrangement from Islam, from its legacy and style, are generated and perpetuated. The educational system is the laboratory where Muslim youth are needed and cut, where their consciousness is molded into a caricature of the West. Here, the Muslim's linkage with his past is severed; his natural curiosity to learn the legacy of the fathers is stymied; here, his willingness to touch with them and spring towards creative representation or *vergegenwartigung*(i.e. the making present and alive again) of Islam is blunted with the doubts the system has injected into every recess of his consciousness.

1. *The Present State of Education in the Muslim World:* Despite the tremendous expansion which has taken place so far, the state of Muslim education is at its worst. As far as Islamization is concerned, the traditional and the secularist schools, and colleges and universities have been more daring in the advocacy of their un-Islamic theses, and never had the captive ear of the overwhelming majority of Muslim youth, as they do today. Since its inception under colonialist administrations, the secularist educational system has assumed tremendous proportions, elbowing out the Islamic system from the field. Islamic education, for the most part, remains a private affair devoid of access to public funds. Where public funds are made available, demands of secularization are imposed in the name of modernism and progress. This usually consists of bifurcating the curriculum into contrasting—nay opposing, sections one Islamic and one modern (sic!). Al-Azhar being the classic example. The Islamic part of the curriculum remains unchanged partly because of convercatism and vested interests, and partly because it is in the secularist plans to keep it out of touch with reality and modernity, so that its graduates would present no competition to those of the secular institutions. That was all thought out and well planned by the colonial strategists. National independence gave the secularist system its greatest boost by adopting it as its own, pouring public funds into it and secularizing it even further in the name of nationalism. The forces of Westernization and secularization and the resultant de-Islamization of teachers and students continue to work full hilt in colleges and universities; and nothing has been done to arrest that aberration. In fact, the situation is worse than under colonialism. A spirit of resistance of searching for liberation and an Islamic solution then animated nearly everyone. Today, there is cynicism and lethargy, mistrust of all leaders; and this is largely due to repeated false promises and disappointments, to the sad example of morally

bankrupt leaders. No Muslims Government no university administration, no private organization is doing anything about the sinking morale of college youth, about their continuing de-Islamization through" "education". The colossal building programme in the affluent countries and the consequent expansion in students, faculty and facilities all serve the secularist cause. Hardly any percentage of the funds are devoted to "modernize" in a genuine sense, i.e. to improve the Islamic quality of education, the Islamic orientation of students and faulty. Everywhere, the race is on at maddening speed toward the Western educational model.

2. *The Lack of Vision*: Despite all claims to the contrary the result achieved is not the Western model, but a caricature of it. Like the Islamic model, the Western educational model rests ultimately on a vision, though different from that of Islam, sand is animated by a will to realize that vision. Buildings and offices, libraries and laboratories, classrooms and auditoria teeming with students and faculty are all material paraphernalia of little worth without the vision. It is of the nature of the vision that it cannot be copied. Only its incidentals can. That is why in nearly two countries of Westernized scularized education, the Muslims have produced nothing—either a school, college or university, nor a generation of scholars—that matches the West in creativity or excellence. The insoluble problem of low standards in Muslim World institutions is a necessary consequence of this lack of vision. There is no genuine search for knowledge without spirit; and spirit is precisely what cannot be copied. It is generated by the vision of self, of world and reality; in short, by religion. Muslim World education lacks this vision. Its leadership does not have the vision of Western man by necessity; and it does not have the vision of Islam by choice, i.e., by ignorance, leziness and unconcern. Educational leadership in the Muslim World has been Philistine, without culture and without cause. Nationalism has inspired the Western universities in the last two hundred years because romanticism has replaced the defunct God of Christianity with the nation as genuine "ultimate reality." For the Muslim, no reality is ultimate but God. Ultimate loyalty to nation

therefore is impossible for him, and this is especially so after his linkage with the legacy and the past had been corroded by doubt.

Look at the highest model of Muslim university teacher the professor with a doctorate from a Western university. He was trained in the West and graduated with a fair or less than fair average. Since he was not Islamically motivated befores hand—i.e., he has not embarked on his expedition to seek knowledge for the sake of Allah ta'ala but for a materialist egotist (at best, nationalist) goal—he did not obtain all the knowledge available to him in the West. Neither did he surpass his Western teachers at their own game. Nor did he like his ancestors who learned and Islamized the sciences of ancient Greece, Persia and India, digest what he learned or seek to rehabilitate it within the Islamic vision of knowledge and truth. Rather, he was satisfied to pass, to obtain the degree to return home and achieve a position of affluence and eminence. The books he read as a student are the ultimate reaches of his knowledge, for now, he has neither time, nor energy nor motivation to push the frontiers of knowledge his training had reached. His living and working conditions add to his distraction form such a distant ideal. Naturally, his students must come out even less motivated as well as less competent than him. for them, the Western ideal had receded even farther. Gradually, the standards sink. Western education in the Muslim World becomes a caricature of its Western prototype.

The materials and methodologies taught are copies of the Western ones but devoid of the vision which animated them at their original home. Without that vision, they become instruments of mediocritization. Unconsciously, these dispirited materials and methodologies exert a sinister de-islamizing influence on the student, by posing as alternatives to the Islamic ones as well as agents of progress and modernization. They make of the graduate of the Muslim World University a typical "sophomore," thinking that he knows but knowing very little indeed.

The very possibility of excellence in the western disciplines is thus removed form the Muslim student. For that possibility requires perception of the totality of knowledge in the field as well as motivation by a driving idea to appropriate and to transecend the totality. The former depends upon the latter; since in order to acquire knowledge of the totality one must be driven by a consuming idea which only commitment to a cause generates. For the Muslim, the cause which is really a cause can be only Islam. Lacking it, the Muslim teachers who studied in the West never reached the totality of knowledge. As teachers in the universities they cannot impart either requisite of excellence to their students. They are content in most cases to copy and to translate the lessthan the totality which they had acquired, dooming their students to a mediocre performance at best.

That teacher in the Muslim world universities are not possessed by the vision of Islam and are not driven by its cause is certainly the greatest calamity of Muslim education. Throughout the Muslim world, students enter the university equipped—as far as the Islamic vision is concerned—with the little knowledge of Islam they acquired at home and / or at the elementary or secondary school. Obviously this constitutes no "vision" and no "cause" Ideologically, therefore, the freshman student enters as a *tabula rasa*. He may come with sentiments, but surely not with ideas. These sentiments, if any, are shipwrecked when confronted with the "ideas" "facts", and the "objective" judgemtns of "science" presented to him in the disciplines. Obviously, he has no defences no vision with which to counter on this ideational level. If he does not graduate a confirmed atheist, secularist or communist, his view of Islam has receded to the realm of personal, subjective and sentimental attachment to family and people. Of Islam as a vibrant ideology replete with the best ideas in relevance to any problem, he has none. On the ideational level, the student in the Muslim World University confronts the alien ideologies presented to him in text book or class room with as miserable defence as a soldier with lance and a word fonfronts one armed with tank and machine gun. Nowhere in the Muslim World is the Islamic vision taught to all students as the Western tradition is taught to high school students in the West i.e., with consistency universality, utmost seriousness and commitment on the part of all. In no Muslim World university is such vision part of the "basic" or "core" studies programme compulsory to all students.

The greatest task confronting the *ummah* in the Fifteenth Century Hijrah is that of solving the problem of education. There can be no hope of a genuine revival of the *ummah* unless the educational system is revamped and its faults corrected. Indeed what is needed is for the system to be formed anew. The present dualism in Muslim education, if brifurcation into an Islamic and a secular system must be removed and abolished once and for all. The two system must be united and integrated; and the emergent system must be infused with the spirit of Islam. It must become an integral part of the Ideological programme of Islam. It should not be allowed to remain an imitation of the West, nor left to find its own way. Nor may it be tolerated to serve merely the economic pragmatic needs of the students for professional knowledge, personal advancement, or material gain. The educational system must be endowed with a mission; and that mission cannot be other than that of imparting the Islamic vision, of cultivating the will to realize it in space and time. Such a task is indeed difficult to perform and may be costly. But the *ummah* in its totality spends a far percentage of its "Gross National Product" of its annual budget than most other *ummah* in the world today. Even in those affluent countries where the budgets of education are significant

the expenditure is for the most part on buildings and administration rather then on education activities proper. The *ummah* must spend far more on education than it presently does, in order to attract to it the best minds, to help them maintain the dignity Allah *ta'ala* has bestowed them as "men of knowledge" or "seekers" after it.

Uniting the Two Systems of Education

The Islamic system of education consisting of elementary and secondary *madrasahs* as well as of college level *kulliyyahs* or *jami-ahs* ought to be united with the secular system of public schools and universities. The union should bring to the new unified system the advantages of both; namely, the financial resources of the state of which the former was deprived, and autonomy which the latter hardly ever enjoyed. Union of the two systems should be the proper occasion to eliminate their disadvantages namely, the inadequacy of archaic text-books and inexperienced teachers in the one, and the mimicry of the secular West in its methods and ideals in the other.

The advantage may be gathered by the new system if the respective governments agree to appropriate for it the necessary funds without exercising stifling control. The steps must be taken to make the new educational system financially secure, if not wholly independent, by promoting endowments whose income would fund the system or its parts. Such endowments are precisely the *awqaf* which the Sariah recognized and protected for the welfare of the *ummah.* It was the *waqf* of each *madrasah* that made it autonomous in the past, and thus enabled its teachers and students to seek knowledge for the sake of Allah *ta'ala* alone—the necessary condition for any successful search for the truth. And it was the *waqf* institution which gave the *madrasah* the first legal or corporate personality in history. It was the *waqf* based *madrasah* that constituted the model emulated by Oxford, Combridge. Paris and Cologne universities when they were founded eight centuries ago.

Because of the explosion of knowledge as well as of student numbers education may be too expensive now a days to be funded by *waqf* endowments alone. A yearly portion of public funds may well be necessary. However, the state ought to develop the wisdom necessary to negotiate with the educators the amount of the subsidy and trust them to make the best use possible of it. If state universities in the West could do this, it is anything but presumption to claim that Muslims acting under Quranic injunctions are incapable of same. There can be neither good nor future in an *ummah* which does not respect its learned songs and daughters, which does not exert itself to transit to them the cultural and spiritual legacy of the ancoestors, which does not enable its youth to add to and enrich their tradition. It is a sign of tyranny when the state does not trust its educators to do their job without policing the income and expenditure of their educational establishments. And it is a sure sign of decay when educators have to be told by the political rulers what to teach and what not to teach the youth.

Instilling the Vision of Islam

The Union of the two system is expected to do more than bring means to the Isalmic system and autonomy to the secular. It is expected to bring Islamic knowledge to the secular and modern knowledge to the Islamic system. As regards elementary and secondary education, the crime of the entrusting Muslim youths to missionaries or non-Muslim educators must be stopped. Every Muslim youth is entitled to receive full instruction in the religion, ethic, law, history, and culture of Islam. The *ummah* or any section of it is legally responsible, and in the eye of God criminally indictable if it failed, to give that basic instruction in Islam to every Muslim child.

The same is even more true in the case of adult education. The child's spirit is protected by his parents or guardian who will see to it that he commit no act odious to Islam; or violate any provision of the *shari'as*. The adult, on the other hand, is free. He is the target of anti-Islamic propaganda in and outside the university. In the college class room and in the assigned readings, he is constantly presented with alien ideologies in the name of science and modern knowledge. Anti-Islamic ideas and options for conduct are claimed to continue scientific truth, to be based on objective fact. In his tender years Islam was presented to the Muslim student with the voice of parental authority. His mind was not mature enough to understand or appreciate "objective" claims. His attachment to the Islamic position therefore was born out of sentiment, not of reasoned conviction. Evidently, his commitment to Islam cannot withstand the onslaught of "scientific" "objective" and "modern" truth. This is why in the absence of any counter presentation of the Islamic claims a presentation made with the same force of objectivity and scientificality the same appeal of modernity, the Muslim college student succumbs to the secular claim and converts to it. So begins the process of de-Islamization in Muslim universities. After four years of such alienating influence, within the university, and an equal if not superior influence stemming from the mass media has peers and society, the Islamic consciousness of the Muslim is ravaged. No wonder that he becomes a cultural Philistine a cynic who is at home neither in Islam nor in the West, ready to be swayed by anyone who caters to his whimseg of the moment.

1. *Compulsory study of Islamic Civilization*: The only possible antidote to this de-islamization on the university level is the compulsory four-year study of Islamic civilization. Every student in the university ought to undertake this course of study regardless of his major. The fact that he is a citizen, a member of the *ummah* imposes upon him to acquire a viable amount of knowledge of the *ummah* legacy, an adequate command of the *ummah's* spirit and familiarity with its civilization. It is not possible to be civil without such knowledge. Even if the student belongs to a non-Muslim minority, it does not absolve him from fulfilling this basic requirement. Since he and/or his parents have opted to be citizens of the Islamic state, he must acquire the necessary familiarity with the civilization to which his home-state belongs, the spirit and hope which move it and his fellow countrymen. No person may be left without acculturation in Islam, without "socialization" or integration into its society. Only such study can immunize him against invading ideologies : for it would enable him to meet argument with argument, objective evidence with objective evidence. Only such study can prepare him for genuine participation in the cultural life and progress of the *ummah*, for only through it will he learn the logique of Islam, the essence of Islamic civilization, and hence the direction into which the *ummah* is going, or hoping to go.

The study of civilization is the only way to grow in the

person a sense of his identity. No one may be said to be self-conscious who does not know his forefathers; and that is to say, who does not know the spirit which animated them, their achievements in the arts and sciences, in their political and economic life, in their social organization, in their esthetic experience; who is unmoved by their travails and tragedies, their glories and victories; who is uninspired by their hopes. The consciousness of self-identity is not achieved except when such knowledge of one's provenance and background is contrasted with knowledge of other peoples and groups of other civilizations. To know one-self is to know how one is different from others, not in material needs or utilitarian realities, but in the view of the world, in moral judgment, in spiritual hope. This is all the domain of Islam, of the culture and civilization which Islam built and sustained through the generations. It is achievable only through the study of Islam and its civilization, and the comparative study of other religions and civilizations. Today, to be "modern " is to be civilizationaly conscious; i.e., to be conscious of the nature of one's civilizational heritage, of the essence which produced its various manifestations of its distinction from other steams of civilizational history, and of its pull and direction for the future. Without such knowledge, one cannot be the subject of his own fate and certainly one cannot survive in this world. Unllike the past the civilizational forces contending in this century can reach and overtake any one without invasion or military occupation of his land. They can subvert his mind, convert him to their world view, neutralize and contain him as a puppet whether he is aware or not. Certainly, these forces are contending with one another to dominate the world. And it is the decision of Muslims today whether Islam will be one of the victors tomorrow; whether or not they will be the subjects of history or merely its objects. Indeed the civilizational battle now in progress in the world scene, will not leave anyone unscathed. Every human is bound to be transformed by one conterder or another, unless he himself instantiates the countender civilization and is therefore a transformer of others.

It is unbecoming of Muslims to argue that Islamic civilization will remain alive as long as it is taught in the departments or institutes of Islamic study in the universities. Indeed, it is indicative of their decadence that Muslims have instituted "departments of Islamic studies" in their universities. These are always copies of departments of Orientalistic studies in Western universities, where the study of Isalm is the specialization of the few whom society needs for administering its relations with the Muslim World.

Knowledge of Islam and of its civilization is not meant for the few. The vision of Islam is not meant for, or needed by the specialist alone. It is for all humans and it is designed to elevate all those who are possessed by it to higher level of existence. Islam abhors the division of humans into clerics and lay; it insists that all man are to know, teach and observe the truth. The vision of Islam is needed to defend the whole people against the alien ideologies invading their consciousness. Unless everybody is immunized against the disease the *ummah* will become the victim. Moreover, Islam is the comprehensive religion whose vision is relevant to every human activity, to every endeavour, whether physical, social, economic, political, cultural, or spiritual. It is not an other worldly religion like Christainity and Buddhism content to direct "divinity" affairs and leave the rest to Caesar. Nothing is said or done in any shop or factory, office or at home, theater or field and a *fortiori,* in any class room or laboratory of the university to which Islam is not relevant. The vision of Islam is therefore truncated—and hence dead—if it is cultivated only in one department or faculty. It must be the guiding, determining first principle of every discipline.

What is needed therefore is a four-year course of study to be part of the "basic" or "core" programme for all students, regardless of their majors no professions. It should seek to give the Muslim student knowledge of the first principles of Islam as essence of Islamic civilization in the first year; of the historical achievements of Islamic civilization as manifestations in space-time of the first principles of Islam in the second year; of how Islamic civilization ocmpars and contrasts with other civilizations in essence and manifestation, in the third year; and of how Islamic civilization is the only viable option in dealing with the fundamental problems of Muslims and non-Muslims in the contemporary world, in the fourth year.

2. *Islamization of Modern Knowledge*: It would be a great step forward if Muslim World universities and colleges were to institute compulsory courses in Islamic Civilization as part of their basic studies programme for all students. This would provide the students with faith in their own religion and heritage and give them the confidence in themselves to enable them to face and surmount their present difficulties as well as to forge ahead towards the goal assigned to them by Allah *taala.* But it is not enough.

In order to forge ahead toward this Islamic goal and thus make the word of Allah supreme in space and time, knowledge of the world is absolutely indispensanble. This knowledge is the goal of the disciplines. Before Muslims went into decay and slumber they had developed, the disciplines, established and clarified the relevance of Islam, of its world view and values, to everyone of them. They integrated them successfully into the main corpus of Islamic knowledge. They made wonderful contributions in all fields, and they utilized that knowledge efficiently to promote their Islamic ideals. During their slumber, non-Musllims have taken the legacy of Muslim scientists and men of knowledge, integrated it into their own world view, developed the disciplines, added significant contributions to them and utilized the new knowledge to their advantage. Today non-Muslims are the indisputed masters of all the disciplines. In Muslim World universities, it is their books, their achievements, their world view, their problems and their ideals which are being taught to Muslim youth Muslim youth are being westernized on account of this.

This situation must change. Muslims ought to master all the modern disciplines, understand them completely, and achieve and absolute command of all that they have to offer. Then, they ought to integrate their certain achievements into the corpus of

Islamic knowledge by eliminating, amending, reinterpreting and adapting its components as the world view of Islam and its values dictate. They should determine the exact relevance of Islam to the philosophy--the method and objectives—of the discipline and blaze forth a new way in which the reformed discipline can serve the ideals of Islam. Finally, by their example as pioneers, they ought to teach the new generation of Muslims and non-muslims how to follow in their footsteps, push the frontiers of human knowledge ever farther, discover new layers of the patterns of Allah *ta'ala* in creation, and establish new paths for making His will and commandments realized in history.

The task of Islamizing knowledge, (inconcrate terms, to Islamized the disciplines or better, to produce university level textbooks recasting some twenty disciplines in accordance with the Islamic vision) is also the most difficult. No Muslim has yet contemplated it enough to discern its prerequisites, or to articulate its consitutive steps and measures. All that our previous reformers had thought of was to acquire the knowledge and power of the West. They were not even aware of the conflict of Western knowledge with the vision of Islam. It is our present generation that first discovered the conflict as we lived it in our own intellectual lives. But the spiritual torture the conflict has inflicted upon us caused us to wake up in panic, fully aware of the rape of the Islamic soul taking place before our very eyes in the Muslim World universities. That is why we are alerting the Muslim World to the evil and seeking for the first time in history to elaborate a plan to arrest it, to combat its effects, and to re-launch Islamic education on its proper track, leading to its predestined goal.

It is most regrettable that the Muslim World is still devoid of a center where thinking on this high level takes place. What is needed is a university which acts as headquarters for Islamic thought-where the disciplines undergo Islamization and the process gets tested in the class and seminar rooms of the undergraduate and graduate programmes of study. Untill the Islamic university of Islamabad entered into collaboration with the International Institute of Islamic Thought, not one educational institution in the Muslim World had moved a finger to Islamize knowledge, to produce Islamic textbooks for college use in the disciplines, or the tools of research necessary for the writing of these textbooks. And yet, everywhere in the Muslim World one hears of the need to Islamize education its men and institutions, its curricula and textbooks. On the official level where the power to decide lies, one finds little more than lip service, either made by the ignorant or designed to meslead the masses.

This tasks is the noblest of all tasks, the highest instantiation of the divine *iradah,* the first and categorical imperative of all morality. The world religions the West and Communism did not begin to grow, to develop and achieve what they did without such a cause animating and driving their adherents. The least argument is that Muslims too, should lend their souls to determination by a cause if they want to stop being the objects of history and become its subjects. And yet, Islam is not another "ism" on a par with these movements; nor does is present its claim as its own, as a dogma personally experienced and subjectively appropriated, which can only be adopted or dropped arbitrarily. The claim of Islam is a rational, necessary and a critical claim. It has universal validity an ought-claim and title to the acknowledgment and acquiescence of mankind. As rational claim it can be met only with counter-argument which the Islamic adherent should welcome and to which he should respond with evidence. No part of the Islamic claim no relevance of islam to any discipline may be accepted without convincing evidence. But when the Islamic vision has made its claims and established it for the most exacting scholarship, when it has substantiated it for the most fastidious consciousness, then it can be rejected and / or resisted only out of irrationality of malice. The former is the prerogative of the ignorant, the mentally deranged; the latter, that of the committed enemy. Both constitute what Islam calls *jahiliyyah.*

This is then the great task facing Muslim intellectuals and leaders : To recast the whole legacy of human knowledge from the standpoint of islam. The vision of Islam would not be a vision unless it is a vision of something, namely, life, reality, the world. That content is the object of study of the various disciplines. To recast knowledge as Islam relates to it, is to Islamize it, i.e., to redefine and reorder the data, to rethink the reasoning and relating of the data, to re-evaluate the conclusions, to re-project the goals—and to do so in such a was as to make the disciplines enrich the vision and serve the cause of Islam. To this end, the methodological categories of Islam namely the unity of truth, the unity of knowledge, the unity of humanity, the unity, of life the relic character of creation the subservience of creation to man and of man to God must replace, the western categories and determine the perception and ordering of reality. So too, the values of Islam, namely the usefulness of knowledge for man's felicity the blossoming of man's faculties, the remoulding of creation so as to concretize the devine patterns, the building of culture and civilization, of human monuments in knowledge and wisdom, heroism and virtue, pietism and saintliness, should replace the western values and direct the learning activity in every field.

To elaborate and articulate more precisely the foregoing principles is the purpose of the following section :

Shortcomings of Traditional Methodology

In consequence of the terrible devastation which non-Muslims inflicted upon the *ummah* in the sixth and seventh centuries of the Hijrah—the Tatar invasion from the East and the Crusader invasion from the West—Muslim leaders lost their nerves their confidence in themselves. Thinking their world consigned to doom, they became over-conservative and they sought to preserve their identity and most precious possession, viz., Islam, by proscribing all innovation and advocating a strict adherence to the shariah. It was then that they abandoned the major source of creativity in the law—*ijtihad.* They declared its gates closed. Treating the shari-ah as perfected in the works of the ancestors, they declared any departure from it an innovation, and every innovation undesirable and condemnable. As electroted by the schools, to the *shari'ah* was to become frozen and as such to safeguard and survival of Islam. The survival of Islam, and indeed, Muslim victory and expansion in Russia, the Balkans, Central and Southeast Europe in the eighth to twelfth centuries did not undo the conservative measures. The universal adoption of *tasawwuf* and its *tariqahs* or ways, helped the Muslims to overcome their difficulties in the absence of *ijtihad* and source of creativity. The *shari'ah* therefore remained a closed system until modern times, when modern science and technology gave the West the power to confront and defeat the Muslims.

In modern times the West undid the Ottoman conquests in Europe, occupied and colonized and fragmented the whole of the Muslim world except Turkey proper, from where the Western powers were driven by force, Yaman and central and west Arabia which provided little incentive for colonization. The western powers exploited Muslim weakness to the utmost possible and contributed in major fashion to the present malaise of the Muslim World described in the first pages of this essay. In response to the defeats, tragedies and crises which the West had imposed upon the Muslim World in course of the last two centuries, Muslim leaders in Egypt, Turkey and India have tried to Westernize the *ummah* in the hope of making it politically, economically and militarily viable. The attempt has proven itself to be a failure wherever it was made. Indeed, it continues to be a failure today, the more striking the more consistently it was applied, as in Turkey and Egypt. In the former, it prepared the way for Mustafa Kamal to abolish all Islamic institutions and reject every traditional Islamic principle affecting public life. The whole Islamic system was to be replaced by the Western. Today, after two generations (sixty years) of westernization, Turkey is just as weak and poor in respects as other Muslim countries. Westernization has somewhat successed in de-Islimizing one class of society, but did nothing else. In the latter, Egypt where westernization was less consistently pursued, a western system was implanted and the traditional Islamic system was permitted to function alongside. The two systems competed with each other; and, despite the tremendous advantages the Western system enjoyed public funds, government support and favors—both failed to achieve public funds, government supported and favors—both failed to achieve excellence. They succeeded in weakening each other.

1. *fiqh and fiqih (s); Ijtihad and Mujtahid (s):* Today, the term *fiqh* means possession of knowledge of the *shariah* according to a given school; and its derivative *fiqh* refers to the person endowed with knowledge. General *fqih* and its derivative would apply to possession of knowledge of the *shari'ah* in all schools of law. Such knowledge presupposes command of the arabic language, of the judgmental *(hukmi)* passages of the Quran and *Sunnah.* Evidently, it is a technical meaning, highly restricted when compared with that of the Quranic term *faqaha* or *tafaqqaha,* repeated in numerous verses, which point to intellection and understanding, to grasping the essence and reasoning, in short, to knowledge of Islam as a whole. The movement of the term from this general connotation to the narrow technical one is itself an index of the *ummah's* outgrowth of the need for a general meaning capable of containing its creative tendencies and varied activities. It is a sign of conservativism and narrowing of vision.

Moreover, the early *faqih(s)* of the *ummah*—namely, the Prophet's companions, their successors, the *tabiun,* and the great founders of the schools (RRA)—were preeminently knowledgeable in all matters affecting the lives of Muslims. The *faqih* (s) of the classical period were real encyclopaedists, masters of practically all the disciplines from literature and law to astronomy and medicine. They were themselves professional men who knew Islam not only as law, ideal or theory, out equally as millions of humans lived it in actual practice. The highest Islamic qualification ever, namely, *al dhawq al shari,* or the intuitive knowledge of the purposes of the law, was well within their grasp. If they were the models of creative handling of the Muslims' problems on account of their superb competence, certainly neither the knowledge nor the wisdom of today's *faqih-* graduate equip him adequately to assume their responsibilities.

Within the traditional system itself, several attempt at self-reform were made, the most daring of which was proposed by Mohammad 'Abduh, and his teacher, Jamaluddin al Afghani. Although awakened Muslims everywhere approved their call to reopen the gates of *ijtihad,* the measure failed for two reasons: First, the traditional qualifications required of the *mujtahids* remained the same and thus restricted the practice of *ijtihad* to the graduates of the traditional *madrasah,* i.e., to those who saw no need for it. For, the graduates of the traditional schools were precisely the recipients of an education which convinced them that the methodology was absolutely adequate and that the problem of the Muslim World was merely one of human reluctance to realize the values of Islam. Secondly, the understanding of the *mujtahid* as necessarily the *faqih*, i. e., the person whose training has enabled him to translate all problems into legal terms, to make pronouncement upon them under the categories of the law, contained or subsumed the problems of modernity under those categories. This restricted *itjtihad* still further by concentrating all its effort upon *ifta* or the pronouncement of juristic verdicts upon specific actions which Muslims have done or propose to do in their daily lives. Almost by definition, as it were, the traditional *faqih* or *mujtahid* was incapable of looking at the problems as awhole, lost as he was in determining the exact correspondence of given deeds to norms and rules already specified in one or more schools. The situation called for a new methodology of which the traditional *mujtahids* were incapable of conceiving for reopening our very understanding of *usul,* or sources of Islamic knowledge.

2. The Opposition of Wahy to 'Aql : Perhaps the most tragic development in the intellectual history of the *ummah* is the alienation of *wahy* and *'aql* from each other. It was the advent of Greek logic and its influence upon some Muslims who were all too anxious to utilize the methods it provide to convince non-Muslims of the truths of Islam which set them on the path leading to such alienation. Hellenized Christians and Jews lived for centuries under the dichotomy; and many had brought it into the *ummah* with them when they converted to Islam. It was al

Farabi who gave it its classical statement in his *ihsa al Ulam.* Since then, the principle has been upheld by the philosophers against the *mutakallimun.* It was accepted by some later *mutakallimun* who were content to elaborate the faith defensively. And it dominated the field of intellectual discussion in the age of decline, especially under the influence of *tasawwuf* which advocated a purely intuitive, and often esoteric methodology, and hence, found no fault with such estrangement between reason and revelation.

The separation of *wahy* and *'aql* is utterly unacceptable. It is inimical to the whole spirit of Islam, opposed to the central appeal of the Qura'ns to reason, to weigh rationally all matters, to favour the more reasonable, the more median course. Unlike those religions which sought to overwhelm man's understanding, to overpower man's conscience so as to surrender to the irrational, or even the absurd, the call of Islam was rational and critical. Invariably, it invited men to use their intelligence, to apply their critical faculties to all claims, to consider the alternative, always to be cogent, coherent, to say nothing but the truth of which one is absolutely certain, always to seek correspondence with reality. Such exhortastions, injunctions and commands are practically found on every page of the Quran. Without reason, the truths of revelation cannot be appreciated. Neither would they be recognized for what they are—namely, divine — and acknowledged as such. The claims of revelation would be indistinguishable from other claims including the absurd. When acceptance of revelation is based not on reason, it is subjective, arbitrary, whimsical. No religious thesis based upon personal whimsy could claim the acquiescence of mankind , or of any significant part of it for a long time. The Muslims exaggerated emphasis on the intuitive at the cost of reason opened the gates of corruption of the faith. By not distinguishing it rationally from the absurd, superstition and old wives' tales found their way into it. Just as surely, the overemphasis of "reason" at the cost of intuitive faich corrupted the "life of reason" by reducing it to materialism, utilitarianism, mechanism and meaninglessness.

3. *Separation of Thought from Action :* In the early period of Islamic history, the leader was the thinker and the thinker was the leader. The vision of Islam was dominated, and the zeal to realize it in history determined all conduct. It was the preoccupation of the whole community of Islam. Every conscious Muslim sought to probe reality for materials and opportunities to undergo rekneading into the Islamic patterns. The *faqih* was at the same *imam mujtahid, qari, muhaddith, teacher, mutakallim,* as well as political leader, army general, farmer or businessman and professional. If he felt weak in any aspect, everybody around him was eager to step in and make up the deficiency. Everybody gave freely all that he had to the cause, and everybody felt strong with the strength of others. Muslims were so closely associated with one another that the weakness of any one of them was quickly overcome by the solidarity and total experience of all. Since Islamic was by nature oriented towards reality, this association with concrete living and doing provided the laboratory in which Islamic thought tried its creative ideas. Equally, it anchored thought in reality compelled it to keep its gazc focussed upon the real commonweal of living men and women. There is no evidence in the records of that period of any significant speculative thought. The reason is not that they were incapable of it, but that their priorities were the healthy and rational ones of bringing enlightenment, virtue and prosperity to the masses of people.

On the other hand, the actual life of the people, being object of continuing thought on the part of the leaders, had the benefit of their creative ideas. Adequate thought was applied to the problems the *ummah* met, and the solutions fitted the requisites of the situations. The *ummah* prospered; for her welfare was constantly in view of the best minds, and the solutions projected by them were put to practice and implemented because the same minds commanded the executive power, or were closely associated with those who did.

Later, this unity between thought and action was broken. The moment they were separated from one another, each began to deteriorate. Political leadership and the men of power moved from one crisis to another without the benefit of thought, without consulting the learned and obtaining their wisdom. The result was bungling which alienated the wise subjects and isolated the leaders still more. Put on the defensive, the political leaders perpetrated still more and greater mistakes. On the other hand, the thinkers estranged and removed from active engagement in the *ummah's* affairs, recoursed to the ideal as grounds or their condemnation of political authority. Some began to indulge in affirming the normative over and against the actual. Those whose condemnation carried political consequence were subjected to persecution by the leadership in power. Those thinkers whose condemnation did not , were encouraged to soar still higher away from reality. Other thinkers began to compromise the normative in their association with the political leadership. Increased tension led to polarity and this brought about the ruin of both thought and action. Whereas action became tyrannical and succession to power violent, thought having abandoned empirical reality, the real commonweal of the people, contented itself with commentaries on older works or took to mystical flight in Sufi speculation. Soon, the whole *ummah* became impervious to its own political leadership. The long succession of tyrants, corrupt leaders, throne-usurpers and caliphal puppets manipulated by powerful sultans, demoralized the *ummah* and repulsed it from the political scene. The Sufi brotherhoods received the people with open arms. They provided them with spiritual self-disciplining and cultivation of mystical experience, and thus compensated them for their loss on the scene of history. Religion provided an escape from the tyranny which none could bear.

Soon, while the sultans reigned without challenge, the greatest mental energies of the *ummah* were channelled toward the spiritual, personal and subjective values contemplated by *tasawwuf.* The equivalence and controvertibility of the spiritual and the worldly characteristic of the early period disappeared. In its place came the pursuit of the spiritual at the cost of the worldly, of the other world at the cost of this world. Losing its anchor in the actual experiences of the *ummah,* Muslim thought became conservative and literal in law, speculative in Qur'anic exegesis and world view, world denying in ethics and politics, esoteric in the sciences of nature. The great thinkers, jurists and saints all looked down upon political authority and action as something beneath them, in itself contemptible. First resistance to it, and then complete disregard for it, became the first conditions of virtue. The *ummah* seemed to have lost the balance between the personal and the public values so sublimely exemplified by the Prophet (SAAS) in his life.

4. *Cultural and Religious Dualism : Al sirat al mustaqim,* the straight forward path which was the hope of all and the practice of early Muslims was a single, unitary path, stemming from the vision of Islam and integrating a; of man's tendencies and activities in to one integral surge toward Islamic self- realization in history. In the period of decay and because of estrangement between thoughts and action, the path split into two: the way of the world and the way of God or virtue. This bifurcation of the Islamic life into two paths in constant opposition to each other — the one praiseworthy and involving all the religious and ethical values; the other condemnable and involving the material world with all its values corrupted and destroyed both. Both paths were transferred. The former became an empty spirituality, similar to the vacuous spirituality of Christian and Buddhist motherhood. For a spirituality that does not concern itself with the empirical welfare of the masses, which does not seek to actualize justice in the rough and tumble of the market places of the world, must be subjective, bent upon the religious interest of the adherent alone. Such a spirituality is egotistic even when it calls for a spirituality arts: for its prime concern is the state of consciousness of the practitioner. The others and their welfare are for it tools and instruments of self-trial, self-purification and self - ennoblement. No wonder that this spirituality fell to the lure of gnosis and the mystical experience; and it became the prey of superstition and miracle- mongering. It never occurred to the *shaykh* (s) who founded the Sufi *tariqahs* and the great minds that provided them with their ideological foundations, that their brotherhoods

would aberrate in such manner and develop and ethic and a hope which run counter to Islam.

The path of the world, on the other hand, developed its own immoral system, absolved as it were from the moral requirements which the representatives of the religion of Islam declared the specialized pursuit of another class of Muslims. Without moral values as internal to and constitutive of it, the system was bound to deteriorate and become the prize for anyone who could contend for it successfully. Government, political leadership or office thus became an instrument for self- glorification and the brute exercise of power, or for extortion of moral and material benefits from the people. When, in the modern period, the foreign colonial enemy attacked, invaded and occupied the land, the masses put up little resistance. The battle, they had already become convinced, was not theirs. Finally, when the colonial administrations set up another educational system and began to favour a style of life, of thought and activity alien to that of the masses, they regarded it as something *deja vu,* condemnable and contemptible but not worthy of total uprising of the *ummah* in a holy war *(jihad).*

First Principles of Islamic Methodology

As prereqisite for the removal of dualism from the educational system, which is in turn a prerequisite for the removal of dualism from life, for the solution of the malaise of the *ummah,* knowledge ought to be Islamized. While avoiding the pitfalls and shortcomings of traditional methodology, Islamization of knowledge ought to observe a number of principles which constitute the essence of Islam. To recast the disciplines under the framework of Islam means subjection of their theory and method, their principles and goals to the followings:

1. The Unity of Allah (SWT)

The unity of Allah *(subhanahu wa ta'ala)* is the first principle of Islam and of everything Islamic. It is the principles that Allah is indeed Allah; that no other being is Allah; and that He is absolutely One, absolutely transcedant, metaphysically and axiologically ultimate; that everything else is ontically separate and different from Him and is His creation. He is the Creator by whose command everything that is has come to be, and every event that happens has come to happen. He is the source of all goodness and beauty. His will is the law of nature, as well as the law of morality. His worship and praise is due from all creatures, above all from humans, whom Allah has created in the best of forms and endowed them with the faculties with which to recognize Him and acknowledge His works, as well as the capacity to transform creation so as to fulfil therein His ethical and esthetic patterns.

To think and live in consciousness of divine unity is to do so in a world enchanted and alive sine everything in it is there by Allah's act, is sustained by His providence, and is tending by nature ever forward toward realization of His will. In such a word, nothing is happen-stance; nothing is futile or devoid of meaning. In Allah's creation nothing is but according to a precise measure which Allah has ordained for it. To be part of such a word to recognize one's infinite complex of relations with all creatures; above all, to acknowledge one's creatureliness, one's indebtedness to Allah, and to gave Him His due of love and obedience. To be a Muslim is to have Allah constantly present in one's consciousness. And since He is the Creator and the Judge, to be Islamic means to do all and everything as He has directed and for His sake. All good and all happiness, as all life and all energy, are his gifts. In the Islamic life, these are acknowledged and used as such, while in Islamic thought, He is the First, the ultimate cause and end, of everything. As such His being and activity are the first constitutive and regulative principles of all knowledge. Whether the object of knowledge is the microcosm of the atom or the macrocosm of the stars, the depth of the self, the conduct of society or the march of history, Islamic knowledge regards the object of knowledge as materially caused by the antecedent constituents of the situation whence that object proceeded, but the actual discharge of casuality which brought about the object out of an infinity of other possible objects to which those same constituents might have led, as the initiative of the Divine being, issuing from a divine command. Likewise, Islamic knowledge regards every object of knowledge as fulfilling an end willed by Allah, or serving another end which is so willed, so that the casual hierarchy of the universe is at once a hierarchy of ends at the top of which stands the divine will, willing the end of every individual being, of every series of ends, and of the hierarchy as a whole. Islamic knowledge recognizes that there is neither being, nor truth, nor value outside the chains and complex of same in which Allah *taala* is cause and end, both immediate and ultimate; that whatever is conceived of, known or evaluated outside the divinely ordained nexus in in existent, false or value-free, or merely misrepresented as standing outside that nexus.

2. The Unity of Creation

(a) Cosmic Order—From the unity of Allah (SWT), the unity of His creation follows with logical necessity. As He has said in the Holy Quran, "If there were in heaven and earth other gods than God, both heaven and earth would have fallen into chaos"(21:22). If there were more than one ultimate reality, ultimate reality would not be ultimate. Moreover, the universe would then have to follow different orders; and it it did, it would not be the ordered universe we know. Nor would it be possible for us humans to know a universe in which more than one order obtains. Nor would it be possible for us humans to know a universe in which more than one order obtains. Cosmic order, it must be remembered, is that under which we discern objects as substances, qualities, relations and events. It is the consistency or unity of cosmic order that enables us to cognize the permanence of substances as order, neither things nor causes and consequents would be the same.

Creation is an integral whole precisely because it is the work of one Creator whose order and design has infused every part of it. Cosmic order consists of the laws of nature. These operate throughout the universe and permeate every part or aspect of it. The material, the spatial, the biological, the psychic, the social and the esthetic—all reality obeys and fulfills these laws. All laws are the *suntan* (patterns) of Allah *ta ala* in His creation. Allah *ta'ala* is not merely the source of these laws; or, having once designed nature according to them and established their working in nature, operates and /or controls them no more. He is not a retired God, but eternally living and active. Therefore, every being in the cosmos, and every event that takes place, are so by His command. At any stage of its existence, every being has built within it the dynamic power to change. This dynamic power comes from God and is sustained by Him. Furthermore, this power is not necessarily bound to produce the result with which it is associated. It is by Allah's command that a particular effect is caused by the causes usually associated with it allah (SWT) may operate a cause to bring about its effect immediately; but He may and does operate a cause by means of other causes, so that what seems to us to be an inexorable chain of causes is just as much divine causing as a single çause; For our part, as humans, we trust Allah *ta'ala* or His cosmic order, that give a cause, its effect will follow. As al -Ghazali and Hume had found out despite their ideological differences, there is no necessity to any casual connection. Indeed, what we call causality is mere "following upon " and repetition, leading us to believe that a cause is usually followed by its effect. Such faith has nothing to stand upon except the benevolence of the divine Being. For Allah *ta'ala* seeks not to cheat or misguide; He is a benevolent Creator, Who ordered things in the universe to make it livable and comprehensible to us, to make it possible for us to exercise our moral options and prove our ethical worth in the deed.

(b) *Creation : A kingdom of Ends*—Allah *ta'ala* created everything and to do so with precise measure (25:2). This measure assigns to everything its nature, its relations to other beings, and the course of its existence. Equally, the divine measure subjects everything not only to the system of causes described above, but also to a system of ends. everything has a *raison de'tre,* a purpose which its being serves. This purpose is never final, but always subject to other purposes with which it constitutes a finalistic nexus which ends only in God. For only he is the ultimate End, the final purpose, unto whom everything returns. His will makes every good good.

Everything that is, therefore, us at once related in a cause-effect relationship to everything else, as well as in a finalistic, or means-to-end relationship as well. For both the metaphysical and the axiological relationships terminate with God.The network of each is infinite. Certainly, both are open for human inspection, for human knowledge and appreciation. Being infinite, however, humans can know only a portion of the relationship, led, as its were, by a pocket spotlight in a dark jungle. But is their prerogative and duty to press ever forward in its exploration and discovery. To discover and establish those relations is to establish for knowledge and appreciation the immutable patterns of Allah (SWT).

That all things in creation serve a purpose and that all purposes are interrelates means and ends to one another makes the world one telic system, vibrant and alive, full of meaning. The birds in the sky, the stars in the firmament, the fishes in the depth of oceans, the plants and the elements—all constitute integral parts of the system. No part of it is inert or evil, since every being has a function and a role in the life of the whole. Together, they make an organic body whose members and organs are interrelated in ways which humans are only now coming to discover for science, but only in very limited parts of nature. Muslims knew all too well that creation was organic, that every part of it serves some end or another, even if that was not known to them. This knowledge is a consequence of their faith. Confronted with the wolf devouring the lamb, the bird eating the butterfly or the human body feeding the worms in the earth, they assumed all being to be good, fulfilling in its natural activity a divine purpose and serving a system of purposes which culminates in the divine will. The Muslims was not free to ascribe anything to accident, to blind fate. Earthquakes and pestilences, drought and tragedy, the Muslim regards as ordained by Allah. However tragic or painful, the Muslim accepts these events, as Gods, effects; willed by Him for a good cause which he may not discern presently. As effects of Allah, the Muslim is never overwhelmed by them because he knows Allah, the Author of them, to be at once His beneficent Protector. He therefore assumes them to be tests, ordained by Allah to try him, calling for the greatest firmness, faith and optimism in the final outcome. This aspect of the faith of Islam is precisely what humans need in face of tragedy.

Allah's ordaining of this world as one in which causes are followed by their effects, where causes converge on everything from an infinite scope, and where effects diverge from every event in infinite scope, and where the same infinite interrelationships exist and bind everything together in a system of ends, is itself meant to provide a theater for man's life and ethical endeavour. The theater is not its own end; nor is it the property and exclusive domain of man. Since man is created for a life of service to His Creator, the world is His grant to him. Man's duty is therefore to work out the divine patterns in it, but to safeguard it from deterioration and indeed to improve it.

(c) *Taskhir* (Subservience) of Creation to man—Allah *ta'ala* has granted the world as a temporary gift and theater to man. He has made everything in it subservient to him; i.e., capable of being used by man for his nourishment, enjoyment and comfort. Such use may be immediate as in the case of nourishment and enjoyment, or mediate as when the forces of nature are utilized to produce the goods men need. Between the objects of creation and human usufruct there is a built—in concordance. Creation has the needs of humanity built into it, its objects being meant to serve those needs. The whole range of nature is capable of receiving man's efficacy, of suffering change at his initiative, of transformation into any pattern man desires. Humankind can dry up the seas or utilize the sum, move the mountains and cultivate the deserts, or lay the whole world waste. They can fill the world with beauty and enable everything to prosper, or fill it with ugliness and destroy everything. The subservience of creation to man knows no limits. Allah *ta'ala* has willed it so. The causal and finalistic interconnections of the objects of creation are substance of this subservience which would be futile and meaningless without them. Man would quickly lose interest in creation and give up any attempt to transform it into the ought-patterns revealed by Allah, if he could not depend on causes to bring about their effects, or the means not to be good for the ends. Such would be an inert, immovable and unchargeable world, or a world for fools.

3. *The Unity of Truth and the Unity of Knowledge:* Reason may certainly have its illusions and aberrations as well as its uncertainties. Its capacity for self-criticism gives it a fair degree of protection; but wherever ultimate truth and reality are concerned, its human predicament leaves it in need of corroboration by the infallible source of revelation. Once the questions of first or ultimate principles are settled, then reason acquires new vigour with which it can overcome the problems confronting it. Its basic presuppositions must all be apodeictically certain. Some are so by self-evidence; others are the common experience of humanity at large. There are others however, which are capable of an ought necessity only; they are capable of being perceived as true only by those who have the requisite degree of wisdom, or maturity of religious or ethical vision, and who are on that account expected to see the reality as it is. Hence, recognition of such truths and values may not be mathematically universal, but it enjoys a different kind of necessity, an ought-to-be necessity or *Sollensnotwendigkeit.* Where reason does not enjoy apodeictic certainty, the light of faith can provide this certainty and in fact cast illuminating light on all other presuppositions, and support with additional certainty the whole world view built upon them. this light of faith is definitely epistemological, and comes as the apogee of reasonableness, not its opposite. Between it and the apodeictically certain presuppositions, there is affinity, harmony, correspondence and complementarity. At least in Islam, unlike the other religions which are dogmatic through and through, faith is never irrational in its role and contribution. it does not stand above reason, just as reason does not stand above faith. The

perception of reason and faith as diametrical opposites, and of man having to choose between them is not Islamic. That "the Hews require a sign [miracle] and the Greeks seek after wisdom. But we preach Christ crucified, unto the Jews a stumbling block [skandalon] and unto the Greeks foolishness.... The foolishness of God is wiser than men..... Not many wise men... are called: but God has chosen the foolish things of the world to confound the wise;... the weak things... to confound the mighty; and base things of the world, and things which are despised hath God chosen, yea, things which are not to bring to nought things there are"(Corinthians 1:22-28) may be Jewish or Christian or Hindu, but it is the antithesis of the Islamic position.

As concerns the theory of knowledge, the position of Islam may best be described as the unity of truth. This unity devolves from God's absolute unity, and is convertible with it. *Al Haqq* ("the truth") is the name of God. If God is indeed God, as Islam affirms, then the truth cannot be many. God knows the truth and, in His revelation, He tells it as it is. What He conveys in the revelation cannot be different from reality, since He is the Creator of all reality as well as of all truth. The truth which is the object of reason is embodied in the laws of nature. These are the patterns of God in creation, His *sunan* which are constant and unchangeable, and hence are possible to discover, to establish and to use for the benefit of humanity. This logical equivalence of reason, truth, and reality with the facts of revelation is the most critical principle epistemology has ever known. This equivalence is based on three principles underlying all Islamic knowledge.

First, the unity of truth prescribes that no claim on behalf of revelation may be made which goes counter to reality. The propositions which revelation is supposed to teach must be true; i.e., they must correspond to reality and agree with it. It is inconceivable that God may be ignorant, or that He may seek to cheat misguide His creature. His statements, therefore, given expressly to guide and instruct, cannot oppose reality. Whatever they may claim must accord with reality. Wherever, such variation from reality occurs, the Muslim is rightly cautioned by the doctrine of the unity of truth to reconsider his understanding of revelation.. the doctrine guards him against overhasty interpretation, exaggerated allegorical interpretation and eisegesis, or the reading into the material of any esoteric meaning *(batin)* which is arbitrarily assumed on the authority of someone. The meanings of the Islamic revelation are eternally anchored in two solid rocks: Arabic lexicography and syntax which remain unchanged since the revelation of Quran and reality.

Second, the unity of truth prescribes that no contradiction, difference or variation between reason and revelation is ultimate; that there is no overarching principle, fact or understanding which can contain, solve and remove the contradiction. In one's investigation of nature and attempt to discover the patterns of laws the Creator in the universe, it is certainly possible to make mistakes, to fall under illusion and to think one has grasped the truth while being in error. Such would create discrepancy between revelation and reason. The unity of truth rejects such discrepancy as illusory and demands of the enquirer to reconsider, to reinvestigate the data. The cause of the discrepancy may well be in the findings of reason, in which case it would be salutary to send the investigator back to the data for re- examination. And it may well be in his understanding of revelation, in which case it would be equally salutory to send him back to its data for review.

Third, the unity of truth, or the identity of the laws of nature with the patterns of the Creator, prescribes that no inquiry into the nature of creation or any part of it may be lossed and concluded. A critical attitude to all human claims, and an active search for the laws of nature which is never ultimately conclusive, are at once necessary conditions of Islamicity and of genuine science. Under this view, the strongest conclusion is always tentative, valid only until new evidence has questioned, refuted or verified it. The highest wisdom, the most certain pronouncement, must always be followed with the affirmation. (Allah Knows better!).

4. The Unity of Life

(a) *the divine Amanal*—In a passage of Quran, allah *ta'ala* said : " and when [after creating heaven and earth] Allah told the angels that He was about to create a vicegerent and to assign him to the earth, the angels pleaded: 'would you place on earth persons who will do evil and shed blood while we praise and adore you constantly?" Allah replied: 'I have an ulterior purpose which you do not know.' [Having created Adam] Allah taught him the names of all things, showed him to the angels and asked them to name the things of nature. They could not and answered, 'Praise be to You. We know only what You have taught us. Yours is the knowledge and the wisdom.' Allah asked Adam to tell the names, which he did.... then Allah asked the angels to prostrate themselves to Adam." (2;30-34). In other passages concerning the creation of man, Allah *ta'ala* said:..." We offered Our trust to heaven and earth and mountains. But they feared and withdrew and refused to accept it. Man, however, agreed to carry it (33: 72). I have not created men and jinn but to serve me... (51:56). Allah created heaven and earth.... that you [human kind] may prove yourselves ethically worthy by your deeds (11:7). Praised be He.... Who created life and death that you may prove yourselves ethically worthy but your deeds(67:1-2).

The foregoing passages of the Quran answer for all time the question of whether or not man's being has a reason which explains it. Islam affirms with all possible emphasis that man has a raison d'etre and that is the service of Allah *ta'ala*. The divine will is of two kinds, a kind that is realized necessarily, and that is the divine patterns on the basis of which creation runs. These patterns are the laws of nature. They are immutable and their fulfillment is cosmic. In addition to revelation, they are known by reason. Allah *ta'ala* enjoined upon man to seek them, to understand them, to establish them for knowledge, and to utilize them to his advantage. The second kind is realized only in freedom, only when they are fulfilled in a condition where both fulfillment and violation or non-fulfillment are distinct possibilities. These are the moral laws. They co-exist with the laws of nature; i.e., they are always realized in a context of things, persons and relations in the empirical world, but they belong to a different order from the empirical. They are a priori. Whether or not they enter the real situation and become fulfilled therein depends upon the situation's fulfillment or other wise of their own peculiar requirements. They demand the free exercise of a personal will.. Devoid of such will, "heaven and earth and mountains" were incapable of carrying the divine *amanah* (trust). Only man carried it; for he alone is capable of such moral freedom. His capacity puts him above the angels. For they do not enjoy the freedom to obey and disobey. That is why Allah commanded them to prostrate themselves before man. For their lack of moral freedom, they are inferior to man. They are perfect and can only obey Allah's orders. They praise and serve Him constantly, and never disobey. Thus the obedience of man is worthier than the obedience of the angles, precisely because it is done by a person who is well capable of doing otherwise. For such a person, to turn away from the way of evil, the way of the lesser good, the way of the material or utilitarian or selfish good, and opt freely to do that which the moral law demands, is to realize a higher value. The moral life is a higher, superior, nobler nd greater kind of life. The higher part of the divine will does not enter history and become real unless human beings chose to realize it in freedom. Man is therefore a cosmic bridge between the higher echelons of the divine will and historical reality. Evidently, his being is of tremendous significance.

(b) The *Khilafah*—Man's carrying of the divine amanah constitutes his khilafh or vicegerency to god. His *khilafah* consists in the fulfillment of the moral laws. These and the religious laws are one. The latter to command a few ritual. But these have aspects which are not merely religious or otherworldly, but which are quite this-worldly in their character and effect. The whole rest of the corpus of religious or moral laws consists of actual practices of living, of being and doing. What they add to the actual practices is a quality, a perspective a way of discharging those self-same practices. It is commonplace for men to desire, to grow to acquire and possess, to love to marry and proscreate, to seize and exercise power etc. Islam wishes these activities to continue. It does not like Christianity or Buddhism, condemn and wish them to stop. All it seeks is to have humankind enter into these actions with different motivation, and to perform them in a different way. The different motivation is for them to be willed for the sake of God; and the different way is to do them justly and righteously to have them bring about their utilitarian or moral objective without entailing any undesirable, unjust or immoral consequence.

The aforementioned unity follows from the fact that Islam does not separate the sacred or religious from the secular. In its view, there is one reality only, not two as in the case of religions which bifurate life into a sacred sector and secular sector. Nothing is as such sacred except Allah; and no act is, as such, religious. Islam regards everything as secular and profane; it is the manner of doing it that fulfills or does not fulfill the religious or more requirement. Events or human deeds could be good or evil, virtuous or vicious, depending on whether they bring about justice righteousness, beauty, happiness or otherwise. To be religious, therefore, does not mean to withdraw from the usual processes of life, nor to perform deeds which are utterly devoid of utilitarian value. The whole matter of religion is a quality of the very practices of living. On this account, Islam remains imbdedded in the very processes of life and history. There is neither piety nor virtue, and certainly no Islam, outside of these processes. Christianity and Buddhism may regard religion as doing other things than the processes of life and history, and they may prescribe self-mortification and asceticism, monkery combat and even arrest of those very processes. They do so because in their view the processes of life and history stand condemned as evil and doomed. For Christianity believes creation is "fallen" and "evil" and "hopeless" and prescribes faith and the *imitation christi* as salvation from them. Likewise, Buddhism believes creation is evil, "*tanha*" full of nothing but pain and suffering and prescribes self and life-denial as salvation from the processes of life and history.

Islam denies such a priori axioms condemning life and history.

In its view creation is as such good, brought about by Allah (SWT)for a good purpose, namely, that it may be affirmed with devotion to Him and justice to mankind. Involvement in its processes is at the root of Islam's view of man. Allah (SWT) has appointed him to achieve who objectives. First humans should transform creation into the objectives. First, humans should transform creation into the divine patterns, i.e., so rearrange its material so as to make them fully and beneficially subserve human needs the material (food shelter, comfort, procteation) as well as the moral (intellectual, esthetic). Second, in the very act of transforming creation humans, ought to instantiate the ethical values by choosing to enter into those acts of transformation in an way that is; in a way which fulfills the requirements of devotion to Allah (AWT) and justice to mankind.

The content of the divine *amanah* and therefore of *khilafah,* is the development and establishment of culture and civilization. To institute peace and assurance of life and property, to organize humans into an ordered society capable of producing food, of processing, storing and distributing it to all in adequate quantities and quality to provide shelter, warmth and comfort communication and ease to build and make available the tools necessary to realize these goals and, finally, to furnish opportunities for education and self-realization, for recreation and esthetic enjoyment, this is the core content of *khilafah.* It is equivalent to the making of culture and civilization to the affirmation and promotion of life and the world. *Allah ta'ala* commands all this to be done and declares it to be the very reason for His creation of the world. The divine ulterior motive in all this is that humans may prove themselves ethically worthy in doing it. They can do so be entering into their routines of action for His sake and maintaining the balance of justice throughout their actions. Rightly, Muslims understand *khilafah* as predominantly political. The Qur'an repeatedly associated *khilafah* with establishment of political power (7:73), the reassurance of security and peace (24:55), the vanquishing of enemies and the replacement of their regime by that of the vicegerents (7 :128; 10:14, 73). Political action i.e. participation in the political process as in election or *bay'ah* of the ruler, giving continual counsel and advice to the chief of state and his ministers monitoring their actions, criticizing and even impeaching them—all these are not only desirable, but prime religious and ethical duties. Failure to perform such duties is, as the Prophet (SAAS) said to lapse into *jahiliyyah*. On the other hand, to be part of the policito-economic body of Islam is integral to the faith itself. Abu Bakr and the sahabah (RAA) fought those who wanted to secede from the former while keeping the latter as apostates who have rejected the whole of Islam. Unlike Christianity, which regards the political process as the depth of evil and counsels against involvement in it, Islam regards it of the essence and prohibits withdrawal. The same is true a fortiori of culture and civilization. Islam regards building them as the very business of religion. All the more contrasting with the norms of Islam, therefore, is the disengagement of the Muslim masses from the political process in the period of decay.

(c) *Comprehensiveness*—The will of Islam to culture and civilization is comprehensive, as it must be if it is meant seriously. This comprehensiveness is at the foundation of the comprehensiveness of the *shari'ah*. Every aspect of human life is affected and this affection is the relevance of Islam to it. This relevance may be clear or unclear, hard as in the shari'ah injunctions and prohibitions its *wajibat* and *muharraman;* or soft as in its categorizations of *mandub, makruh, and mubah*. But nothing escapes Islam's relevance. True, the area of the *mubah* (permissible) is wide. But its width is not a sign of Islam's irrelecance, but of its fall outside the realm of strict enforcement, whether coercively as in the case of *wajib* and *haram* or by moral authority as in the case of *mandub* and *makrah*. Beyond that realm stands the realm of culture and life- style which is just as important for Islam as that of strict enforcement. In fact, strict enforcement depends upon proper acculturation which is its presupposition, and without which it is unthinkable. Nothing is enforcible to which the masses have already not been acculturated, of which they are not already convinced.

It is therefore the duty of the Muslim thinker to Islamize i.e., to define and apply the relevance of Islam to every single item in human living. The Qur'an has already done so in a number of areas of human activity normally assigned the status of "soft enforcement" or neutrality; e.g., greeting, soft voice, door-knocking before entry, quick exit after food, gentleness to parents and elders, etc. The Prophet (SAAS) did his best to complete the application by his teaching and example in the areas of how to eat and drink, to keep clean, to recreate oneself, to treat one's neighbour, etc. The style of life which Islam had instituted in the early period in elaboration or extension of these Quranic and Sunnatic directives, needs today to be redefined recrystallized, complemented so as to extend to those activities which were not known or common then or to apply more firmly to those areas which modernity had raised from the status of laxury or marginality to that of necessity. The areas of social intercourse of travel and transportation, of recreation of the audio and visual arts, of mass communications, for example, are especially needy of such extension of coverage by the relevance of Islam.

5. *The Unity of Humanity*: Being the unity of the Creator, the divine unity must stand in absolutely the same creatorly relation to all humans. The converse of this relation is that all humans must stand in absolutely the same freaturely relation to the Creator. In so far as their being is concerned, they cannot be ontically plural without this plurality implying an equal plurality in the Creator. Certainly, humans can and do have different characteristics such as race, colour, physical build, personality, language style and culture. None can have ontological value; i.e. constitute the person it qualifies as a different being. None of them can effect the person's creately status before Allah (SWT). Their value remains accidental to the person's being God's creature. By determining the personality and/or conduct of their processor-ethnic characteristics may and very often do bring about his moral felicity or ruin. But their determination of the ethical outcome is never final or ultimate. For it is never ultimately impossible that a person with any imaginable combination of such characteristics

be morally worthy, or unworthy. The inner core which is constitutive of the person's being must therefore remain somewhat free of them, capable of following their determinative power or doing otherwise, i.e. of channeling their causal efficiency to other ends.

The foregoing argument is the reason underlying the divine statement of the Qur'an "O People, We have created you [all] of a single pair, a male and female [namely, Adam and Eve; and We have constituted you into tribes and nations that you may know one another, Nobler among you in the estimate of Allah is the more virtuous" (49:13). Belonging to one gender or another, to "tribes and nations" or one ethnicity or another is perhaps the most obvious characterization of, and first differentiation among, humans. Second, come language, physiognomy intelligence, dexterity, body strength, which are less fixed at birth and more apt to undergo change. Third, the readily changeable characteristics of personality which constitute the virtues and vices: from wisdom and knowledge piety and patience, to ignorance and foolishness faithlessness and rebellion. All these constitute human personality or life style, at least in its foundation and base. The rest of personality and life style is what is built up as habit or judgment, tendency or temperament reputation history or tradition of that personality through the accumulation of its own deeds. All of them are constitutive and determinative of the human person. But they differ widely from predetermination before birth and hence immutability, to acquisition in various stages of life and hence growth and development, or change and abolition. Humans are most apt to mistake the values of these characteristic's the nature of the roles they play in the life of the person. In history, no other human facts have determined judgement of persons and groups more than the first order of characteristics, namely, gender and ethnicity. And yet these are the most innocent because they are the least dependent upon moral decision and action, the least susceptible to change. In most cases, their immedetiacy and obviousness mislead judgment to take them as antic and to differentiate and discriminate on their basis. That is why the Qur'an picked them first and sought to demolish all judgments dependent upon them. These characteristics are God's work, necessary and unchangeable, created by God merely for the purpose of identification. They are to be regarded solely as "passport" or "identity card," saying absolutely nothing about the moral character or value of the carrier. This is the meaning of the verse if its terms are taken literally. If the term "know" is taken figuratively, than the Qur'an would be telling us that gender and ethnic characteristics were created by God to the end of humans finding in them mutual complementation and cooperation.

Hence, all humans are one and the same. On this ground the universalism of Islam is based. All humans are one in God's eye except as their deeds distinguish them in moral virtue, in cultural or civilizational achievement. If these deeds are dependent upon group or personal characteristics to determine of facilitate human undertaking of them, it is a moral duty to grow, develop, change or radically alter those characteristics. And it is always possible to do so. The door to such cultivation or alteration is never closed. On the other hand, where judgment does take place on the basis of the immutable characteristics a moral even namely, ethnovotrism is committed. The impliations of such crime are ominous; the unity of humanity is violated, and divine unity is violated as well. Nothing is more odious to Allah (SWT) than *shrik* (i.e. associations or polytheism) ; and nothing less than *shirk* is the implication of ethnocentrism. Nothing has been more productive of hostility war and bloodshed among humans than ethnocentrism. Religion and all sorts of causes have been paraded as causes of various conflicts among groups of humans. In reality, nearly all conflicts among groups are ultimately reducible to ethnocentric decisions made on the basis of the immutable characteristics of a so-called "enemy".

With ethnocentrism, of which racism and nationalism are the commonplace expressions, Islam can have no compromise. The conflict between them is insulate as the damage which ethnocentrism inflicts upon the human spirit—whether as subject or object of discrimination—is irreparable.

To condemn ethnocentrism as Islam does is not to condemn patriotism. The latter means the attitude of love and endearment, of appreciation of the life and value of the group, of self-preparation to undergo any exertion or sacrifice, including lying one's life, for its defence. As such, patriotism is not only not an evil but a positive good enjoined by Islam. It is both a religious and ethical duty to love and serve, to defend one's people and land against aggression and injustice. Ethnocentrism, however, is far removed from patriotism. Its essence is to assume the advantage of the ethnic entity as ultimate criterion of good and evil; and its most common expression is to hold the ethnic entity superior to mankind because of the innate characteristics of its members, to regard and pursue that advantage at the cost of any other. It is because ethnocentrism makes such assumption that it is possible for it to command the absolute loyalty of the adherent. The claim it makes is the claim of ultimate reality. The committed ethnocentrist, whether Jew German, French or Russian, genuinely assumes the Jewish people, Germany, France or Russia to be ultimate realities constituting ultimate criteria of good and evil. What Zionism built in the psyche of the Jewish people what Hegel, Fichte, Nietzsche and other Romantic thinkers built in the psyche of the German people as to what is "Deutschland" what Rousseau, Fustel de Coulanges and others had built in that of the French people as to what is la *Nation* or *la France* was nothing short of a mystique which bloated the Jewish People, Germany and France into something approximating the ultimate reality of religious faith. The pride and inspiration which those mystical entities command, the moving appeal which they exercise upon the heart and imagination of the adherent, are indeed those of a reality that is mysterious tremendous, fascinating, transcendent and ultimate.

The Muslim is the person who believes the exact opposite precisely because his God is absolutely the only God of all, the premise which necessitates his assumption of the unities referred to above as well as the unity of humanity. A Muslim nationalist or racist is therefore a contradiction in terms; and the Muslim who claims commitment to nationalism is either a *manafiq or zindiq* (a non-Muslim pretending to be one) or one whose commitment is so superficial that it cannot withstand the lure of bribe or personal advangate. That is also the reason why the careers of the overwhelming majority of so-called committed Muslim nationalist leaders had left much to be desired by way of consistency and fidelity.

In modern times, knowledge of man has nearly all been based upon ethnic entity as ultimate definiens of humanity; and knowledge of society, upon ethnic entity as first and ultimate ground of social order and organization. The universalism of the Enlightenments had never been given a chance of implementation before it was repudiated in favuor of the ethnocentric approach of romanticism. Indeed the universalism of the Enlightenments was theoretical and suspicious, considering that even in the hands of the prinece of thc movement, Immanuel Kant, the various peoples of mankind were graded as superior and inferior on the basis of traditional European prejudice, and the innate characteristics of Asians, Africans and Europeans. Romanticism swept over the whole of the West wiped out every trace of rationlist or Christian universalism, and provided the greatest impetus for the humanities, the arts and the social sciences. Man was defined by the thinkers as a function of facts, faculties and forces which spring and nourish themselves from a land mystically conceived, from a race or people or blood mysteriously standing in an infinite dimension of time, and from a tradition whose roots run infinitely as to depth and extension in both space and time. Furthermore, these are understood not by reason but grasped by feeling, immediate experience and intuition. Their most eloquent and clearest expression is to be found in the arts, especially in music painting and literature. Even religion was reconceived by these romantic thinkers, notably Schlciermacher, as founded solely on the ineffable experience of the adherent i.e. his personal feeling, after conceding the point to its detractors that it is irrational and arbitrary and of the same nature as "illusion" and "opium."

The Western humanities continued to speak of "man" and

"humanity." But in their romanticised understanding, these terms denoted Western man and Western humanity. If they did not exclude the billion "blacks" the billion "browns" and the billion "yellows" of Asia, Africa and Latin American, it counted them only as approximations of humanity which may be colonized, exploited and used for the welfare of Western humanity. Certainly they ought to be studied; but they ought to be so as specimens of an age that once was Western, and thus contribute to the Western man's historical (evolutionary) understanding of himself.

Ethnocentrism is internally divisive; for it is always possible to find within any defined group sub-groups which reveal a greater concentration of innate characteristics than the larger group. Such "facts" could then furnish the base for a smaller group to call itself an ethnic entity endowed with a stronger particularism. Hence besides separating the Westerners from the rest of the world with which they were coming into more intensive contact because of the development of industry and transportation, romanticism divided the West into mutually hostile and competitive nations, each seeking its "national interest" as if it were the criterion of all good and evil. The nations of the West learnt from and readily accepted the findings of one another. The romantic insights, analyses and expressions of one nation were quickly acknowledged as true of another, adopted and applied as if they were one's own.

The Western social sciences—history, geography economics, political science, sociology and anthropology—were all developed under the impetus provided by romanticism. All of them each in its own way, are based upon the ethnocentric view that the nation or ethnic entity in its well defined geography and demography but infinite and woozy history, is the ultimate unit of analysis and value. When they speak of "society" or "social order," they mean their own national entity or order. Some say it openly on their first pages others leave it unsaid as their most basic needless-to-be said assumption. Sociology boldly affirms the ethnocentrist thesis because it deals directly with, society and social order.

Political science follows. Western geography can conceive of the world only as a satellite to the West a world revolving around England, America, France, Germany, or Italy as its heart and core, depending on the author and place of publication. Western economics was at its earlier stages impertinent enough to claim for itself the status of a universal science. But it was put back in its place as a Western analysis of a Western nation by the arch-romanticists and ethnocentrist of Europe, the Nazis. The same bombastic claims made on behalf of the discipline by Karl Marx were denied in practice by Lenin and Khrushec. However, their regime has not yet permitted a statement to this effect to appear in print; but it allowed a fair measure of ethnocentric (in this case, national-socialistic) declarations to be included in the new U.S.S.R. constitution of 1978.

Finally, anthropology is the boldest of all. In its view, "humanity" means ethnicity and is logically equivalent to and convertible with it. In the last two centuries, its effect has been to whip up humankind into a frenzy of ethnocentric consciousness by singling out one subgroup after another, and contracting for it an ideology and exiology out of that group's innate characteristics or what its advocates have fabricated and declared to be innate and particular to that ethnic group. Instead of identifying and emphasizing what is universally human, its whole concern is to identify, to develop and to below up to great proportion the particular.

Islam recognizes the family as the constitute unit of social order; and buttress its extended form with legislation regarding inheritance and dependence to enable the largest possible family membership to eat from the same kitchen, and hence economically; mutually to support the social, emotional and mental health and prosperity of the members. Beyond the family, Islam recognizes humanity, the universal social order. Man's membership in this order is its concern in the social sciences. Human groupings between the family and humankind, namely, the country, or region, the people or nation. Islam regards purely as administrative units which are absolutely irrelevant to the definition of good and evil, to the interpretation and application of the shariah. The arts, the humanities and the social sciences of the modern West must therefore be totally recast. A new foundation of first principles should be given them which are concordant with the universalism of Islam. And they ought to receive from the Islamic thinker a new exiology—viz., Islamic values and ends—as ultimate objectives for guiding social research.

IV. The Workplan

The objectives of the workplan are the following :

(1) To master the disciplines.
(2) To master the Islamic legacy;
(3) To establish the specific relevance of Islam to each area of modern knowledge.
(4) To seek ways for creative synthesis between the legacy and modern knowledge.
(5) To launch Islamic thought on the trajectory which leads it to fulfillment of the divine patterns of Allah (SWT).

To realize thee objectives, a number of steps must be taken. Their logical order defines the order of priority belonging to each step.

A. *The necessary Steps Leading to Islamization of Knowledge.*

Step 1. Mastery of the Western Discipline; Categories Breakdown.

The disciplines, as they stand today in their most advanced state in the West, must be broken down into categories, principles,, methodologies, problems and themes. Such breakdown must reflect the "table of contents" of a classic textbook of the discipline's methodology, or the syllabus of a course in the discipline which all graduate courses in that discipline assume their students to have taken and mastered. Such breakdown will not be couched in technical terms, nor in chapters' titles. It would have to be couched in sentence-form, making clear what the technical terms mean, and explaining the categories, principles, problems and dominant themes of the discipline in its Western and higher form.

Step 2. Discipline Survey

Every discipline ought to be surveyed and essays written on it to lay bare the broad outlines of its genesis and historical development, the growth of its methodology, the widening of its field of vision, the main contributions its great votaries have made. An annotated bibliography of the most important works should conclude the survey for each discipline. It should include, in categorized and ordered form, all books and articles upon which knowledge of the discipline stands, and without which no mastery of it may be achieved.

This step has for purpose to ascertain Muslim understanding and mastery of the discipline as it developed in the West. Clearly substantiated and amply annotated and footnoted, the discipline survey would constitute a base of common understanding for specialists on the discipline which they are expected to Islamize. Since disciplines in the West today have become "many splendored things" because of the explosion of knowledge, it would be necessary for Islamic scholars dealing with that discipline to touch base and agree together on the identity, history, topography and frontiers of the object of their Islamization efforts.

Step 3. Mastery of the Islamic legacy. The Anthology

Before any elaboration of the specific relevance of Islam to the discipline, it is necessary to discover what the legacy of Islam had to say on the discipline. The legacy of the ancestors must remain for us the starting point of the relevance of Islam. Our Islamization of the discipline would be all the poorer if it did not take the legacy into account and did not benefit from the insights of the ancestors. However, the contribution of the legacy to the discipline is not ready for the modern researcher to obtain, to read or to understand. Indeed, the modern researcher is not equipped even to search in the legacy for Islam's contribution to the discipline. The reason is that the categories of the modern discipline, sometimes even its very name, are unknown as such in the legacy. The Western trained Muslim scholar is too often defeated by the inaccessibility of the legacy. He is strongly tempted to give up in despair, judging that the legacy is silent on the matter in hand whereas the fact is that he is unfamiliar with the legacy's categories under which the sort of material relevant to his discipline is classified. Moreover, the Western trained Muslim scholar has neither the time nor the energy requisite for successful exploration of the vast and colossal works of the legacy of Islamic learning.

On the other hand, the traditionally trained Muslim scholars, masters of the Islamic legacy, can neither discover nor can establish the relevance of the legacy to the modern disciplines because of their ignorance of those disciplines. This is so despite their expertise in the legacy. They are unfamiliar with the topics, the problems and themes of the modern disciplines, Therefore, it is necessary to instruct them in what is needed and then turn them loose on the legacy to draw from it what is pertinent. For this, the products of steps 1 and 2 serve the purpose, by familiarizing the experts with the modern disciplines and thus providing them with a criterion of relevance which they can use in their searches.

This step involves the preparation of several volumes of anthologies of selected readings from the legacy for each modern discipline, arranged according to the categories of that discipline. These anthologies would give the modern Muslim scholar ready access to the legacy in the area of his spaceialization. They would present in a topical order familiar to him, the best that the legacy has contributed to the range of issues which are the main objects of his disciplined study. Since the modern Muslim disciplinarian has neither time nor know-how to reach the legacy by himself (in most cases he does not even know he language of the legacy). no familiarity with the legacy—let alone the mastery of it, is possible for him without these anthologies.

Step 4. Mastery of the Islamic legacy: The Analysis

In order to bring the achievements of the Islamic legacy

closer to the understanding of the modern Western trained scholar, it is necessary to do more than merely to present in anthological form, pages of materials dealing with a given subject. The ancestors had done their own work of relating the Islamic vision to the problems which faced them. And they did so under influence of all sorts of factors and forces which pressed upon them for attention. In order to understand their crystallization of the Islamic vision, their works must needs be analyzed against their historical background, and the relations of the problem at issue with the other departments of human life and thought identified and exposed. Historical analysis of the contributions of the legacy will undoubtedly illuminate numerous area of the Islamic vision itself. It is conducive to a better understanding of the vision to learn how the ancestors understood and were moved by it; how they translated it into prescriptions for action and a style for conduct; how is helped them overcome and solve their peculiar difficulties and problems.

Such analyses of the contributions of the Islamic legacy cannot be undertaken at random. A hierarchy of priorities ought to be established and Islamic scholars invited to undertake them in order. Above all the main principles, the major problems, the continuing themes—those issues which promise relevance to the problems of the present, ought to be the object of Islamic educational and research strategy.

Step 5. Establishment of the Specific Relevance of Islam to the Disciplines

The foregoing four steps amount to posing the problem before the Islamic thinker. Together, they sum up for him the development of the discipline which Muslims have missed during their slumber. Equally they should inform him with the greatest authority and clarity possible of the contribution of the Islamic legacy to the areas studied by the disciplines, and generally, to the general goals of the discipline. These material will have to be made more specific by translating them into principles on a level with the modern discipline in generality, of theorization, of reference and application. In this regard, the nature of the modern discipline, its constituent methods, principles, problems, objectives and hope, its achievement and shortcomings—all of these should be related to the Islamic legacy; and the legacy's specific relevance to each must be deduced from the general contribution. Three major questions must be posed and answers to them found. The first is, What did the Islamic legacy of learning, from the Quran to the modernists, contribute to the whole range of issues envisaged by the discipline? The second is, How does the Islamic legacy's contribution to the discipline compare or contrast with the achievement of the discipline? Where has the legacy fulfilled, fallen short of or transcended the vision and scope of the discipline ? The third is, Given the areas or issues in which the Islamic legacy has given little or nothing, in which direction may Muslim effort be henceforth exerted in order to fill the discrepancy, to reformulate the problem, to enlarge the vision ?

Step 6. Critical Assessment of the Modern Discipline: The State of the Art

Now that both the modern discipline and the Islamic legacy have been exposed, their methodologies, principles, themes, problems and achievements have been identified, surveyed and analyzed, and finally, now that the specific relevance of Islam to the discipline has been clarified and established, the discipline should be subjected to critical analysis from the standpoint of Islam. This is a major step in the Islamization of knowledge. All the previous five steps seems to lead to it as a sort of *preparation*. In its historical development, the circumstantial factors which determined the discipline to be what it is must be identified and exposed. Its methodology—what is regards as its data and problems, their classification and categorization; what is regards as its theory, the first principles under which it treats its problems—must be analyzed and tested for reductionism, adequacy, reasonableness and consistency with the five-fold unity which Islam teaches. The discipline's dominant problems and persistent themes ought to be analyzed for their assumptions, their importance and relationship to the essential vision of the discipline. The discipline's ultimate purpose ought to be critically related to its methodology as well as to its front line objectives. Has it fulfilled the vision of its own founders? Has it realized its role in the total enterprise of knowledge seeking that is the human quest? Has it achieved the human expectation of it as part of the general human quest? Has it established for the understanding and for history the divine patterns of creation it was meant to establish? The answers to these questions should give a genuine state-of-the-art report on the discipline from the standpoint of Islam, as well as to shed the necessary light upon the areas where one or another kind of Islamic correction, amendment, addition or elimination is necessary.

Step 7. Critical Assessment of the Islamic legacy: The State of the Art

By the Islamic legacy we first mean the Holy Quran , the word of Allah (SWT) and the *sunnah* of the Prophet Mohammed (SAAS). These are not object of criticism or of assessment. The divine status of the Quran and the normativeness of the *sunnah* are beyond question. Muslim understanding of these two sources however is not. Rather, it is subject to both assessment and criticism in terms of the principles which the two revelatory sources provide. So too is everything else in the legacy, which may be derived from either of the two two sources by human intellectual endeavour. This human element needs to be reviewed because it is not playing the dynamic role in Muslim life which it once did, and which it is always supposed to play. The relevance of our human understanding of the revaluation to the various problems of the present must be subject to critic from three areas of reference: First, the Islamic vision in so far as it can be established from the sources of revelation directly and from its concrete instantiation in history by the Prophet (SAAS), his companions and their descendants (RAA); Second, the present needs of the *ummah* around the world; and Third, all modern knowledge represented by the discipline. If the legacy is found to be adequate or erring, it should be corrected by our present endeavour. If it is adequate, further development and creative re-crystallization are necessary for the future. At any rate, no islamic stand is viable today which does not relate to the legacy of Islam.

To do so, it must be based upon through knowledge of the legacy in its strength and weakness. Moreover, today's and tomorrow's Islamic stand must assume a form that is continues with the legacy, rather than a radical departure from it.

The task of assessing the Islamic legacy's contribution in each field of human activity, must therefore fall upon the shoulders of the expert in that activity. They are the monitors of Muslim need in that field and they are the masters of the modern discipline studying that activity. Certainly, they should be assisted by the experts in the legacy in order to guarantee the most adequate and correct understanding of it possible.

Step 8. Survey of the Ummah's Major Problems

Awakening from its slumber the *ummah* is today confronted with formidable problems on all fronts. Its economic, social and political problems which are overpowering by any standard are "iceberg tops" of its deeper- lying malaise on the intellectual and moral levels. The whole "iceberg," or complex of causes, manifestations, dialectic with other phenomena and consequences of the *ummah's* problems, require empirical survey and critical analysis. The wisdom of the discipline should be brought to bear upon the *ummah* problems, i.e., to enable the Muslims to understand them correctly, to assess with precision their effect upon the life of the *ummah*, and to chart out exactly their influence upon the cause of Islam in the world. No Muslims disciplinarian may pursue his disciplined study as pure, ivory-tower, intellectual curiosity; as it were, in isolation from the *ummah's,* existential realities or from its hopes and aspirations. The prayer to Allah (SWT) to grant us a "useful knowledge" must apply to our disciplinarian pursuits, by bending our gaze to the problems at hand. Above all, the problem of disciplines and of our educational institutions, viz, the persistence of their de-Islamization and the progress of our re- Islamization attempts. Simultaneously, our attention must be devoted to the main problems affecting the *ummah's* political, social, economic, intellectual, cultural, moral and spiritual problems; indeed, the *ummah's* problems in every department of human endeavour.

Step 9. Survey of the Problems of Humankind

It is an intrinsic part of the Islamic vision to bear responsibility to only for the welfare of the *ummah* but for that of the whole human race. Indeed, the *amanah* of Allah (SWT) encompasses the whole universe; and man's responsibility must accord therewith. It is true that the *ummah* is in many respects backward and non- developed by comparison to other *umam.* But in respect of possessing the truth, the ideological statement of it which is most conducive to religious, ethical, and material prosperity at the same time, the *ummah* is second to none. Because of Islam, the *ummah* alone possesses the vision requisite for the felicity of human kind, for history to be as Allah (SWT) has desired it to be.

Hence, the Islamic thinker is called upon to confront the problems facing the world today and to contend for their solution according too Islam. As carrier of the Islamic vision, the *ummah* is today the only viable speaker for the human masses of the earth whose cause is lost between imperialist—colonialists and revolutionaries seeking to throw off their yokes. Ethnocentrism is ravaging inter human relations worldwide. Alcohol and other drugs, sexual promiscuity and deterioration of the family ethic, illiteracy and laziness, militarism and armament build up, the rape of nature and the threat to the earth's ecological balance have been doing the rest without effective check from any source. Certainly these problems constitute another area of reference for Islamic thought, planning and action, that is of crucial importance to the *ummah's* felicity as well as to the felicity of humankind. To solve these problems and to lead humankind to felicity, that is to prosperity with justice and dignity, cannot be separated from the Islamic hope.

Step 10. Creative Analyses and Syntheses

Having understood and mastered the modern disciplines as well as the islamic legacy. having assessed their strengths and weak-nesses; having established the relevance of Islam to the specific areas of inquiry of the disciplines; having identified and grasped the problems facing the *ummah* in it march in history as the *khulafe* of Allah on earth; and having understood the larger problem of humankind from the standpoint of Islam which enjoins upon the Muslims to be *shuhada ala al nas* in human history, the stage is now set for the Islamic mind to make its creative leap. A new road must be blazed for Islam in the fifteenth century if it is to resume its world leadership and continue its salutary and civilizing role in human affairs.

A creative synthesis must be struck between the Islamic legacy and the modern disciplines which would bridge over the gap of centuries of no-development. The legacy of Islamic learning must become continuous with the modern achievement and start to move the frontiers of knowledge to more distant horizons than the modern disciplines have envisaged. The creative synthesis must maintain its relevance to the *ummah's* reality by addressing itself to its problems which have already been identified and analyzed. Indeed, it must provide efficacious solutions to the problems of the whole world as well as address the ever-new issues presented by Islamic hope. What are the specific contents of that hope in every department of human life and how does the new synthesis move the *ummah* and humankind forward in its realization of that hope?

Given the specific relevance of the legacy to a certain topic or problem, and give the particular character of the pertinent issue, what options are legitimate for the Muslim to pursue ? Certainly, in every case, a vast array of options are possible, which approximate or stand at a distance from the Islamic ideal; which are more or less effective; which generate or retard movement toward Islam's ultimate goals. Which of these options is possible, necessary or indispensable, desirable, legitimate? By what criteria may the specific relevance of Islam (its *shariah,* its ethic, its culture and spirit) to the problem in hand be ascertained? By what methods may the efficacy of the solutions proposed be measured ? By what principles may the contribution of the creative synthesis be projected, tested and evaluated; the proper emendations and corrections introduced, and their progress and efficacy monitored and evaluated?

Step 11. Recasting the Disciplines under the Framework of Islam: The University Textbook

By nature, the Islamically determined minds will not all reach the same solutions, or choose the same options in their determination of the relevance of Islam to the present and future existence of the *ummah.* Such diversity will not be undesirable, but highly welcome. We need scores of diverse critical analysis by the Islamically committed and modern- disciplined in order to enrich the *ummah's* consciousness of it own desiderata and goals. In fact, the *ummah* may not be said to have recaptured its dualism of the first centuries of the Hijrah unless Islam itself becomes again for all Muslims a cauldron constantly bubbling with new ideas in which Allah's patterns may be objectified in nature; an infinite mine of ethical and creative options in which His divine values and commandments may be concretized and instantiates in history.

It is out of a plenum of such new insights into the meaning of Islam, of creative options for the realization of that meaning, that the desired college or university text book may be written for the discipline. The essays representing individual breakthrough in any topic, branch or problem must pile high in order to provide a " back ground vision," or "field of relevance" from which the Islamic vision for the discipline may be drawn.

Islamization of the discipline is not fulfilled by one textbook, even if competing perfectly with the foregoing requirement. Scores of textbooks are needed to develop the intellectuals stamina of Muslim minds. Above all, numerous books are immediately needed to fill the educational needs of the various university levels (freshman, sophomore, junior, senior and graduate). More books are needed to satisfy the Muslims needs which are infinite and to project and crystallize the vision of Islam which is equally infinite. However, priority dictates that our first efforts be devoted to the production of a standard textbook in each discipline which would state definitively the relevance of the Islamic vision to that discipline- and serve as a general guide or future Islamic minds to follow. Hopefully, it need not be said that any attempt to preempty the production of the university text book by opting over the foregoing steps is bound to result in mediocrity. The Prophet Mohammed (SAAS) commanded us to do anything that we enter upon doing, *perfecly.* The university textbook is truly the final end of the long process of Islamization of the disciplines. It is the work which crowns the long search of all foregoing steps.

Step 12. Dissemination of Islamized Knowledge

It would be idle, even if great, should all these works be produced by Islamic scholars and be kept in the privacy of their personal collections. And it would be a great pity if they should remain known only to a closed circle of their authors' acquaintances and friends, or utilized by the educational institutions of their neighbourhoods or countries alone. Whatever is produced for the same of Allah (AWT) belongs to the whole *Ummah* The benefit of it will not win Allah's blessing unless it is brought to and is appropriate by the greatest number of His creatures. Although Muslims may, and indeed should, be materially rewarded for their intellectual effort, the work of thought in Islam cannot be copy-righted, i.e. monopolized for profit. The fact that it is produced for the sake of Allah (SWT) imposes upon it always to remain available to whomsoever wishes to invest in the paper, ink and binding necessary to carry it.

Secondly, the intellectual work to be produced in the foregoing steps in intended as something by which the Muslims of the world— nay, humankind—are to be awakened, enlightened and enriched. They are the readers, or "consumers" of the product. However, being Islamic, executed for same of Allah (SWT), and carrying within it the vision of islam itself, it is expected to do more than to inform. In presence of the vision of Islam human consciousness should lose its poise, become astir, and generate new energies hitherto unknown. Under its spell, the subject is expected to become an instrument of the divine will, and to be ready to press forward and achieve in God's name what he had never dreamt of achieving before.

That is why the work plan calls for measures to place every one of the works produced under the foregoing steps in the hand of every muslim university academician free of change. To such academician, the given article, essay, pamphlet, anthology or books should come as a personal invitation to join in this enterprise, become a "producer" of better works in consequence of his appropriation of the product in hand. Equally, to place such products in the hand of all Muslim thinkers is the greatest reward possible in this world. This is not to obviate the need for the material rewards; but for the scholar determined by the vision of Islam and devoted to seek *wajh Allah ta'ala* there can be no greater reward than to plant that vision in the heart and mind of another human; no greater duty than to nurture that vision in the consciousness of the muslims of the world.

Thirdly, the products of this workplan should be officially presented to the universities and colleges of the Muslim World with the request to consider them for possible adoption as required readings in the pertinent course of instruction. Naturally, they would have to be translated to the languages of instruction in the various countries of the Muslim World.

Other Necessary Aids to Islamization of Knowledge

1. *Conferences and seminar:* A series of conferences and seminars should be held between experts in the relevant fields designed to solve any problems transcending any single disciple. The *ummah's* problems mostly fall in this category requiring all the light numerous disciplines could shed on them at the same time. Another series of conferences should be held between scholars specialized in various aspects or areas within one and the same discipline in order to assist one another in their respective tasks.

2. *Classroom Workshops for Faculty Training:* Once the textbook and the literature preceding it in steps 1 - 12 have been produced, it is necessary for the teaching faculty to be trained in their use. The experts who produced these works should be given the opportunity to meet the faculty and discuss with them the unwritten presuppositions, the unprojected effects of the theories, principles or solutions they have included in their essays and books. In addition, such meetings would explore the pedagogical issues of materials—presentation and thus help the faculty to achieve the ultimate goal efficiently.

16

Islamization Through Art: Implications for Education

LOIS LAMYA' AL-FARUQI

(Abstract: Defines the role of the arts in Islamic education, and highlights the areas which — economic, political, spiritual and artisitc — need to be revitalised for initiating the process of Islamisation).

I. The Present Situation

In recent centuries, we Muslims have been taught to despise the arts, both those of the visual (or seen) and the aural (or heard) variety. In fact, it would not be an overstatement to say that the field of art is a "disaster area" today in Muslim education and Muslim life. Many of us grew up in the Muslim world with the lesson that poetry was mere "play on words", that the visual arts distracted from prayer and meditation, and that music was a stimulant to fornication. This disdain for the arts came from two sources.

First, let us delineate the internal source, that which was created by the Muslims themselves. Probably there is no argument with the statement that recent centuries of Muslim history comprise a period of decline, with only occasional bright spots of reform and progressive activity. We shall not go into the many and varied reasons for that decline at this time. What is important for us to remember here, in defining the role of the arts in Islamic education, is that in any period of decline a people loses not only its economic and political powers and creativity, but also its spiritual and artistic vitality. This has certainly been evident in the Muslim world.

Political rivalries and economic failures in recent times have been coupled with a corresponding deterioration in the confidence and vigour that in better times characterized the spiritual, the social, and the artistic achievements. Many debates have been waged whether the decline of material and political aspects of civilization brought spiritual decline, or vice versa. Whatever, the outcome of that debate, we know that in recent centuries the powers of the Muslims weakened, and this was accompanied by a comparable decline in their aesthetic appreciation and their artistic creativity. As a concomitant of this decline, many literati, architects, sculptors, craftsmen, singers and instrumentalists lent themselves to sentimental, naturalistic and even sensual art tendencies. The Muslims gradually found themselves less and less able to distinguish between the good and the bad in new art expressions; and as a result, they tended to question the validity or worth of all art. Puritanical reformers, who always flourish in times of decline, supported them in their art "cop out", though of course for entirely different reasons.

It was on such a scene that the European colonialists entered the muslim world. These alien peoples contributed the external source for further exacerbation of the problem. Because they came from entirely different backgrounds, they were seldom able to understand the Islamic art works with which they came in contact in the colonized areas. They could see them only through eyes dominated by their own cultural values and styles. As examples of Western-European-Christian art, of course, the Islamic items were always found wanting by these non-Muslim aliens. In addition, not a few of them realized the political and even missionary advantages of wooing us into forgetting our aesthetic tradition and adopting that of the European conquerors. What better and more unobtrusive way was there to cut the Muslim people off from their roots than to encourage them to think that their artistic pursuits were at best inconsequential, while, at worst, they were morally debilitating? What better way to cut us off aesthetically from our relationship with the Qur'an, that divine product of literary art in Islamic culture, than to encourage us in the idea that our literature was deficient and inferior to that of Western Europe. We, in our weakened condition, were not able to withstand this onslaught or to counter it by explaining to Muslims and non-Muslims alike the significance of Islamic art and its relationship to the Qur'an and *tawhid.* For the most part, we failed to recognize the ways in which European arts were incongruous to the Muslim world view, however fitting they may have been to that of Western Christianity.

With these internal and external pressures opposing the Islamic arts, it is not surprising that every field of aristic endeavour in recent times discloses few outstanding products which can match those of earlier centuries. Few Muslims today can talk intelligently about either the aural or visual arts, and many of those who do speak about art, hold a blind intellectual commitment to the premises of Western art while maintaining a school boyish attachment to the understanding of their Islamic faith. They seem completely unaware of the incongruity of this schizophrenic combination. Except for literature, public as well as private educational institutions in the Muslim world ignore the Islamic arts. Even literature is often down-graded by modernist educators and men of letters who call for the teaching and translation of the great works of European literature, instead of encouraging knowledge of the classics of the Islamic heritage—above all, of the Qur'an. Except in literature, contemporary writers on Islamic art are generally non-Muslim Westerners who have done admirable work in collecting and preserving Islamic art works but who have, almost without exception, failed to see the art creation of the Muslim peoples except as poor substitutes for western art. Even where art is included in the curricula of institutions for general education, or schools for professionals, it is almost always training in European art which is provided. From the earliest grades, the child is taught that figural drawings are art, and that the abstract designs of Islamic art are somehow an extraneous matter to be ignored. Every art exhibit or museum of contemporary art in the Muslim world comprises a collection of local caricatures of Western art which have little if any interest or appeal for the Muslim populace.

Perhaps some of you would say this is all as it should be. You would maintain that appreciation of and creation in the arts are degrading pastimes which undermine the religious purity of the individual and of the society. In order to deal with such a position and determine whether it is valid or not, it is necessary to understand what functions or benefits art might have for a society. Only then can we ascertain what role, if any, it should play in the future education curriculum being planned for Muslim communities around the world, and what steps should be taken to establish that role.

II. Functions of Art in Muslim Society

1. The most important function of art for the Muslim community rests in its ability to reinforce the message of *tawhid.* But how can a painting, a building, or a performance of music reinforce a religious truth? In order to answer this question, we must remember that *tawhid* is a message of monotheism which admits of no confusion between the creator and the created world. Allah, *subhanahu wa to'ala,* is so utterly other than His creation that when the Muslim of the past sought to express his deepest thoughts and convictions in an aesthetic way, he never chose the naturalistic portrayal of man and nature as subject matter or content of his art. Since the Qur'an tells us : "No vision can grasp Him..." (Holy Qur'an 6:103), the Muslim realized the futility and even blasphemy of visually depicting God. Likewise his ideas about the nature of existence and man could not successfully be expressed with characteral portraits or realistic scenes from nature. He needed to create a new way of directing man's thoughts toward transcendence. His solution involved the creation of intricate pattern known as arabesques. This solution was not a lifeless reaction to prohibitions and legal pronouncements. Instead it constituted a positive and creative answer to a problem of expression.

The intricate patterns known as arabesques are made up from a rich vocabulary to geometric figures, stylized plant motifs, and calligraphy. Even human and animal figures were sometimes used on a metal platter or in a miniature painting, but the artist of the Muslim world always felt impelled, whether consciously or unconsciously, to de-humanize and to de-naturalize those figures.

In poetry or epic the Muslim's aim was not the portrayal of an individual human's character or psychological yearnings. In music, since his mind was transcendence oriented, mood depiction and "tone painting" were never the goal. In fact, any sensuous or naturalistic portrayal would have offended the Muslim's religious as well as his religiously-determined artistic sensitivity.

Content (that is, the subject matter and motifs utilized in the art work) is not the only aspect of Islamic art that reinforces the message of *tawhid.* The structure or form (in other words, the way in which the subject-matter and motifs are organized) is equally representative of the translation of the Islamic religious message into aesthetic language. Islamic art evidences distinctive structures which are repeated in all the media—in the visual arts, in music, in literature, in architecture. Regardless of which of these structures is chosen by the sculptor, the architect, the weaver, the calligrapher, the poet, the musician, the architect, the aim of the arabesque is always to give the viewer or listener the impression of an infinite pattern. The limitlessness of Allah, which is proclaimed in His *sifat* or attributes, is thereby re-emphasized in visual and aural patterns.

These arabesque designs convey no feeling of beginning or end, whether produced for a carpet, a ceramics panel, a musical performance, or a building design. In all of them the pattern gives the impression of a necessary continuation beyond the limits of the art work. The central medallion of the carpet in Illustration 1, for example, is found in replica medallions at top and bottom. Additional partial medallions at right and left edges of the main field convey the impression of a pattern which can be continued *ad infinitum.* In Illustration 2 a similar effect is conveyed by the brass plated door made for the 14th century madrasah of Sultan Hasan in Cairo. A Qur'anic recitation or *qasidah* chanted or sung is always a series of beautiful literary-melodic phrases, none of which gives a feeling of finality. Another *ayah,* another *bayt* is always possible in this open-ended artistic expression.

Even the three-dimensional architectural monuments of the Muslim artists express infinite patterns. For example, Illustration 3 shows the never-ending aisle and arch patterns which meet the eye of any visitor to the Mosque of Cordova. These aisles and arches are repeated to vision as one looks down the aisles, across the aisles and even diagonally as the gaze is directed toward the corners of the building. In the Shahzadah Mosque of Istanbul, Turkey, another substantiation of the architectural arabesque is found. There one is made aware of the architect's intention to create, not a succession arches or aisles, but a succession of spaces. From the central domed area, additional semi-domes, exhedrae and window opening create a virtual explosion of space.

As an example of infinite pattern, the arabesque is also multi-centred. Illustration 4 gives evidence in ceramic decoration of this characteristic of Islamic design. One may choose any one of the floral hexagons as a starting point for viewing. Satisfying in itself as an arabesque of floral and leaf motifs. The diamond-shaped calligraphy motifs could be added as another step in a succession of ever-expanding designs. To begin from the floral hexagons is, however, an arbitrary decision. One could just as well choose the calligraphic diamond with its symmetrical repetition of the word "Allah" as a centre of attention and aesthetic interest. Moving from the centre, another pattern can be made by adding the geometric quadrilaterals as its four sides. Continuing in the search for additional arabesqe design two triangles could be included in our pattern. Then the floral hexagons could be added to create still another pattern for appreciation. The discovery can continue to the end of the arabesque panel and even beyond in the imagination of the spectator. One of the triangles could act as still another centre for pattern creation and thereby provide further examples of interlocking infinite patterns which are the "translation" into sensory media of the Islamic message of *tawhid.*

2. A second role that Islamic art can play for the Muslim community is to "open the door" to depths of meanings, to intuitions, which are difficult to achieve through discursive explanation. Anyone who has heard a verbal explanation of the idea of universal brotherhood which Islam teaches and experienced as well the feeling of universal brotherhood as he stands shoulder to shoulder

with his Muslim brothers in prayer, can testify to the immediacy and depth of understanding which the sensory experience can provide to the discursive message. The effect of a finely done art work, whether appreciated by the eye or the ear, will provide the same heightened translation of the discursive lesson to the sensitive spectator. A Muslim will not fail to be moved as he or she reads a passage describing some episode in the Prophet's life. Yet compare the depth of feeling and understanding which a beautifully chanted poem about the Prophet can evoke in the same Muslim believer.

As another example, let us consider that often repeated message of the holy Qur'an to take heed of the marvels of creation. The perfectly co-ordinated functioning of the sun and the moon (Qur'an 10:5), of night and day (10:6; 17:12), of the rain and the seasons (41:39; 45:5), of the animal species (45:4)—all of these reveal Allah's expert and masterful hand in creation,

> "Is there (not) in these
> An adjuration (or evidence)
> For those who understand?" (89:5)

They are surely "Signs for those who believe" (45:3). Suppose we were to couple such discursive statements with contemplation of an intricate arabesque in which interlocking patterns of beautiful and varied shapes cause our eyes to move in fascination from one coloured motif to the next in never-ending succession, we would find in the arabesque a beautiful reminder of Allah's mastery in creation. To recall this perfection, which is present in the tiniest crystal and largest galaxy of stars, produces a powerful effect on the Muslim believer. It draws him irresistibly to a contemplation of Allah's transcendence and produces a feeling of wonder and awe for His unlimited perfection and ability. We could not help but deepen or understanding of Allah's message by the contemplation of Islamic art if we have been taught to understand these arabesqe patterns, whether in two-or three-dimensional forms, as subtle metaphoric or symbolic representations of these deepest teachings of our faith.

3. The premise that the forms and patterns found in Islamic art are suggestive of our deepest convictions brings us to a third important function of art, that of psychological refreshment. No doubt the daily life of every individual brings many disappointments and many impressions of the futility of his efforts. Anyone of us may begin to doubt the good of striving and question the relation of this striving to the whole pattern of destiny. When surrounded by the aural and visual patterns of Islamic art, whether exemplified in the beautiful recitation of the Qur'an, performances of *taqasim* musical arabesques, Islamically inspired buildings, or two-dimensional patterns in colour and shape, the sensitive Muslim who has been trained in perceiving the intricate patterns of an aural or visual arabesque and in relating them to his world- and God-view, will not fail to be psychologically refreshed. These patterns and their myriad varieties are a reminder of the limitless power of the Transcendent who controls all, despite the seeming futility and transience of daily experience. When a Muslim perceives the forms revealed in this art as reminder of the complex and well-ordered precision of God, he (or she) find his (or her) faith in the significance of life renewed. He is reminded that he is not an insignificant and helpless pawn in history but an integral instrument of destiny and of Allah's plan for creation. In restores his rapport with the universe, and allows him to return to the sometimes petty tasks of everyday life, knowing that he can, through them, contribute his share toward the good and toward the realization of Allah's will.

4. Fourthly, the Islamic arts can contribute to the unity of our lives as Muslims by integrating our leisure occupations, relaxations and entertainments with other aspects of our lives. It is the contention of most Muslims that Islam prescribes for not only religious duties but for the cultural, social, economic and political life as well. In fact, Islam is described as not so much a religion in that limited sense so often given to the concept in the West, but as a complete way of life. If this is true, the means for joy, relaxation and entertainment should be as permeated by *tawhid* as any other aspect of life. Yet we have thought little of providing for any age group the means for Islamic entertainment. We leave the leisure

hours of our children and adults to be dominated by whatever the television, the movies or the radio can offer. And more often than not what those media offer contributes not merely neutral influences but has actually negative effects on the personalities and the ideas of the viewers or listeners. No one needs to be reminded of the damaging effects of the exploitation of violence and sex which are standard ingredients of entertainment in the 1980's. Every newspaper and magazine carries articles on this problem. When will we wake up to the fact that preaching *tawhid* on Friday will have little results if we live and play non-*tawhid* for the rest of the week? The Islamic arts can serve a valuable function if they are encouraged to flourish as an avenue for refreshment and entertainment.

5. A fifth way in which the arts can fulfil an important role in the Islamic community, whether in Western nations or in the Muslim world, is to aid in the Islamic education of children. Every educator knows how difficult it is to reach most children with a message that is purely discursive, i.e., a purely verbal explanation. Yet up to now our educational institutions have taken little initiative in utilizing art for propagating the message of *tawhid*—or any other message advocated by an Islamic society—among children. Where can we find a school in the Muslim world, not to speak of one serving our Islamically deprived children of North America and Europe, where a beautifully inlaid metal tray is brought to class in order that the children may learn to appreciate an arabesque pattern? Where in any of our schools or colleges can we point to a course in art education which deals with Islamic, not Western, art? Where, in any of the Muslim countries, is calligraphy, as an artistic expression, cultivated by our children? Where can our young people learn an appreciation of the past heritage of Islamic art or develop an aesthetic taste to help them judge between the good and bad in contemporary art? Unable to discern which examples are truly representative and fitting sensory expression of *tawhid* and which are cheap imitations which depend on sensual, not sensory, stimulation, the average Muslim, uneducated as he is, in the appreciation or creation of his art, can only depend on unreliable "gut feelings" for discriminating between works of art. Often he takes the easier

but less responsible course of discarding all art as unsuitable. If our children continue to be raised in a non-Islamic atmosphere without training in their schools to counter the alien influences, there seems to be little doubt that the adults of tomorrow will have little chance to cultivate even "gut feelings" for their artistic tradition. We will have thereby destroyed another link in the chain of the unity of our lives.

III. Implications for Education

We see then that a vital and well-understood Islamic art tradition can play an important role in the Islamization of the Muslim peoples. Realizing this, what suggestions can we make to those who are involved with plans for the improvement of education throughout the Muslim world? What are the needs of the Muslim community in art education? What are the steps which must be taken before aesthetic training can become an important factor in counteracting the de-Islamization of Muslims and in furthering the well-rounded and unified life of the Muslim community?

1. First of all, there is a need to remove our old prejudices against the arts, to open our minds to discover the valid gains to be derived from that art which is truly a reflection or "translation" of Islamic ideals and the Islamic message. We cannot go on "sticking our heads in the sand" in order to avoid the difficult job of discerning which art is suitable and which art is incompatible with Islamic thought and culture. We must remember that the artistic propensity of human beings is as old as historical records of the activities of man. If we neglect to direct and guide the course of that propensity, we cannot count on its remaining dormant. On the contrary, it will be stimulated by other agencies or people or ideologies which have far less noble aims to promote.

2. Secondly, our educational institutions or their supporters need to initiate a research programme which would help us characterize those kinds of artistic products which are suitable to the message of *tawhid* and to the renaissance of the Muslim peoples. This can only be done with a thorough study of the Qur'an and the *Hadith*. Such a study should not be merely concerned with discovering

what prohibitions and prescriptions are clearly spelled out in those sources for Islamic guidance; it should equally be involved in discovering in what more subtle ways the Qur'an itself, as a supreme example of Islamic literary art, points the way for those content and formal characteristics which should be encouraged in all the Islamic arts. But how can this be achieved if we leave the field of research on Islamic art to non-Muslim historians? As everyone knows, the history of Islamic art is at present almost a purely western discipline. Of course, no one needs to remind the reader of the misconceptions of the nature of Islamic art that fill the works of these scholars, despite their thoroughness and their intelligence.

3. A third requirement for a viable art education programme for Muslims is the preparation of new textbooks and art materials for students of various age levels. To be effective, these books and materials should not only contain discursive statements about the arts. They must be equally replete in attractive illustrations of examples and suggestions for actual creative projects in which the students can actively participate. Non-Muslim scholars will never—can never—do this job for us.

4. At the same time as we produce teaching materials for Islamic art, we must train teachers for elementary, secondary, and college courses in art. How can Western educational institutions train these people for us, when they view Islamic art either as a primitive aesthetic expression which has not yet reached the skill or perfection of Western art, or as one which could not blossom because of an inhibiting prohibition against figural art? Teachers trained by such philosophies will kill the art of the Muslims instead of encouraging it.

Unless we achieve success in teacher training, we can never hope to cultivate an appreciation of the legacy of Islamic art among the Muslims. Nor can we train an audience for art which would be perceptive enough to demand contemporary works which are truly Islamic or to choose between the suitable and unsuitable in contemporary art works. Without such aesthetically-aware Muslims, the benefits described above that the arts can provide will be lost to our Muslim communities.

5. A fifth suggestion for art education in a Muslim society involves stimulating the creation of art products. One way to achieve this is through the proper training of professionals. At present, art education is either totally Western, even when conducted in our Muslim world universities, or it is taught haphazardly by the "guru" method, without encouragement or support from public or private sources. Those persons who defy public opposition to art and artists are forced to go abroad for professional training. Of course, when they return, they find themselves still more estranged from their societies because of their non-Islamic art training in Russia, Western Europe or America. Only a very few of them manage to "digest" their foreign training and then go on to produce artistic works which can be called "Islamic" in content and form.

We cannot expect every educational establishment in the Muslim world will provide professional training in music, architecture and the visual arts; but it is not too much to suggest that each Muslim country provides, in one of its institutions, a sound programme for professionals in the various arts, a programme based on Islamic aesthetic principles. The training of the school children at all levels will have the effect of creating for the future a discerning audience for Islamic works of art. This in itself will serve as a second stimulus for new creative efforts since appreciation and commissions and jobs will be forthcoming from an enlightened patronage. Another means for stimulating the creation of new art products which are representative of the characteristics of Islamic art would be to hold international symposia or seminars for artists which would foster and encourage their interest in the principles of truly Islamic art. Exhibits, lectures and panel discussions connected with the seminars should be designed to show the artists, as well as the public, how the various arts can be related to *tawhid.* These seminars would provide adult education in the characteristics of content and form which reveal that relationship as it applies to each of the arts and in each of the countries where Muslims represent a sizable portion of the population. There could be no more healthy encouragement to pan-Islamic awareness and solidarity. There could be no more convincing proof to both artists and non-professionals attending that Islam is operative in every aspect of a Muslim's life.

FEASIBILITY OF COMMERCIAL BANKING WITHOUT RATE OF INTEREST AND ITS SOCIO-ECONOMIC SIGNIFICANCE

Rates of interest are a critical factor in all functions of modern commercial banking; they are used for attracting deposits and in determining the investment policy of banks. In each case they measure the reward for 'waiting' or 'parting from liquidity' and for 'risk-bearing'.

The rate of interest varies with the period of waiting (parting from liquidity) as well as the degree of risk. Generally the greater the time span involved or the higher the risk assumed, other things being equal, the higher is the rate of interest. In this manner the rates of interest paid on deposits and the rates charged on lending money also determine the profitability of banks.

In view of the strategic position of rates of interest in commercial banking, and also because an exchange economy has several structures of rates of interest, it is questioned whether commercial banking can be viable without a rate of interest. If so, what will be the *modus operandi* of commercial banks in accordance with Islamic Shari'ah?

The purpose of this paper is to demonstrate that commercial banking without rate of interest is not only commercially feasible; but it can produce better socio-economic results.

Islamic Shari'ah and the Rate of Interest

Islamic Shari'ah is quite clear on the prohibition of rate of interest. For example, Qur'an, ayhas: 2:275; 2:276; 2:278; 2:279; 3:130; 4:161 and 30:39 do not make any distinction between production loans and consumption loans; between compound rate of interest and simple rate of interest; between high or low rates of interest. They denounce outright any type of interest, in any form or at any rate.

The present distinction of 'usury' and 'interest' has been coined to suit the transformation in the meaning of interest so that it may be acceptable to Christian canon law. Islamic Shari'ah, however, does not accept any such codification of interest-bearing loans by treating them as new norms. Thus instead of searching for scope for the transformation of the meaning of Ribah, a positive approach is to take Islamic Shari'ah as a fixed axiom, and consider the banking principles and practices as a variable factor.

This approach is not ambiguous. Banking principles and practices have never been fixed. They have undergone changes over time and have been altered to suit the special circumstances and needs of different countries. A recent example is the 'banking revolution' of 1960 in the U.S.A., where the banks have shifted their operation from 'banking' to 'non-banking' business — from short-term deposits and loans to long-term deposits and loans ; from investment in mortgages to direct investment in real estate. For increasing their profitability and ensuring stability and growth, commercial banks now depend upon non-banking and non-financial business.

Moreover, banks of the advanced industrialized countries, in their quest for more profits and better investment opportunities, have crossed their own national boundaries and are operating in different social, political and economic conditions after adjusting changes in their principles and policies to fit into the specific requirements of developing countries.

Furthermore, banks in almost all countries of the world function under an imposed molecular structure and pedestrian operating technology. The legal restrictions encompass, in most countries, all manner of government control including direct intervention in the prerogatives of commercial and development banks. The government exercises control in entry, merger and branching, portfolio regulation of rates and deposits — time, saving, and demand and usury laws.

The chief feature of banking legislation is that there is no uniformity. It differs from country to country, yet the banks have shaped their operation to suit the legal requirements. The principles and policies of commercial banks have been designed within the legal framework of each country.

Hence in, subordinating banking principles and practice to Islamic shari'ah, we are not adopting any exceptional course. The molecular structure of Ribah-free commercial banks and their behaviour must be determined by the Law of the Qur'an.

According to Islamic Shari'ah, Ribah-free Banks (RFBs) are not debarred from earning profit ; but this should not be through the medium of rates of interest. In earning profit either by trade or by any other 'legitimate' means, RFBs will observe all those precautions which modern banks follow by ensuring safety and liquidity of funds. There will thus be a departure only in means and in methods, but not in the objective of earning profits. Modern commercial banks make a selection of assets from the available menu of investment material according to their liability characteristics and legal framework; RFBs will choose investment avenues according to their own liability characteristics and the framework of the Shari'ah.

Economic Feasibility of Banking without Rates of Interest

It is, however, contended that this will not be commercially and financially viable proposition, mainly because the lending of money is one of the essentials functions of modern banks. A bank that does not lend money is not a bank in the true sense of word. Besides, in an exchange economy financial transactions especially borrowing and lending without a 'price' (rate of interest) are simply unimaginable.

Undoubtedly, borrowing and lending of money are essential functions of commercial banks that cannot be achieved without rate of interest. But every bank has its own technique, style, method and procedure for borrowing and lending. RFBs, will perform these functions without rates of interest. The channels open to them are many and varied through which they can diversity their activities.

In the first instance, it should be remembered that Islam forbids 'interest', but not business on credit. In fact credit is not only allowed in Islam but a code of conduct for credit transactions has been prescribed in ayhas 2:280 and 2:282, which insist on the uses of credit instruments with proper witnesses.

Moreover there are still further areas where RFBs can move freely. One is trading operations. The Qur'an has not only made lawful for its followers trade and commerce, but has encouraged them to pursue these vigorously. This provides ample scope to ensure alternative channels of income through profit-sharing in trade, commerce and industry.

Secondly in forbidding interest Islam has not illegalized all those transactions from which fixed income may accrue without labour. It has made lawful that income which accrues from the rent of property or from the rent of agricultural land. This means that RFBs will be free to buy and sell land an buildings ; or they may rent housing and commercial real estate. In trade or in any other type of commercial activity, RFBs will not enter into stock hoarding, speculation and forward dealings, as these are forbidden in Islam.

RFBs will also be free to perform the general agency functions of banks and earn commission and fees by offering safe-vaults, trusteeship, and the transfer and remittance of foreign exchange. Charges for these services will be based on the cost of service, without any element of rate of interest. Again, in buying and selling foreign exchange they must avoid forward dealings.

Thus by combining banking and non-banking functions, which are in line with modern trends in commercial banking, RFBs can have a definite and regular flow of income to meet their operating expenditures and also to earn profits.

Within the permitted area outlined above, it is possible to carve out commercially viable Saving and Investment Plans for RFBs. A broad sketch of such plans is given below :

(a) Viable Saving Plans for RFBs

In the broadest sense, like other commercial banks, RFBs will mobilize financial resources from a large variety of 'surplus units' in the economy, comprising business, household and government, and will re-lend them to an equally broad spectrum of private and public users of capital.

The performance of the first function — mobilization of savings— of any financial institution depends on its ability to design saving schemes to cater to the needs of large numbers of people in different social and economic strata of society.

This is because savings are made with definite but varying motives where the rate interest does not play any important role. Financial institutions, therefore, direct their efforts to devise saving plans to meet the expectations and objectives of purposeful savings. A number of empirical studies and surveys on the competitive nature of banks and financial institutions have also shown that competitive devices intended to attract savings do not make use of price (rate of interest).

In an imperfect capital market, differentiation in saving schemes is created by adding new features, such as linking a savings scheme with Life Insurance, or with Investment Trusts or a Housing Scheme, cash-box scheme, Monthly deposit schemes and so on. Other factors determining the ability of a saving institution are the quality of service, location, salesmanship and persuasive efforts of the institution.

RBFs will therefore be offering three types of Deposit Scheme, with the distinctive feature that none of them will bear rate of interest. They are Demand Deposit Schemes, Short-term Deposit Plans (Joint Venture Accounts), and Long Term Deposit Plans.

Demand Deposit Schemes are offered by all commercial banks without any rate of interest. Practices, however, vary regarding the conditions of maintaining a minimum balance, imposing service changes and so on. RFBs can conveniently adopt this type of deposit scheme.

The Joint-Venture Accounts of RFBs will be based on their 'Joint Venture Business', explained elsewhere in this paper. Deposits under this scheme will be accepted for a term-of-trading period — which may range from a week to a year. The Depositors will share the profit earned in a specific trading period.

Long-term Deposit Schemes will be linked with a Unit Investment Plan or with a Housing Scheme of RFBs. Under the Unit Investment Plan, the depositor will be required to deposit a lump sum or pay a stipulates sum in instalments. The operation of the Unit Investment Plan will be on the pattern of Mutual Saving Banks and Credit Unions in the U.S.A. People borrowing from this fund will not be charged any interest, but they will lose their entitlement to a share of the profits. The same principle will be applied in the Housing Scheme. Those who are taking a loan for houses or buying a house from the RFBs Real Estate have to become members of a 'Unit Investment Plan.'

(b) Trading and Investment Operation of RFBs

The problem of RFBs does not end with the designing of attractive saving schemes; it actually starts with the mobilization of savings. Resources mobilized by RFBs will be their liability, and they must bring corresponding assets to : (a) meet the *de facto* and *de jure* requirements of cash, (b) fulfil the expectations of the depositors, (c) cover administrative costs, (d) yield a surplus to satisfy the share-holders and also to plough back a part of it for further growth and expansion.

To meet the above requirements, modern banks divide their assets into three categories : primary reserve, secondary reserve, and earning assets. The main purpose of this division is to ensure profitability with liquidity. The primary reserve is meant to meet the liquidity requirements of the bank. It consists of cash, and cash balances with the Central Bank of the country.

Secondary reserves of modern commercial banks consist of securities of short-term low risk, highly marketable obligations which can be converted into cash quickly. Besides ensuring liquidity, these securities, which consist mainly of Treasury Bills, also yield some income even in the shortest period. Earning assets are the main source of medium and long-term investment. A major part of these assets are long-term loans, the duration of which is matched with the duration of the liabilities of commercial banks.

RFBs will also divide their reserves on a similar pattern. They will have no problem in their primary reserve area because it is a non-earning part of assets. But substantial assets should not be kept in this form. A problem is bound to arise in the management of the secondary reserve. RFBs cannot have liquidity through short-term government securities or commercial papers, because they are all interest bearing. An alternative source of income for them should be through short-term trading operations such as consignment business, joint-ventures and factoring.

Their earning assets should comprise profit-sharing in business, and permanent ownership and direct investment in real estate (residential and commercial).

The above areas of trading and investment operations are now becoming accepted channels of outlets for funds of commercial banks. As was pointed out earlier, since 1960 commercial banks' willingness to take risks and to switching over from interest-free demand deposits to costlier time deposits has made them equally venturesome in commercial financing. They have expanded into higher risk business, such as accounts, receivable financing (secured by inventories or real estate). Some of the leading banks have also entered into 'factoring' and direct investment in real estate. Hence the investment and trading patterns of RFBs will be in line with the current trend of modern banking.

(c) The Competitive Vigour of RFBs

Thus by drawing on viable saving and investment plans, RFBs will compete, both for the mobilization of savings and in the procurement of assets, with the traditional commercial banks and with other saving institutions.

The competitive vigour of any financial institution, however, depends upon the quality of its products, service and salesmanship. Like all other saving institutions, RFBs will be alert in creating product differentiation by adding features in their Saving Schemes, in the performance of service and salesmanship.

Since the organization and policies of RFBs have been conceived on sound banking principles, let us feel sure that in an imperfect capital market their will be a section of savers and users of funds that will be attracted by the quality of the products and services offered by RFBs ; just as there is a group of depositors and borrowers of capital which is attracted by the terms and conditions of rates of interest offered by traditional types of commercial banking.

THE SOCIO-ECONOMIC SIGNIFICANCE OF BANKING WITHOUT RATES OF INTEREST

The operation of modern financial institutions is based on the simple logic that risk in production process is inevitable and that it should be borne by every participant in proportion to his ability and willingness. Thus, to relate the degree of risk to the rate of return, borrowing firms (the users of capital) issue several types of security, to suit the nature and circumstances of different types of investor.

The purpose of issuing interest-bearing obligation is to suit the investment requirements of 'defensive investors' who put their chief emphasis upon the avoidance of any serious losses. The great majority of security holders, specially institutional investors, belong to this category.

However, the contractual nature of loan operations implies that the borrower should pay a stipulated rate of interest irrespective of changes in his financial capacity and that too without knowing the free loans will also enhance the economic and social welfare of the community.

Conclusion

The above study has shown that a financially viable and socially effective banking system is feasible without rates of interest. Alternative flows of operational income and investment income have been suggested in this study, but not as a ruse or subtle manoeuvre to circumvent the rate of interest by such devices used in the past as *bay'al-wafa* or *mukhat'tarah.* The broad outline of the banking system without rates of interest have been carved out by adopting such permissible business practices as *muzaraah, musaqh, mugharsah* and *Qirad/Mudaraabh.*

The organization of RFBs will be based on the Islamic Shari'ah. Their operation activities, apart from their productive efficiency, will ensure: (a) allocative efficiency, (b) absence of exploitation of depositors, borrowers and other clients, (c) adaptability to change in the demand for banking.

It would be wrong to say that RFBs will ultimately succumb to the rigidity of Shari'ah and a scarcity of suitable interest-free investment opportunities. It is true that the operation of RFBs will not be free from problems. But the problems are opportunities in disguise. As they are, these opportunities will permeate the entire fabric of the banking system without rates of interest. One of the problems will be their proliferation, especially arising through the limited availability of suitable investment opportunities without rates of interest. But problems concerning growth are confronted by every type of institutions, to which RFBs will be no exception. As with other firms and institutions, these will be solved through a continuous search for investment opportunities. In this paper we have suggested the pattern in which a commercially viable system of banking without rates of interest can be organized.

REFERENCES

1. Ismail R alFaruqi, "Islam and Art", *Studia Islamica*, Fasc. 37, pp. 81-109.

2. Lois Lamya al-Faruqi, *Aesthetic experience and the Islamic arts*, Delhi, in press.
3. My another article, "Developments and the Islamic Arts," Islam and development, *Proceedings of the Annual Convention of the Association of the Muslim Social Scientists*, 1977, pp. 27-35.

Revised and edited; originally published in *Islamic Culture*, Jan. 1982.